grow

organic

FRUIT AND VEGETABLES
FRESH FROM YOUR GARDEN

grow

organic

FRUIT AND VEGETABLES
FRESH FROM YOUR GARDEN

NICK HAMILTON

NEW
HOLLAND

First published in 2007 by New Holland Publishers (UK) Ltd
London • Cape Town • Sydney • Auckland
Garfield House, 86–88 Edgware Road, London W2 2EA, United Kingdom
www.newhollandpublishers.com
80 McKenzie Street, Cape Town 8001, South Africa
Unit 1, 66 Gibbes Street, Chatswood, NSW 2067, Australia
218 Lake Road, Northcote, Auckland, New Zealand

ISBN 978 1 84537 718 2
1 3 5 7 9 10 8 6 4 2

Editorial Direction: Rosemary Wilkinson
Senior Editors: Caroline Blake, Naomi Waters
Production: Marion Storz
Design: Casebourne Rose Design Associates
Photography: Sue Rose
Illustration: Sue Rose
Reproduction by Pica Digital Pte. Ltd., Singapore
Printed and bound in India by Replika Press

The paper used to produce this book is sourced from sustainable forests.

CONTENTS

Introduction

I have been gardening organically for most of
my life. My interest in edible gardening began when I first grew
vegetables in the back garden of my parents' semi-detached
house as a ten-year-old. I simply didn't have any inorganic
material, so I had to make do with next to nothing.

My father was my main source of inspiration, being a horticulturalist himself, and he taught me all the basics that would inspire me to grow vegetables, fruit, herbs and ornamentals organically. After school, there was never any question in my mind that I would go on to horticultural college. Following a compulsory year of work experience at the government-run Lea Valley Experimental Station (where I was involved in growing a wide range of new varieties under protection), I enrolled at Writtle College in Essex. I studied commercial horticulture, which gave me a broad overview of all things horticultural within the growing spectrum. I covered the production of fruit and vegetables, as well ornamentals, but on a commercial scale and in a commercial way. This gave me enough basic knowledge to adapt these ideas for growing on an amateur scale. I was greatly helped in this quest by working with my father in the gardens at Barnsdale, where we have been producing organically grown fruit, vegetables and herbs for well over 20 years now. The garden is diverse, having productive as well as ornamental areas, with a good proportion of trees. Our beneficial wildlife population is at a very healthy level, which helps greatly with our organic pest controls.

Pushing the boundaries

A lot of what we know in gardening is learned by trial and error. I have gained as much knowledge from the many disasters we have had as from the successes. Since the death of my father in 1996, my wife Sue and I have taken over the running of the Barnsdale garden, which is now open to the public. We are still pushing the boundaries by trying new things with fruit, vegetables and herbs. We want to find ways of extending the cropping season, to test planting distances in order to get more crops into smaller spaces, as well as trialling varieties for seed companies. Ultimately, we really enjoy sitting down at the dinner table and eating seasonal produce that has been picked fresh from the garden, and has been grown in the best possible way.

Natural selection

Organic gardening is all about producing the best produce in the best possible way for ourselves, our children and the environment in which we live. Organic gardening used to be considered the preserve of hippies, but it now uses techniques at the cutting-edge of horticulture, and encourages productive growing methods. Organic growers have been espousing for many years what only now seems to be becoming obvious. We want to grow our produce in tune with nature, by harnessing all the good things that the earth has to offer. It is entirely possible to align this ethos with the highly productive techniques that we have learned over hundreds of years of growing fruit, vegetables and herbs.

A helping hand

I have put all of my experience and "know-how" into this book, in a way that can be simply understood by novice gardeners. It is not full of jargon and technical writing, but instead offers simple-to-follow, accurate and precise techniques that

will guide you through the growing of over 660 varieties of fruit, vegetables and herbs. The most important aspect of growing produce is the soil in which it grows, which is why the book begins there and then follows onto the materials that can be used for improving the soil – the nutrients and fertilizers available to organic growers. The first chapter then finishes with two of my favourite subjects: composting and propagation. The bulk of the book covers all the information required to successfully grow fruit, vegetables and herbs.

This book is intended to be used as a reference guide before, during and after your crops are grown. We will follow the crop from its initial propagation through planting, harvesting and storage, as well as comprehensively covering the varieties available for each crop. If your crop is going to survive, it is vital to understand the problems that you might face. The chapter on pests and diseases not only explains the symptoms, but also details the measures available to organic growers to combat these problems. And you will find many of my special tips scattered throughout the book.

I really hope this book encourages you to embrace organic gardening, and offers practical support and dynamic inspiration. Most importantly, I want to make sure that the journey from your garden to your table is swift and rewarding.

chapter 1

the organic
APPROACH

Soil types • Soil conditioners

• Nutrients • Trace elements

• Crop rotation • Composting

• Propagation

Before you think about what to grow,

it is important to know what type of soil you have and how best to manage that soil to get the best yields from the crops to be grown in it. The type of soil will not only dictate what can be successfully grown, but also the timing of those crops. For example, most herbs require a free-draining soil, while brassicas like a firm, heavy soil with plenty of nutrients. There is more to soil than most gardeners realize and for organic gardens it is where the real difference lies, as this is where most of the work is carried out. Inorganic gardeners will rely on artificial fertilizers to get the best yield, without worrying too much about the structure of their soils, the natural nutrient levels or the amounts of micro-organisms and wildlife present in their soil. To an organic gardener, the soil is the basis from which everything will be nourished, and therefore the most important point at which to start.

Soil is formed in layers, of which the topsoil is the most important for the cultivation of crops. It has been formed over many years by the addition – naturally or otherwise – of animal droppings, along with dead and decaying plant matter. This layer contains the highest level of nutrients and organisms, as well as the best structure, so this is where we need our plants to be placing their roots.

The second layer is called subsoil, which is generally opposite to topsoil in every way. It has little or no nutrients, few organisms and a very poor structure. Yet, this was how the topsoil began life and shows quite clearly how nature will guide the organic gardener towards the best methods for the best results. The final layer of soil is the parent matter, and this is the layer from which the other two above it were formed. In most cases, this layer is too low to worry most gardeners.

The thickness of the top two layers of soil is not standard and will vary enormously from area to area, and garden to garden; in fact, it can vary within a garden. It is the topsoil that needs to be as thick as possible to provide an area that will grow a wide diversity of crops. Therefore, if you are trying to work with a thin layer of topsoil, the simple answer is to work plenty of organic matter into it. This will raise the level, giving more soil to work with. Incorporate organic matter into the subsoil, improving it and making a better environment for the micro-organisms and wildlife to continue improving it.

Please note that when I mention soil type in the following pages, I am referring to the topsoil only.

SOIL TYPES

There are five main types of soil: clay, silt, sand, chalk and peat. It is unlikely that your soil will contain just one of these types, as it will generally be a mixture of two or three. Your soil type will refer to the highest proportion of one of these five in the soil.

Clay This type of soil is hard to work, because it is usually very heavy and becomes wet and soggy very easily. It is a cold soil that sticks together easily when wet, and is poorly drained. This poor drainage occurs because the soil particles of clay are very small and sit together very closely, not allowing many air spaces between them. Water will filter down through the soil gradually, causing a backlog of water and creating a wet and boggy soil. Another problem associated with small soil particles and very little air space is that the soil will compact very easily. You should stay off this type of soil as much as possible, and certainly during wet periods. Poor air spaces in the soil will also inhibit wildlife and create a difficult structure for roots to push through, especially for root crops such as carrots and parsnips.

The great advantage with clay is that it is naturally a very fertile soil as the nutrients are held onto within the soil. It can also be manipulated, over time, into whatever soil structure you require by the addition of various materials. Organic matter is one of the best materials to add to a clay soil, as this will improve the soil drainage by adding bulk and raising the soil level, as well as adding nutrients. Adding coarse grit or sharp sand will also help to improve drainage by opening up air spaces.

There is also a method called "flocculation", which means the binding together of smaller particles to create a bigger one, thereby improving drainage and structure. This is achieved by adding lime – or gypsum in more alkaline soils – to the soil. If the soil is improved, the levels of micro-organisms and wildlife will also naturally increase.

The final way of improving a heavy clay soil is not to walk on it. Either use boards to walk on, which will spread the weight, or implement the 1.2 m (4 ft) bed system, where you do not walk on the cultivated soil, but carry out all your work from the pathways on either side.

Silt This is a very similar soil to clay, and has all its characteristics – good and bad. The soil particles that make up this soil are small, but not as small as clay, so the soil is slightly better drained. However, it still sticks to your boots when wet. The easiest way to distinguish between the two is to rub moist soil between finger and thumb. A clay soil will feel sticky, while a silt soil will feel silky smooth.

Sand The large particles of this soil make it dry and fast-draining, but very hungry. It is ideal for growing root crops, as their long tap roots can push through the large particles and air spaces easily. However, it is very poor for brassicas, as they like a rich, heavy soil filled with nutrients. As the soil is free-draining, it will remain workable for virtually the whole year. It can also be used for growing early crops, as it warms up very quickly in the spring.

Sandy soil can be improved, and its moisture content increased, by mulching crops with organic matter. This will be taken into the soil by wildlife, as well as natural decomposition, and can be forked in at the end of the crop. The mulch will help to prevent water loss by evaporation from the soil surface, and the organic content of the soil will be improved. Prior to mulching, it is essential to dig in plenty of well-rotted organic matter each year, not only as bulk that will help to conserve moisture in the soil, but also as an invaluable source of available nutrients to the plants. Finally, the soil can be improved by growing green manures, some of which will fix nitrogen in the soil, making it more readily available for the crops to be grown on it. They will also add bulk to the soil. Another bonus is the fact that, while growing, the green manure will prevent leaching of nutrients from the soil during wet weather.

Chalk This type of soil is very similar in its characteristics to sand, although it will generally have a high stone content. Since it has a larger particle size, it will be slightly more free-draining and certainly hungrier. The soil will also invariably be alkaline, although this high pH should not pose a problem for most vegetables.

Peat An unmistakable soil, generally black or very dark brown in colour. It is a soil that can be very poorly drained or very well-drained, depending on the peat type and the area you live in. Some peaty areas are below sea level, which makes them difficult to drain and generally very boggy. It is a spongy material, which has decomposed over millions of years. It holds water well, meaning that most peat soils will become waterlogged, particularly in the winter. There is no need to add a lot of extra organic matter to it, as it is organic matter. Peat soils are almost always acidic, and therefore need lime added to grow most edible crops. It will also be low in nutrient levels, so organic fertilizers will play an important part in the growing process.

SOIL CONDITIONERS

All soil types have good and bad points, but they can all be easily improved by adding various soil conditioners. The following are all types of organic matter that can be incorporated into the soil to improve it:

Farmyard manure This includes cow and horse manure that has been well-rotted before incorporating it into the soil. It will add bulk to the soil, improving drainage on heavy soils and retaining moisture in a lighter one. It will also add vital nutrients to the soil. In towns it is harder to come by than if you live in the country, and it can be smelly and disliked by close neighbours. The most important factor, however, for the organic gardener is to ensure that any farmyard manure is obtained from a clean farm, because the cleaner the farm, the less likelihood of the manure coming infested with weed seeds.

Garden compost Obviously, the easiest organic matter to come by as it is generally produced on site. The quality is controllable and the nutrient levels should be balanced, if the heap is managed correctly. The most important factor, however, is that it is free.

Green composts These are the by-product of recycling. When our rubbish is taken away by the refuse collectors, all the materials that will not biodegrade quickly are removed, and the rest is composted in big heaps. It is then bagged up and sold back to us at a greatly inflated price. Due to the complete lack of control over what is discarded, the end result is a compost that can have very variable nutrient levels, which only makes it suitable as a soil conditioner. It must be more practical to cut out the middle man, save all that unnecessary waste of energy and compost it ourselves.

Leaf mould Depending on where you live and how many trees you have in your garden, this is either an easy material to come by or nigh-on impossible to get. It makes an excellent soil conditioner, but can take between one and three years to break down, depending on the types of leaves collected. They take such a long time to rot down because of the amount of lignin (fibrous tissue) in the leaves. Due to the period of time it takes to compost and the excellent, consistent nutrient levels produced, I prefer to use it as a seed or potting compost, as opposed to using it on the soil.

Spent mushroom compost This is actually well-rotted horse manure that has had its pH raised to make it alkaline – a condition that is favoured by mushrooms. Be aware of the pH of your soil, as too much of this compost may raise the pH to a level beyond what your crops prefer.

Seaweed If you live by the coast, this makes an excellent soil conditioner and can be dug fresh into the soil, as it rots down very quickly. Although the nutrient levels may be variable, it does contain vital trace elements.

Peat This has little or no nutrients in it, so should only be incorporated into the soil to add bulk.

Green manures These are very good for the soil, as some will fix nitrogen in the soil as they grow. They will also add vital organic bulk.

Sheep manure You have to be keen to use sheep manure, as it is collected by hand and bucket. As the sheep are free range, there is only the manure and no straw. The manure will add vital nutrients to the soil, but no bulk. It can also be used for liquid feed.

Chicken manure Only use manure from free-range chickens and ensure that it is well-composted. Otherwise, it will be too powerful and can burn off your crops.

Pig manure A little bit more of an awkward one as the manure must come from organic farms, but it is worth the effort as it has a high nutrient content.

Adding organic matter to the soil will not only improve the structure and water-holding capabilities of the soil, but will also benefit from the fact that worms in the soil can convert it into something the crops can use. These worms are essential to break down the organic matter by ingesting it and then releasing pellets that make the nutrients more easily available to the plants. The worms will also improve the drainage and aeration of the soil.

All of these soil conditioners can be incorporated into the soil in three ways: double-digging, single-digging or mechanically.

Double-digging is used to improve the soil to the deepest level, by working organic matter down to a depth of about 40 cm (16 in). Firstly, dig out a trench 120 cm (4 ft) wide, 30 cm (12 in) across and about 20 cm (8 in) deep, with any soil that has been dug out going into a wheelbarrow and then dropped at the end of the area to be dug. Plenty of well-rotted manure is then put into the bottom of the trench, and this is forked into the subsoil,

going down about 20 cm (8 in). Once this has been done, a trench of identical proportions is dug out directly behind the first one and the soil is then thrown into the empty first trench, adding plenty of organic matter as it goes. The process is then repeated until the last trench, when the soil originally removed from the first trench is used to fill that.

Single-digging uses exactly the same principles as double-digging, only the manure is put at the bottom of the trench and not dug in.

Mechanical cultivation uses a rotovator or cultivator that is run over the soil, after a generous layer of well-rotted manure or compost has been placed onto the surface. This method should not be used too often, as the spinning blades can smear the soil – particularly with clay and silt soils – creating a pan that will prevent water passage, causing potential waterlogging problems.

There is also a range of organic materials that can be used to mulch the soil that will eventually be incorporated, either by the soil wildlife, or by forking in the old material before topping up with fresh mulch.

Shreddings No garden should be without a shredder, as it can recycle virtually all the waste from a garden. The woody material will take a while to break down and, when incorporated, it will add bulk to the soil but little or no nutrients.

Wood-based products This refers to bark, wood chip, shavings etc. They have the same properties as shreddings, but ensure that the product does not come from treated timber.

Farmyard manure, garden compost, green composts and leaf mould These can all be used as mulches as well.

Before applying any soil conditioner or fertilizer, it is important to understand the nutrient requirements of fruit, vegetables and herbs. All of these plants will obtain 96 per cent of their nutrient requirement from the air around us, so we are only looking to top up that remaining four per cent. Although this is a small amount, it can make or break a crop, so it is of vital importance. There are two types of nutrient, the major nutrients consisting mainly of nitrogen (N), phosphorus (P) and potassium (K) and trace elements,

which are not needed by the plants in such a big quantity, but are still vitally important for a healthy crop. The percentage given with each nutrient heading below is that needed by a plant for healthy growth within the four-per-cent requirement.

NUTRIENTS

Nitrogen (N)   1.5%

Responsible for the vegetative growth of leaves and shoots. A lack of nitrogen will cause stunting of growth, resulting in smaller crops, while too much will cause the plant to grow too quickly. As a result of this rapid growth, the shoots will be soft and weak and therefore more susceptible to pest and disease attack. The older leaves become yellow quickly. To rectify this, apply a high-nitrogen fertilizer – dried blood, hoof and horn, chicken manure, nettles or well-rotted organic matter.

Phosphorus (P)   0.15%

This is responsible for good root growth. The obvious result of a lack of phosphates is stunting of the plant caused by a bad root system. The older leaves have a distinct blue colour when deficient. Rectify with bone meal.

Potassium (K)   1.5%

Required in the same quantities as nitrogen. It is responsible for the size, quantity and quality of flowers and fruits. Deficiency shows in fewer and smaller flowers or fruits, and stunted plants. An excess can result in the plants being unable to take up magnesium. If the soil is deficient in potassium, the edges of older leaves become yellow and then brown, or the leaves become bluish and then bronze. Rectify with rock potash, some seaweed-based fertilizers, wood ash or comfrey.

Magnesium   0.2%

A constituent of chlorophyll, so deficiency shows as yellowing between the leaf veins. This generally shows in the older leaves first. Deficiency occurs when there is too much potassium in the soil, or when there is not enough organic matter. Rectify with liquid seaweed or liquid animal manures and improve the soil with organic matter.

Calcium   0.5%

This neutralizes certain acids and helps in the manufacture of protein. In a well-managed soil, where organic matter is added on a regular basis, there is rarely a deficiency.

Sulphur   0.1%

Forms part of many plant proteins and is a vital constituent of protein. Sulphur deficiency causes stunting and yellowing of the plant, but it is rare, as there is usually enough in manure and compost to satisfy the plant's needs.

TRACE ELEMENTS

Iron

Deficiency shows as yellowing between the veins on younger leaves. More likely on alkaline soils. Rectify by adding well-rotted manure or compost.

Zinc and Copper

If there is a deficiency, younger leaves are mottled yellow. Control as for iron.

Manganese

Stunting of younger leaves and yellowing between veins, so easy to confuse with iron deficiency. Control as for iron.

Boron

Internal "corkiness" in root crops and brown-heart in celery, cauliflower, broccoli and calabrese. Control as for iron.

Molybdenum

Deformed growth such as "whiptail" in cabbage – leaves become thin and strap-like. The deficiency is usually due to the element being "locked up" in an acid soil. Rectify by adding lime.

For all the trace elements, a regular application of manure or compost will be sufficient to prevent deficiencies occurring. However, if required, liquid seaweed or liquid manure can be used. When liquid manures are put directly onto a soil that has already been watered, this can be done so directly from the water butt or diluted 50:50 for use as a foliar feed. If using comfrey, it needs to be added to a watering can at a ratio of 10–20:1 (water:comfrey).

To make liquid feed, put animal droppings, comfrey or nettles in a hessian sack or permeable bag, with a large stone to weigh the sack down, and leave submerged in a water butt

ORGANIC FERTILIZERS

The percentage of major nutrients shown in the fertilizers below will act as a guide with the coding as follows: N for nitrogen, P for phosphorus and K for potassium.

Blood, fish and bone . . . . .N 3.5, P 8, K 0.5

Pelleted chicken manure . . . . .N 4, P 3.5, K 2.5

Hoof and horn . . . . .N 13

Dried blood . . . . .N 12–14, P small amount

Fish meal . . . . .N 9, P 2.5

Bone meal . . . . .N 3.5, P 22

Rock potash . . . . .K 10.5

Wood ash . . . . .variable

Liquid and dried animal manures . . . . .N 1, P 1, K 1.5

Trace elements . . . . .full range

Liquid seaweed . . . . .N 1.5, P nominal, K 2.5

Liquid animal manures . . . . .N 1, P 1, K 1.5

Comfrey . . . . .N 0.02, P 0.03, K 0.05

or large bucket for about two weeks. After this time, the sack can be removed, the butt covered and the liquid feed used.

CROP ROTATION

For the organic gardener, management of the soil and what goes into it is incredibly important in controlling soil nutrient levels, as well as pests and diseases. It is not a complicated procedure to ensure that your soil does not become starved. You can also eliminate the build up of pests or diseases. Move the crops around your growing area so that heavy feeders, such as brassicas, do not draw all the nutrients from one area of soil over a number of years. It will also ensure that pests overwintering in the soil or on surrounding plants do not have a suitable crop to feed on in the following growing season. This simple, but very effective procedure is called crop rotation. It involves the grouping together of plants that have similar nutrient requirements and are affected by the same pests and diseases, so that they can be moved around in a block from season to season. I have listed companion plants for each of the

vegetables in this book, to make grouping together nice and simple. There are two types of rotation: a three-year and a four-year. The three-year rotation will allow the gardener four beds, but one is planted with permanent crops, such as soft fruit, with the vegetables rotated around this using the remaining three beds. The four-year rotation uses all four beds each season. However, when intercropping brassicas with quick crops of lettuce and spring onions or the like, the crop rotation is not affected, as these crops are in the ground for too short a period of time to be a problem.

This guide to crop-rotation is not, however, the final word, just a guideline. If it is not possible to stick to the rotation requirements exactly, any sort of rotation will do. In this case, doing something is better than nothing.

COMPOSTING

This is by far the easiest form of organic matter to source for use in the garden, as it is at hand, having been produced on site. It will have been produced by recycling waste from the organic garden, the kitchen and the house. The end product should be of even nutrient content, as well as being a good bulky material to improve the soil. If the composting process is carried out correctly in the spring, summer and autumn, it will be possible to convert two lots of raw material into usable compost, with another batch being produced through the remainder of the year. This means that in any one year it is possible to produce three lots of compost for use in the organic garden.

The bacteria within the compost heap will break down the raw material into the finished, friable compost. These bacteria are fuelled by the nitrogen in the heap, so, the more nitrogen, the faster and better they work. In order to aim for three heaps of usable compost per year, it is important to add plenty of material that is high in nitrogen. This material is called an "activator" and needs to be added at regular intervals to the heap. For maximum decomposition, the material added needs to be in thin layers as fine leaf materials, such as grass clippings, will compact down too much, causing anaerobic bacteria to work. Bulkier items will cause the heap to cool, due to the air spaces created.

There are several methods that can be employed in order to compost materials:

Compost bin The best type of compost bin is an enclosed one that will keep all the heat created by the rotting process within the heap, ensuring that the bacteria work to their maximum potential over most of that material. If a slatted side or open-sided bin is used, then the contact with the air will naturally lower the temperature of the outer edge, causing the bacteria in that area to work at a slower rate. To combat this, line the inside of the compost bin with cardboard. This will act as an insulator, as well as ultimately breaking down into the compost itself. If you intend to compost leaves, the easiest method is to knock four posts into the ground and wrap chicken wire around them. As they are slow to compost, there is no need to spend vast sums of money building or buying a closed bin. If needs be, cardboard could be put around the sides and an old carpet or sheet of polythene put over the surface to speed up the process. An enclosed bin with a lid will produce the fastest compost.

Open heap This is where material is just piled into a heap and left to rot. The bacteria in the middle of such a heap will be working fast, but the ones on the outer edges will not. It is a usable method, if you do not have purpose built bins, but it will not create three heaps in a year.

Sheet composting For those without a specific area in which to compost, this method can be employed, as it involves spreading thin layers of compostable material between vegetable rows and leaving it to rot in situ. This will also save on the hard work involved with composting in the first two ways.

Worm composting This method works well in bought bins, as well as homemade ones, and even old dustbins. A small amount of compostable material is placed in the bottom of the bin, with brandling worms, not earthworms, added at this stage. As before, the material is then added in thin layers at regular intervals, with the worms then converting it into usable compost. In specially made bins, this material will fall out of the bottom when ready and can be used immediately. Other bins that do not have this facility will need to be emptied once the worms have worked their way to the top.

If employing any of the first two methods to compost waste materials, then this process is speeded up by regularly turning the bin. This involves either emptying the bin or moving the heap from one place to another, with the intention of mixing up the materials within that heap. This ensures that all the material gets composted at the fastest possible rate. Turning of the heap needs to be carried out once a month during spring, summer and autumn, and probably once every six weeks during the winter.

With all of these composting methods, it is important for the bacteria to work at their best, so maximize the heat in the heap and keep the heap moist. Closed or covered heaps will need water applied to them from time to time. These bacteria also work better in a heap that has an alkaline pH, so applications of lime from time to time will help to keep the pH at a favourable level. However, adding a good mixture of materials to the heap should give the right pH level, but if adding coniferous or evergreen material it may be wise to counterbalance its acidic properties with a handful of lime.

There is a basic list of materials that can be used in an organic compost heap, some fairly obvious and some not:

Garden prunings and hedge clippings
It is possible to put the softer material straight on the heap, although it is generally better to shred it first. Woodier stems will compost much slower as they contain lignin, which the bacteria find hard to break down, so these will definitely need shredding first. Be aware of conifers and evergreens, as these will tend to make the compost more acidic.

Wood ash If you have a wood burner, then all the ash produced can be added to the heap. However, if the ash contains material from a coal and wood fire, be warned that too much will acidify the heap. Wood ash will provide the heap with a good source of potassium.

Dried blood This will be available from a garden centre or DIY store, generally in powder form. It contains readily available nitrogen, so it is an excellent activator for bacteria.

Fabrics, feathers, human and animal hair All of these materials contain available nitrogen, so they are activators. However, they are slow to break down. Before adding them to the heap, cut or rip them into small pieces or strips so that they can be broken down more easily.

Bracken A fairly rampant plant that is usually found in woodlands, but a good bulking-up material for a compost heap. Due to its high lignin content, it needs to be shredded first.

Newspaper and cardboard Available in most households, only use paper and cardboard that contains only black print on white paper or non-coloured card. Although usable, newspaper and cardboard do not really add anything to the heap, so are probably better used for something else in the garden, such as being put into a bean trench or made into sweet-pea tubes.

Brassica stems These are very thick and slow to break down, so will need to be shredded first.

Grass clippings Most of us have these to dispose of each week during the growing season. The clippings are an excellent activator. However, ensure that regular but thin layers are put onto the heap, as too thick a layer will cause anaerobic bacteria to work, creating a smelly and slimy mess that rots slowly.

Hay and straw Hay is better than straw, as it contains more nutrients and rots down quicker, with both needing to be well-moistened before adding to the heap.

Spent hops If you live close to a brewery, then I'm sure they would be more than happy for you to take these away. They add bulk and valuable nutrients to a heap.

Raw vegetable scraps After lawn clippings, this is probably the most popular material going into the compost bin.

Comfrey leaves (Symphytum officinale) As with shredders, every garden should also have a patch of comfrey. It is an invaluable crop for the organic gardener, as the leaves, when regularly cut, are an activator for the compost heap as well as being a valuable source of potassium and phosphate. The leaves can also be put into water to create a liquid feed.

Rhubarb leaves Although we eat the stems, the leaves are generally discarded as they are poisonous to eat. They are perfectly safe to compost.

Potato haulm Once the crop has been harvested, all the tops, or haulms, can be put onto the heap to compost down. If there has been blight on a particular variety, ensure that these haulms are only composted on heaps in an enclosed bin.

Nettles Another crop that no garden should be without is a small patch of nettles. Not only are they an excellent host for beneficial insects, but put on the compost heap they also act as an activator. They are high in nitrogen and other minerals.

General garden waste and old cut flowers All material removed from plants, such as leaves and dead flowers etc can be composted – even diseased and pest-infected material (unless advised not to do so in the pest and disease section of this book). The heat generated in most compost heaps, and certainly enclosed heaps, has been found to be high enough to kill most diseases, spores, pests and their eggs. Always shred anything that is not soft, to maximise the rate of decomposition.

Tree leaves Leaves are very slow to rot down, as they comprise mainly lignin. They take a minimum of one year, but normally two or three years, to totally decompose. As leaf mould makes an excellent seed or potting compost, it is better to compost these separately in a purpose-built leaf bin.

Seaweed If you live near the coast, there should always be a good supply of seaweed. It makes an excellent activator for the compost heap, being high in nitrogen, potassium and most trace elements.

Cow and horse manure High in nitrogen, so it makes an excellent activator, as well as adding bulk.

Sheep manure This is also an excellent activator, being high in nitrogen and most nutrients.

Poultry manure It contains much higher rates of nitrogen than other manures and will make a fiery compost.

Pet manure Small-animal manures from rabbits, hamsters, gerbils, guinea pigs, etc are fine to add to the heap, whereas cat and dog manure – although adding valuable nutrients to a compost heap – also contain other organisms that can be harmful to humans and especially children. They also smell foul, so they are best kept off the heap.

Urine Ideal if you are potty training a child. Urine is an excellent activator for the compost heap, as it is very high in nitrogen and potassium.

Weeds Only compost annual weeds that are not in flower and perennial weeds that have been lifted and left on the top of the ground to totally wilt and dry, before adding them to your heap. If annuals are coming up to flower, cut off the flower buds and add the rest of the plant. Do not add pernicious weeds, such as bindweed, couch grass etc to the compost heap.

Items that should not be added to a compost heap include:

Soil This does not add anything to the heap and is much better-suited for growing crops in.

Glass, plastic, metal and stone None of these will decompose, so they are useless in the heap.

Dog and cat manure As already mentioned, not really suited to a compost heap.

Cooked vegetables These tend to putrefy in a compost heap and will only act as an attractant to rats.

Meat and fish Cooked or raw, these will have the same effect as the above.

Pernicious weeds One thing we do not want to do is spread these weeds around the garden.

Weeds in flower or seeding For the same reasons as above.

Wood products Slow to break down, so they should be composted in a separate heap and used for mulching.

When ready, the compost should almost look like soil and smell like nectar to any organic gardener. It can then be added to the vegetable plot, fruit orchard or herb garden.

PROPAGATION

This is a subject that wrongly strikes fear into the hearts of many organic gardeners. The methods used are quite simple and very successful. For fruit, vegetables and herbs, we are going to look at the main methods: seeds, cuttings and division. We will not look at grafting fruit trees onto rootstocks, as this is something that most gardeners would not attempt.

Sowing seeds

This is undoubtedly the most commonly used propagation method for vegetables and many herbs. Three basic methods are used: sowing into trays, sowing into modules and sowing directly into prepared soil.

Traditionally, seed trays have been used and these are still popular for the crops that have a more erratic or difficult germination. A seed tray is overfilled with compost and each end is lifted and dropped back onto the bench to settle the compost into the tray. Using a firming board (a piece of wood exactly the same size as the inside of the seed tray), or a straight edge, level the compost off the top of the tray. Press the firming board down onto the compost gently, just to firm it a little. This gives enough room for the topping to be applied, covering the seed.

Water the compost well with a watering can and rose, as this will prevent the seed from being washed to one end of the tray. Sow the seed thinly and evenly across the surface of the compost, and then cover with vermiculite. I find vermiculite better than other products. Vermiculite is best because it breaks down in the soil (eventually) and does not form a hard crust on the surface of the tray, like peat.

This tray can then be put into a propagator with artificial heat or can be left to one side on the greenhouse benching or windowsill. The unheated seeds will germinate, but this will happen a lot slower than with ones kept in a propagator. Once big enough to handle, the seedlings can be pricked out into pots or modules and grown on.

The next and newer method is to use module trays. These are trays with individual cells that act as mini pots, with the number of cells per tray depending on the size of each cell. For the propagation of vegetables and herbs, I would usually look to use trays consisting of somewhere in the region of 54 to 77 cells, but no smaller. The tray of cells is overfilled, tapped and levelled as for seed trays. It is necessary to make a small indentation in the compost of each cell. I find a cane cap on the end of a pencil is ideal. The seed can be sown into this indentation; usually one to three seeds per cell. After germination, the weaker ones are removed.

The plugs, as these mini-plants are called, can be planted out directly from the module tray without the need for pricking out or potting on. This system is used for varieties that germinate readily as there is a lot of space and compost taken up if the seeds fail.

The multi-sowing method of growing vegetables also uses modules. It is carried out in exactly the same way as mentioned above, but between five and seven seeds are dropped into each module and no thinning takes place. These crops are planted out in their little clump and they will mature quickly, pushing each other out of the way, to be harvested as a young, very sweet and tender crop.

The final method is directly sowing into prepared soil, in situ. This is the cheapest method, as it involves no materials, except for the seed. A drill is pulled out to the length required, using either the corner of a hoe, rake or a bit of cane. The drill is a small furrow that will be to the depth recommended for each variety, but is usually 1–2.5 cm (½–1 in) deep. Water the bottom of the drill with a watering can, to prevent watering from overhead and stop the soil from crusting over. The seed is then thinly sown into the bottom of this drill, which is then backfilled with soil and gently firmed.

For all three methods, it is vital to label the seeds. I also recommend adding the date sown and the company providing the seeds on the label for reference. You never know when it might come in useful.

Cuttings

This type of propagation will be used for herbs and some soft fruits. There are three basic methods: softwood, semi-ripe and hardwood cuttings.

Softwood cuttings These are taken when the plant is usually growing at its strongest, producing soft and sap-filled growing tips and sideshoots. It is these soft shoots that are required. Tips of between 5–10 cm (2–4 in) are removed with a pair of sharp secateurs, a knife or a pair of scissors. The length of stem at the base of the cutting is then removed just below the bottom set of leaves with a nice clean, horizontal cut. These basal leaves are then carefully removed, as are the next set above them, leaving no more than half of the total amount of leaves. Insert four such cuttings into an 8 cm (3 in) pot so that the bare stem is pushed right into the compost. Then they should be well watered. A plastic bag can also be fixed over the pot and the cuttings, to retain the moisture. In the summer, they should root within about four weeks, when they can be gently teased apart and potted individually into 8 cm (3 in) pots.

Semi-ripe cuttings These are taken in exactly the same way as for softwood cuttings, except that they can be inserted directly into the ground outside, in a cold frame. Rooting will take longer, but once rooted, they can be lifted and potted on as before.

Hardwood cuttings This is the easiest and cheapest method and can be used to propagate currants. In the autumn or early winter, once all the leaves have fallen, cut a length of stem that is about pencil thickness. Just below a bud, cut horizontally across the stem. Then move about 20 cm (8 in) above this to look for a good bud to cut above, with a slanting cut (ensuring that the bottom of the cut is not below the base of the bud). These cuttings can then be pushed into a cultivated piece of ground, so that only a third of the top is showing and two-thirds of the cutting is buried. Firm in and leave for a year to root. Keep watered throughout the growing season. In the early winter, they can be lifted and planted out into their permanent positions.

Division

A simple method, used for some herbs and soft fruit. Once the plants have become dormant (any time from the end of October until early March) they can be lifted and split up into smaller pieces, before being replanted. You can use your hands to split them, if it is only a small clump. For larger clumps, use two forks pushed into the clump back to back and lever them until the clump splits. This splitting and putting back of smaller pieces revitalises the clumps, so that they produce more of whatever is required. It will also have the added bonus of plantlets left over that can be used elsewhere in the garden, or can be given away to friends and family.

Following these simple techniques will ensure a good propagation and a bountiful yield.

plant organic
FRUIT

Apples • Apricots • Blackberries and
hybrid berries • Blackcurrants
• Blueberries • Cherries • Figs
• Gooseberries • Peaches and
Nectarines • Pears • Plums, Gages and
Damsons • Raspberries • Redcurrants
and Whitecurrants • Strawberries

There can be no better feeling than picking fruit from your own bush, tree, cane or plant, knowing that no harmful substances have been put onto or into it. This is an essential feeling to have, as a lot of work will have gone into achieving the crop. Fresh fruit is an important part of our diet. We are now blessed with a huge selection of modern varieties and a greater understanding of cultivation techniques, so it is important that we enjoy the fruits of our labour.

IMPROVED VARIETIES

The advances in dwarfing rootstock research have been a very important factor in producing fruit trees that have shrunk at the same pace as the gardens of new properties. Since these trees are also producing a bigger crop, most gardens could squeeze in at least one fruit tree. For apples and pears it is usually necessary to have at least two trees, so that one pollinates the other. However, if your garden only has space for one, a "Family Tree" is the choice for you. This apple or pear tree usually has three different varieties grafted onto one stem, with each variety being a pollinator for at least one of the other two. These trees are found not only as bushes, standards and half-standards, but also as fan-trained specimens, which means that they can fit into any spot. Continual horticultural research is making new varieties availabile to amateur gardeners. These varieties not only yield a better crop than their predecessors, but also extend the season at both ends, with some varieties flowering and fruiting very early in the season and some very late.

ALL THE YEAR ROUND

There are shapes of tree and training techniques that have been developed to ensure that fruit can be grown in most gardens, if not in the soil then in containers. This means that, with careful planning, fresh fruit can be available for most months of the year. When fresh fruit is in short supply, stored fruit can be used to plug the gap. Storing fruit is a simple procedure, as the place of storage can be as simple as a garden shed or garage and, if stored correctly, some fruit varieties actually improve in flavour.

BASIC TECHNIQUES

As with vegetables, the basic techniques are the most important factor and they are: soil preparation, vigilance and hygiene. Hygiene is especially important, so that strong-growing trees, bushes and plants do not succumb to pests or diseases so easily. If they do fall prey to pestilence, we should be ready for it and make sure that it is less likely to happen the following year by clearing the problem from site. There are times in the organic fruit garden when you have to look beyond blemishes, misshapen fruit, the odd maggot in an apple, birds stealing a few cherries and all the other pitfalls that face you. But rest assured that these problems and many more are faced by inorganic gardeners every day.

APPLES
Malus domestica

Rosaceae

Without doubt, the apple is the most versatile of all tree fruits.
It can be accommodated in most gardens, in one form or
another, and will produce fruit from midsummer until late
autumn; stored fruit can be made available until spring. They
can be grown in warm and cooler climates, but still perform
better in a sunny and sheltered spot. Through many years of
research and development, there is now an apple variety that is
suited to almost any position, in any soil. Apples will tolerate
most soil types, although their rate of growth is determined by
the rootstock that they are grown on. These range from very
dwarfing, producing a tree of 150–180 cm (5–6 ft) in height, to
vigorous, which will produce a tree that could grow to over

9 m (28 ft) high. Many older varieties are available, as well as newer, more disease-resistant types that can be used for culinary or dessert purposes. The variety of apple that you choose to grow is an important factor when considering the position that it is to be grown in, because early flowering varieties do not suit colder areas or areas that are in a frost pocket. This is because the flowers are likely to be frosted and will not produce fruit, so the answer is to grow mid- or late-season varieties that will flower when the worst of the frost has passed. Apples are not generally self-fertile, so they will need to be pollinated by at least one other apple. It is best to choose apples from the same flowering group (although ones from adjacent groups will suffice in most cases). The shape of the tree will depend on the training method used and this will be dictated by their fruiting habits, as apples can be divided into two groups: the ones that fruit on spurs (spur bearers), and ones that fruit at the tips (tip bearers). These two groups will also dictate the pruning method employed once the tree shape has been formed, although pruning also falls into two groups: winter and summer. Correctly pruned a good range of apple trees will produce an abundant crop of fruit that will be available to eat for up to nine months and these trees should produce an excellent crop of fruit for about 30 years.

DATES

Flowering time April–May

Harvesting August–December

Cropping age 2 years

SITE AND SOIL

Site Warm sunny spot, sheltered in cooler areas. They do not like windy sites. They like rich, fertile soil that is well drained.

pH 6.0–6.5

Fertilizer When planting, apply bone meal to the hole. Once growing, the trees will require blood, fish and bone meal, or pelleted chicken manure, in the spring. Apply it in a wide band where you think the root tips are and not around the tree stem. Continue this annual feeding for 10 years, after which regular applications of the mulches should suffice, unless on poor soil where it will probably have to continue for the life of the tree.

Water The most important time to ensure the trees never go short of water is from the time the small fruitlets start to swell, until they start to show some colour. If you water beyond this time, on a regular basis, it will encourage diseases. Do not water in small doses; water steadily, but continuously for about an hour.

ROOTSTOCKS

M27 (Very dwarfing) Requires permanent staking and should grow on fertile soil with no competition from grass, weeds or any other plant. Produces a good crop early in the life of the tree.

M9 (Dwarfing) Same as M27.

M26 (Dwarfing) Slightly stronger grower than the M9 rootstock. Strong root system; ideal for growing in most soils. Stake for the first two to three years.

MM106 (Semi-dwarfing) Most widely used rootstock. Suitable for growing in fertile and poorer soils as it has a strong root system. Will crop well after two to three years.

MM111 (Vigorous on fertile soils, semi-vigorous on poor soils) Vigorous root system supports a vigorous top. Well-suited to poorer soils and will crop after two to three years.

M25 (Very vigorous) Suitable for orchards and for trees grown on poorer soils. Will not fruit early.

DIMENSIONS

The size of tree is determined by a combination of the variety and the rootstock onto which it is grafted. However, the size is also regulated by the pruning method used, so all sizes given below are for unpruned trees.

Height of tree
M27 1.5–1.8 m (5–6 ft)
M9 2.4–3 m (8–10 ft)
M26 2.4–3.6 m (8–12 ft)
MM106 3.6–5.4 m (12–18 ft)
MM111 6–9 m (20–28 ft)
M25 over 9 m (over 28 ft)

Planting distances
M27 1.2–1.8 m (4–6 ft)
M9 1.8–3 m (6–10 ft)
M26 2.4–4.5 m (8–15 ft)
MM106 3.6–4.5 m (12–15 ft)
MM111 4.5–7.5 m (15–25 ft)
M25 6–9 m (20–28 ft)

AFTER CARE

The most important job after feeding and watering is to keep weeds down, thus eliminating possible competition for the very important moisture. Each year, the trees will require pruning, either in summer or winter, to maintain their shape and to keep them under control. Thin the fruits to one fruit per cluster on normal soils and two fruits per cluster on poorer soils. Pears are somewhat heavier than apples, so it may be necessary to support some of the branches in particularly good fruiting years.

PRUNING

There are two basic categories of pruning: winter and summer. Winter pruning is carried out to encourage growth, so it is used when initially shaping a young tree or rejuvenating an older tree. Once the tree shape has been formed, and the tree is yielding fruit, the requirement for winter pruning is restricted to keeping a good balance between the older growths, while encouraging new shoots that will carry later crops. In this way, the tree will never become tired and unable to produce a decent crop. Summer pruning is carried out to encourage fruiting buds to be formed on the tree. It is generally used on spur-bearing varieties and tree forms that have a restricted growth, such as cordons and espaliers.

TREE FORMS

Bush A rounded head on a stem, usually about 90 cm (3 ft) high. Easy tree to prune and pick. Can be grown on all rootstocks except for MM111 and M25.

Half-standard Same shape as a bush with the classic lollipop look, but stem is about 1.35 m (4½ ft) high. Most pruning and picking carried out with a ladder. Grown on MM106 or MM111 rootstock.

Standard Same shape as the half-standard, but stem about 1.8 m (6 ft) high. All work carried out with a long ladder. Grown on MM111 rootstock.

The pruning of the above forms generally consists of the removal of dead, diseased or crossing branches in the winter and spur-pruning in the summer.

Pyramid Grafted onto a dwarfing rootstock such as M27, M9 or M26, although it can also be grown on MM106, if a taller tree is required. Easy to keep, with some pruning and picking done from the ground and some done with a ladder. About 2.5 m (8 ft) in height.

Espalier Best suited to growing on fences or wires, where it takes up no space. Can be grown as a two- or up to seven-tier tree with 30 cm (12 in) between the lateral branches. Almost all the work is carried out from the ground with each of the branches pruned as if they were individual cordons. Grown on M26 or MM106.

Stepover Shorter version of the espalier, as the leader is removed after only one tier. Usually grown as edging trees to paths and grown to a height where one can "step over" the tree. Grown on M27 or M9 rootstocks.

Fan Takes up hardly any room. Initially, two opposite shoots are trained out from the main stem and winter-pruned to encourage more shoots to form, until the desired shape of about eight main shoots (four on each side) is achieved. Each shoot is then summer pruned as a cordon. Grown on M26 or MM106.

Cordon Two definite forms of training. Firstly, a vertical cordon, sometimes called a minarette, which consists of a single stem that is trained perfectly vertically. All the shoots that come off this stem are spur-pruned in the summer. The other method is called an oblique cordon, which is grown in exactly the same way, only at 45 degrees to the ground. The advantage of the second method is that, because the plant is partially laid down, it reduces the amount of effort the tree puts into growing and increases the effort it puts into fruiting. Both types can be planted at only 75 cm (30 in) apart to maximize cropping space. Grown on M27, M9 and M26 rootstocks.

Festooned Grown like a bush, but the branches are pulled down and tied to the supporting stake with string, to give it a water fountain look. Bent over branches produce lots of fruiting buds around the bend and, as the branches are held down, this also restricts the growth. Grown on M27, M9, M26 and MM106 rootstocks.

Double-"U" cordon Very ornamental. A young, single stemmed tree, a whip, is pruned in the winter 30 cm (12 in) from the ground just above two good buds. Then the following winter the same thing is done again to each of the shoots that sprouted from the last pruning. The four resulting shoots are trained to each resemble the letter "U" giving a double-"U" cordon. Each stem is pruned as an individual cordon. Grown on M27, M9, M26 or MM106 rootstocks.

HARVESTING AND STORAGE

The easiest way to tell, initially, if fruit is ready for harvest is to cup your hand underneath the fruit, gently lift it up and twist slightly. If the fruit comes away from the tree easily then it is ready; if not, then leave it and try again in a few days. After the first year, noting down harvesting dates will give a good guide for future harvests. The earliest varieties are better picked in August, slightly before they are fully ripe. They can then be left to ripen off the tree for two or three days to get the best flavour. Once picked, it is vitally important that the fruits are handled with the utmost care, as they bruise very easily, which will shorten their storage term. Pick the fruit and place it gently into a basket, bucket, or other container that is lined with a soft material, and stack the fruits carefully. At no point should the apples be dropped onto one another. Any apples that are not suitable for storage should be eaten first.

As with all stored produce, it is vital that only perfect fruits are stored, as one rotten apple will quickly infect the rest. After they have passed a close inspection, place the perfect fruits carefully into a clear polythene bag, tie up the top and label it. To allow the fruits to breathe and lengthen their storage time, pierce the bag with a few small holes. An alternative method is to individually wrap each fruit in newspaper or tissue and place them

SPECIAL TIP

To minimize the problems of fruit drop, where the tree will shed a lot of the fruit due to overloading, it is important to thin the fruit. Most trees, in a good year, will set a lot of fruit with some naturally dropping in the early summer. To prevent a further drop that will impact on the yield, remove the central or "King" fruit from each cluster first, as this is generally distorted. Then leave one fruit per cluster, ensuring there are about 10–15 cm (4–6 in) between fruits. If there has been a poor fruit set, two fruitlets can be left per cluster. It does seem harsh, but this will ensure good fruit size and an excellent harvest.

into a tray as a single layer. In both cases, the fruits need to be placed into a dark, cool, frost- and rodent-free store. Check the fruits regularly for signs of rot or disease and remove them.

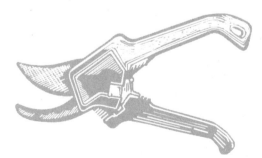

PESTS

Aphid, codling moth, apple sawfly, apple and pear sucker, wasps, birds and the winter moth caterpillar.

DISEASES

Canker, powdery mildew, apple scab, fireblight, bitter pit and brown rot.

DESSERT VARIETIES

Ashmead's Kernel Late-flowering. Pale green fruits, with russetting. Harvest in November and December. Store until February.

Blenheim Orange Can also be used as a cooker and considered to be the best dual-purpose apple there is. Triploid, so requires two pollinators. Mid-season variety ready in November. Orange-yellow fruits with red stripes, russetting and a distinct nutty flavour. Store until February.

Cox's Orange Pippin Not easy to grow. Orange red on green fruits. Superb flavour. Pick in October, store until January.

Crispin Heavy-cropping, mid-season variety. Yellow-green skin and crisp taste. Large apples. Can also be cooked. Harvest in October. Store until April.

Discovery Mid-season. Bright red on yellow fruits. Harvest in August and September. Store until September.

Egremont Russet Compact tree. Flowers early. Golden-brown apples with patches of russetting. Harvest in October. Store until December.

Ellison's Orange Distinct aniseed flavour. Flowers early. Green fruit with red flush and striping. Harvest in September. Store until October.

Greensleeves Excellent pollinator. Produces fruit early in its life. Mid-season flowerer. Harvest in September. Store until October.

Idared As good raw as it is cooked. Flowers early. Harvest red fruits in November. Store until March.

James Grieve Dual-purpose, eating and cooking apple. Mid-season flowerer. Pale yellow fruits, orange-red flush. Harvest in September. Store until October.

Jonagold Requires two pollinators. High-yielding. Mid-season flowerer. Greenish-yellow apple overlaid with red. Harvest in October. Store until March.

Jupiter Distinctive Cox taste. Vigorous grower, if not on a dwarfing rootstock. Mid-season flowerer. Requires two pollinators. Orange-red fruits, on green-yellow. Harvest in November. Store until February.

Laxton's Fortune Early variety. Red-flushed, green fruit. Harvest in September and October. Store until February.

Lord Lambourne Compact tree. Heavy cropper. Early flowering. Green-yellow fruits, with red flush. Harvest in September and October. Store until November.

Pixie Yellow apples, red stripes and orange-red flush. Harvest in October. Store until December or January. Flavour improves in store.

Queen Cox Better fruit colour than Cox. Self-fertile. Harvest in September. Store until January.

Spartan Mid-season flowerer. Purple-red, on yellow. Apples have a heavy bloom. Harvest in October. Store until January.

Sunset Disease-resistant. Mid-season flowerer. Cox flavour. Harvest in October and November. Store until December.

Tydeman's Late Orange Mid-season. Orange-red on yellow fruits, some russetting. Harvest in December. Store until April.

Worcester Pearmain Mid-season. Excellent pollinator. Bright red on yellow fruits. Harvest in September. Store until October.

CULINARY VARIETIES

Bramley's Seedling Vigorous, long-lived variety, best on a dwarfing rootstock. Large green fruits. Requires two pollinators. Mid-season flowerer. Harvest in October. Store until March.

Crawley Beauty Late-flowering. Use for culinary or eating. Green, flushed fruits. Harvest in November and December. Store until April.

Edward VII Good for colder gardens. Late flowering. Yellowish green fruits. Harvest in December. Store until April.

Emneth Early Early flowering. Usually behaves as a biennial. Heavy cropper. Scab and mildew resistant. Harvest in August and September.

Grenadier Compact. Disease-resistant. Mid-season flowerer. Harvest in August and September. Store until October.

Howgate Wonder Late-flowering. Green-yellow fruit, red flushes. Harvest in October. Store until February.

Lanes Prince Albert Mid-season flowerer. Green fruits, some red stripes. Harvest in November. Store until March.

Reverend W. Wilks Early flowering. Enormous pale-green fruits. Harvest in September. Store until November. One of the best for baking.

APRICOTS
Prunus armeniaca

Rosaceae

Apricots are winter hardy, but as they flower early, they are
susceptible to spring frosts so protection is vital. They require
a warm, sunny position to ripen the fruit, so they grow well
on a south-facing wall or fence as a fan. Apricots are akin
to plums and require much the same growing conditions
although, unlike plums, all the varieties are self-fertile, so
only one tree is required in a garden.

DATES

Flowering time February–March

Harvesting July–September

Cropping age 2–3 years

SITE AND SOIL

Site Sunny and sheltered site and a well-drained soil. Not fussy, although a clay or deep loam is preferred.

pH 6.0–6.5

Fertilizer As for apples (*see* page 38).

Water As for apples (*see* page 38).

ROOTSTOCKS

St Julien A (Semi-vigorous) Predominantly used on bush, half-standard, pyramid and fan types.

Torinel (Semi-vigorous) Produces medium-sized trees that crop well.

DIMENSIONS

Height of tree
St Julien A 3.6–3.9 m (12–13 ft)
Torinel 2.7–3 m (9–10 ft)

Planting distances
St Julien A 3.9–5.4 m (13–18 ft)
Torinel 3–3.3 m (10–11 ft)

AFTER CARE

As for plums (see pages 79–80).

PRUNING

As for plums (see page 80).

TREE FORMS

Usually grown as fans, but in warmer areas can be grown as bush, half-standard and pyramid.

HARVESTING AND STORAGE

Harvest when fruit is soft to the touch and comes away easily from the tree. They will store for a few days in a cool area.

PESTS

Aphids, birds, red spider mite and sawfly.

DISEASES

Silverleaf, bacterial canker and rust.

SELECTED VARIETIES

Alfred Some resistance to dieback. Orange fruits during July and August.

Early Moorpark Heavy cropper. Orange fruits. Harvest in July and August.

SPECIAL TIP

It is important that you give apricots the drainage they require, otherwise you could encourage a common problem. They can often suffer from a fungal infection known as "dieback", where stems and branches will start to die back, often from the tip but it can happen from anywhere up the stem or branch. The leaves will wilt, turn yellow and fall off as the stem dies. If left, it will continue down the stem or branch and eventually kill the tree, so prune it out as soon as you spot it.

Flavourcot Compact tree. Orange fruits with red blush. Harvest in August.

Larquen Heavy cropper. Large orange fruits. Harvest in August.

Moorpark Red flushed, orange fruits in August and September.

Petit Muscat Golf-ball-sized, very flavoursome, orange fruits. Harvest in late August.

BLACKBERRIES AND HYBRID BERRIES
Rubus fruticosus

Rosaceae

Blackberries are usually grouped together with the rest of the briar fruits, as they have the same cultivation requirements. This group includes loganberries, tayberries, boysenberries, youngberries and numerous others. There are many instances where blackberries can be picked from wild plants growing in hedgerows, but these are not as sweet as the cultivated forms. To ensure that your plant is healthy, always buy virus-free stock from a reputable supplier. All these varieties are vigorous, so they will require plenty of space in the garden to crop. Their great asset is that they are ready for harvest late in the season, so they tend to follow on nicely from raspberries. Blackberries, as in the wild, grow in most situations, but the hybrids generally require more attention and similar conditions to raspberries.

DATES

Flowering time May–June

Harvesting August–October

Cropping age 1–2 years

SITE AND SOIL

Site Being vigorous growers, blackberries tend to be grown against walls, fences and wires where there is plenty of space. Hybrid berries require a sunny position in well-prepared soil that is moisture-retentive, but free draining. Blackberries are not so particular and will grow in almost any soil and are best in a position that is not in full sun. They will even grow and bear fruit in the shade.

pH 5.5–6.0

Fertilizer Mulch each winter with well-rotted farmyard manure or compost. If necessary apply liquid seaweed to combat iron deficiency.

Water All types benefit from plenty of water.

DIMENSIONS

Planting distances 2.4–3.9 m (8–13 ft) between plants, dependent on variety.

AFTER CARE

Once planted, the canes need to be cut to within 15 cm (6 in) of the ground. The new shoots will then grow up in the spring and these can be trained to one side of the support and tied in. These canes will produce fruit in the following season. As the new canes start to grow in the second year after planting, they can be tied on the opposite side of the support so that they do not get mixed up with the fruiting canes, with these fruiting in year three. On soils that have a pH of over 7.0, briar fruits are likely to suffer from iron deficiency, which shows as yellowing between the leaf veins. This can be easily remedied with liquid seaweed, as a summer foliar feed, and a dressing of seaweed meal in the spring. Mulch around the plants in summer to retain moisture. Pull out unwanted suckers as they appear.

PRUNING

Once the fruiting canes have been harvested, they can be cut down to ground level to re-shoot the following spring.

HARVESTING AND STORAGE

The fruits are ready when they have turned a lovely deep colour and are soft and juicy. They can then be carefully removed from the canes by twisting the stalk slightly so that the central core is not left behind. They can then be frozen, cooked or kept in the fridge for a couple of days, but cannot be stored in any other way.

PESTS

Aphids, birds and raspberry beetle.

DISEASES

Botrytis and spur blight.

SELECTED VARIETIES

Black Butte Enormous fruits, up to 5 cm (2 in) long. Fairly thornless. Harvest from mid-July to late August.

Boysenberry Unusual fruit. Big, purplish-black fruits, naturally sweet flavour. Thornless. Harvest in July and August.

Helen Compact and thornless blackberry. Large fruit. Harvest from early July to late August.

Karaka Black Huge, dark blackberries. Harvest in August and September.

Loch Ness Thornless blackberry. Harvest in mid-August.

Loganberry LY654 Hybrid between a blackberry and a raspberry. Burgundy-red, sweet fruits. Thornless. Harvest from July to September.

Tayberry Buckingham Blackberry and raspberry cross. Bright red fruits turn to deep purple when ready. Harvest in July and August.

Youngberry Vigorous. Mulberry flavoured, square-shaped fruit. Harvest when totally black, from July to September.

BLACKCURRANTS
Ribes nigrum

Grossulariaceae

Younger, better-fruiting stems appear from below ground. Due to their growth habits, blackcurrants are best suited to growing as a bush. They are gross feeders and like a soil that is high in well-rotted organic matter, so before planting it is vital that the ground is prepared properly. It is also possible to grow blackcurrants in containers for up to three years, so that they can be moved under cover for an early crop. When selecting the variety that is best for your garden, bear in mind that some varieties show excellent resistance to many of the pests and diseases that affect this crop, with others having an excellent flavour and vitamin C content.

53

DATES

Flowering time March–April

Harvesting July–September

Cropping age 2 years

SITE AND SOIL

Site Full sun, although they will tolerate semi-shade, in a rich soil prepared with plenty of well-rotted organic matter.

pH 6.5

Fertilizer High nitrogen requirement, so apply blood, fish and bone meal during early spring and mulch with well-rotted compost or manure. Apply fertilizer again in early summer if growth rate has not improved.

SPECIAL TIP

When planting a new blackcurrant bush, bury the stems about 5 cm (2 in) below the level at which they were grown, so that the shoots have somewhere to grow from when the bush is stool-pruned.

Water As the fruits start to swell and show colour, the plants must not go short of water. In dry spells, ensure the soil stays moist.

DIMENSIONS

Planting distances 1.5 m (5 ft) 1.8 m (6 ft) rows

AFTER CARE

Water the soil at the base of the bushes, to minimize spread of disease. Net bushes once the fruits start to colour against birds.

PRUNING

As blackcurrants fruit best on one-year-old shoots, in the first season after an autumn or spring planting there will be hardly any fruit produced, but in the second year there should be a prolific crop. If you have more than one bush then select half to prune right down to the ground and half to leave for the next year's fruit. Then at the end of the next year, prune down the fruited bushes so that the ones stooled the previous year will fruit the next year. In this way, you create a two-year cycle. If there are not enough bushes to do this, then cut down half of the shoots in the bush every other year for the same effect. This will keep the bushes vigorous and producing the maximum crop for at least 20 years.

HARVESTING AND STORAGE

Fruits can be harvested as soon as the strig, on which they hang, is completely ripe. Modern cultivars have had even ripening bred into them. However, the older varieties will have to be harvested by picking off the individual fruits as they ripen.

PESTS

Birds, aphids, big bud mite, sawfly and capsid bug.

DISEASES

Botrytis, mildew and reversion disease.

SELECTED VARIETIES

Baldwin Compact plant. Reasonable yield. Harvest in August and September.

Ben Nevis Frost resistant. Large fruits. Useful on poor soils. Resistant to frost and mildew. Harvest in July and August.

Ben Sarek Compact. Abundant crop. Black fruit in short strigs. Resistant to mildew and frost. Freezes well. Harvest in July and August.

Jostaberry Hybrid between blackcurrant and gooseberry. Blackcurrant fruits, with a blackcurrant flavour, but the size of small gooseberries. Vigorous and thornless. Resistant to mildew and big bud mite. Harvest in July.

Titania Heavy crops of large fruit over a long period. Mildew resistant.

BLUEBERRIES
Vaccinum spp.

Ericaceae

These beautifully flavoured, small blue berries are highly sought after and are delicious when cooked or eaten raw. There are two types: the bilberry and the highbush blueberry. Both have to grow in an acid soil, although they do take well to containers. However, the plants are slow to get going. They will usually start to bear a few fruit from the second or third year, but they do not achieve full production until the sixth or seventh year. Regarded as a fruiting bush, they also have a place in the ornamental garden as they have beautiful white, bell-shaped flowers followed by clusters of blue fruit. In autumn, the leaves turn wonderful shades of red. Most varieties are not self-fertile, so they will require a pollinator.

DATES

Flowering time May

Harvesting July–August

Cropping age 3–8 years

SITE AND SOIL

Site Acid soil with good moisture retention, but not waterlogged. Full sun, but grows in semi-shade.

pH 4.0–5.5

Fertilizer Late winter feed of blood, fish and bone meal.

Water Never let them dry out, but only use rainwater. Mulch plants with bark mulch or pine needles to conserve moisture.

DIMENSIONS

Planting distances 1.8 m (6 ft)

AFTER CARE

Net against birds.

PRUNING

Blueberries fruit on 2–3-year-old wood, so in the first few years just remove the tips of the branches and the weaker shoots to shape the bush. Then, in late February or early March, when the buds are visible, remove some of the older branches that have fruited and are more than four years old. Remove any weak or crossing branches at this stage. Carrying out this procedure on an annual basis will provide a good supply of fruiting branches.

HARVESTING AND STORAGE

The fruits do not ripen all at once and will be at their prime about 7–10 days after they turn blue. At this point, they will come away from the bush very easily.

PESTS

Birds.

DISEASES

Botrytis.

SELECTED VARIETIES

Berkley Vigorous, spreading, high-yielding bush. Very large, light blue berries. Harvest in July. Golden winter stems make a nice feature. Requires a pollinator.

Bluecrop Heavy cropper. Large berries with slightly tart flavour. Harvest in July. Self-fertile, but will crop better if cross-pollinated.

Duke Heavy cropper. Light blue, medium-sized fruits. Harvest in early July. Self-fertile but will crop better if cross-pollinated.

Herbert Best flavour. Very large, dark blue berries. Harvest in August. Requires a pollinator.

Sunshine Blue Dwarf, growing to 90–120 cm (3–4 ft). Tolerant of a higher pH. Pink flowers and large blue berries. Ideal for a container. Self-fertile but will crop better if cross-pollinated.

CHERRIES – SWEET AND ACID

Prunus avium and *Prunus cerasus*

Rosaceae

These two types of cherry have been classed together, as their cultivation techniques are identical, although they differ greatly in the fruits produced. Sweet cherries, as the name implies, are grown for their lovely flavour and can be eaten raw, straight from the tree. However, acid cherries have a much sharper flavour and do not taste good raw, so these are used for cooking, where their flavour is supreme. They also differ in that the acid cherries are less vigorous and therefore much better suited to small, modern gardens. They can be grown as fan-trained trees, whereas the sweet cherries are really suited to growing as bushes or pyramid trees, but can be grown as fans on a dwarfing rootstock. Both are susceptible to frost damage at flowering time, although the sweet cherry is slightly more prone than the acid cherry, which can be grown in cooler positions. Most cherry varieties are self-fertile, although some are not and will require a pollinator.

DATES

Flowering time Late February–March

Harvesting July–September

Cropping age 4–5 years

SITE AND SOIL

Site Sweet cherries require a sheltered spot to minimize frost damage to the flowers. Acid cherries can be grown on north-facing walls or fences, as long as they are not in a frost pocket. Well-drained soil, with clay or deep loam is preferred.

pH 6.0–6.5

Fertilizer Sweet cherries require the most feeding, so apply blood, fish and bone meal or pelleted chicken manure around the tree base in late winter. Acid cherries require more nitrogen, so apply dried blood in the spring. Apply an annual mulch of well-rotted manure or organic matter for both.

Water Cherries suffer from fruit splitting, which is caused by erratic watering, so keep the soil moist, but not waterlogged, and avoid using overhead irrigation (particularly once the fruit has set).

ROOTSTOCKS

Gisela 5 (Semi-dwarfing) Very good for fan, pyramid and bush trees.

Colt (Semi-vigorous) Best for standards and bush trees in larger gardens.

DIMENSIONS

Height of tree
Gisela 5 1.8–2.4 m (6–8 ft)
Colt 3–3.6 m (10–12 ft)

Planting distances
Gisela 5 2.4–3 m (8–10 ft)
Colt 3.6–3.9 m (12–13 ft)

AFTER CARE

During cold weather in the spring, protect the blossom on the trees using fleece. Keep the bases of the trees weed free and water when required. Protect the trees from birds by covering them with netting, just as the first fruits start to ripen.

PRUNING

For standard and bush forms there is very little pruning required, except for clearing out dead, diseased and crossing branches. Cut right back to the main branch. Fan-trained cherries are pruned using the same method as for peaches, so each summer you should let the side-shoots grow until they have achieved four-to-six leaves, and a new shoot is growing at the base. At this point, the growing tip can be removed. In order to channel all the trees efforts into producing fruit, it is important to pinch out any other new growth. In late summer, once all the fruit has been picked, cut out the shoots that have borne fruit and tie in the replacement shoots ready for fruiting the following year. All pruning is done in mid-summer to reduce the risks posed by silverleaf.

TREE FORMS

Standard, bush, pyramid and fan.

HARVESTING AND STORAGE

Sweet and acid cherries come easily away from the tree when ripe. Pull by the stalk and not the fruit. They will keep for a few days in the fridge.

PESTS

Birds, aphids, winter moth caterpillars, sawfly, wasps and red spider mite.

DISEASES

Silverleaf, bacterial canker and rust.

SELECTED VARIETIES

Amber Prolific cropper. Requires a pollinator. Medium-sized, pale yellow skinned fruit. Harvest in July.

Bradbourne Black Large black fruits have dark flesh and juice. Harvest in late July. Can be pollinated by Stella.

Early Rivers Early flowering. Large, black fruits, red flesh. Harvest in mid-June. Can be pollinated by Merton Glory.

Lapins Late flowering. Very large, black fruits, dark juice. Harvest in early August. Self-fertile.

May Duke Early flowering. Red fruits. Harvest in July. Self-fertile, although better if pollinated by Lapins or Merton Premier.

Merton Glory Large yellow fruit, crimson flush and white flesh. Disease resistant. Harvest in June and July. Pollinated by Early Rivers.

Merton Premier Red-black fruit. Harvest in June and July. Pollinate with Lapins or May Duke.

Morello Best acid cherry for culinary use. Large dark red fruits, red flesh. Harvest in August. Self-fertile.

Nabella Acid cherry. Large, round dark red fruits. Harvest in June and July. Self-fertile.

SPECIAL TIP

Only some sweet cherries are self-fertile, with certain varieties being incompatible as pollinators so check varieties before buying. The Morello acid cherry is self-fertile and will also fertilize other sweet cherry varieties that flower at the same time.

Napoleon Yellow fruits overlaid with red. Harvest in July. Pollinated with Lapins, Nabella or Stella.

Rubi High-yielding. Sweet red cherries. Harvest in early July. Self-fertile.

Stella Large, sweet red fruits and red flesh. Harvest in lat July. Self-fertile, but will produce a better crop if pollinated.

FIGS
Ficus carica

Although viewed very much as exotic fruiting plants, figs are easy to grow as long as they can be given a sunny, hot spot where they will get the light levels and heat required for successful fruiting. They are grown outside in temperate climates as fan-trained trees, although they can be grown as half-standards in pots and brought in under protection for the winter. Figs can also be grown in greenhouses if there isn't a suitable place to situate them outside, using the same growing methods as for outdoor figs. In their natural habitat, they will fruit twice a year, but in more temperate climates the best that can be hoped for is one successful crop per year. Given the right position, their soil requirements are very basic, as they originate in areas of poor soil. Giving them too good a soil will encourage too much growth and not enough fruiting. This makes them eminently suitable for growing against a house wall, where they will be planted over the foundations. Unlike a lot of fruiting trees, they are grown on their own roots and not grafted onto a rootstock. They are unlike other fruiting trees listed, as they do not produce a visible flower. Instead, an embryo fruit is produced in the season prior to cropping in temperate climates, and the flower is within this fruit. All figs are self-fertile, so this fruit will simply swell in size until ready for harvest.

DATES

Flowering time Not applicable

Harvesting August–October

Cropping age 3–4 years

SITE AND SOIL

Site Sunny and sheltered position in any soil type that is free draining, but moisture retentive. Ideally, figs prefer a south-facing position. If the soil is too fertile it can be dug out and the bottom of the hole into which the tree is going to be planted can be filled with rubble and even paving slabs or bricks up the sides to restrict the root run, before a mixture of soil and organic matter is replaced around the roots. This will restrict the roots and prevent them growing into the very fertile soil, which would produce plenty of good growth but little in the way of figs.

pH 6.5–7.0

Fertilizer Feed of pelleted chicken manure every other spring for trees with restricted roots. Feed all with a high-potash, seaweed liquid feed in summer.

Water Water regularly.

ROOTSTOCKS

Grown on own roots, so not applicable.

DIMENSIONS

Height of tree
Fan-trained 2–2.4 m (6–8 ft)
Bush or half-standard 6–7.5 m (20–25 ft)

Planting distances
Fan-trained 3.3 m (11 ft)
Bush or half-standard 3 m (10 ft)

AFTER CARE

Water as required and keep the area around the trees weed free. Feed during summer with a high-potash, liquid seaweed mixture.

PRUNING

Figs do not need to be pruned in order to form a fan, but appropriate shoots should be selected and tied in. All pruning is carried out in early spring, when the worst of the severe frosts has passed. Remove a quarter of the oldest wood of an established tree, cutting to within 5–8 cm (2–3 in) of the base, so as to leave a stump from which new, young shoots will grow. Remove all crossing branches and branches growing into the tree and tie in the remaining shoots. With a bush or half-standard tree, the procedure is much the same, but be careful to maintain the shape.

TREE FORMS

Fan, bush and half-standard.

HARVESTING AND STORAGE

The darker skinned fruits will turn purple when ready for harvest, while the lighter-skinned varieties will become yellow. It is possible to store figs by drying or freezing them, but they are much tastier straight from the tree.

PESTS

Birds and red spider mite (with the latter only on greenhouse figs).

DISEASES

Botrytis and canker.

SELECTED VARIETIES

Brown Turkey Hardy. Brown-purple fruits, sweet red flesh. Harvest in August and September.

Brunswick Green-yellow, large fruits ripen about two weeks earlier than Brown Turkey.

White Marseilles Green fruits ripen to yellow with white flesh. Harvest in September. Not as hardy as other varieties.

GOOSEBERRIES
Ribes uva-crispa

Grossulariaceae

For the fruit lover, this plant is a must. Gooseberries produce
the first soft fruits of the year, with a well-cultivated plant
lasting up to 20 years. They are closely allied to redcurrants
and therefore share similar cultivation requirements. There
are many varieties to choose from, with the fruits ranging in
colour from yellow to green and even red. Some plants have
enormous spines, while others are spineless. Certain varieties
have excellent disease resistance, while some have none. As
with redcurrants, gooseberries can also be trained in various
forms including bushes, cordons, fans and standards. All
of this, combined with the fact that they grow well in
containers, means that every garden should have a
gooseberry plant somewhere.

DATES

Flowering time March–April

Harvesting June–July

Cropping age 1–2 years

SITE AND SOIL

Site Avoid planting in frost pockets. Gooseberries do not require particularly fertile soil, but well-rotted organic matter – dug in prior to planting – will be beneficial. They dislike waterlogging, so if this is a problem improve the soil before planting. The plants do not require a lot of direct sunlight, although the dessert varieties will be sweeter if they are exposed to direct sunlight for part of the day.

pH 6.5

Fertilizer Do not over fertilize the ground, as this will encourage the plants to put on plenty of growth, but little fruit. However, they do benefit from an application of rock potash in late winter or early spring. A mulch of well-rotted organic matter each spring should suffice.

Water Keep watered as the fruits start to swell.

DIMENSIONS

Planting distances
Bushes 1.5 m (5 ft); 1.8 m (6 ft) rows
Single cordons 30cm (12 in)
Double cordons 60 cm (24 in)
Triple cordons 90 cm (36 in)
Fans 1.5m (5 ft)

The "arms" of the cordons should be spaced 30 cm (12 in) apart.

AFTER CARE

Pull off suckers growing up from the base of the stem. Mulch each spring, as this will help to conserve moisture and suppress weeds. If frosts are forecast in the spring, cover the plants with fleece to protect the flowers. Net in autumn to protect the fruit buds from attack by bull finches and, as fruit ripens, blackbirds. If there is an over-abundant crop, then thin the fruits by picking alternate ones before they are ready and using them for cooking. Allow the remainder to grow and ripen to their full size.

PRUNING

Pruning is carried out in summer when all the sideshoots are cut back to five leaves, immediately after the crop has been harvested. The diseased and congested branches can also be removed at this time. For cordons and fan-trained gooseberries the sideshoots are pruned back at the same time, down to 8 cm (3 in) from the base, with any secondary shoots coming off these pruned shoots cut back to 2.5 cm (1 in).

HARVESTING AND STORAGE

The thinnings can be harvested before fully ripe for cooking, but the remainder are picked in late summer when fully ripe, to benefit from the full sweetness. The fruits are quite tough and can be sharply pulled to remove them from the bush. Do not store, unless frozen.

PESTS

Aphids, capsid bug, sawfly and birds.

DISEASES

Botrytis, mildew and leaf spot.

SELECTED VARIETIES

Careless Heavy cropper. Culinary. Pale green fruits. Harvest in June. Susceptible to mildew.

Greenfinch Culinary variety. Compact. Bright green fruits. Resistant to mildew and leaf spot.

Invicta Dessert or culinary. Vigorous. Large, pale green berries. Thin in early May for cooking and pick main crop early June. Grown as bush, cordon or fan.

Leveller Dessert. Susceptible to mildew. Very large, oval green fruit, ripening yellow-green. Harvest in June and July.

Martlet Heavy-cropping, red-fruited and hairless dessert variety. Harvest in June and July. Disease resistant.

Pax Dessert variety. Large red fruits. Almost thornless. Mildew resistant. Harvest in June.

Whinham's Industry Dessert or culinary. Suitable for growing on heavier soils and in semi-shade. Susceptible to mildew. Harvest in June and July.

PEACHES AND NECTARINES

Prunus persica and
Prunus persica var *nectarina*

Rosaceae

When talking about peaches it is also possible to use the same information for nectarines, as the same cultivation techniques apply to both. They originate from China and are perfectly winter hardy, although, due to their early season, they can be susceptible to hard, late frosts when in flower. Woven fleece draped over the tree when it is in flower can prevent frost damage. Both peaches and nectarines are self-fertile, so there is no need to have more than one tree if you don't have enough space. There are two distinct types of peaches: the conventional peach cultivar and the compact cultivar. The conventional peach cultivar can be grown against a wall, in a fan shape, or free standing as a bush or pyramid. The compact form is best suited to containers on a warm patio or sheltered part of the garden. To maximise the crop of any peach tree, it is important to give them shelter. Fan-trained types prefer a warm wall, with bushes and pyramids only being grown in warmer areas. They can also be greenhouse-grown in any area. The peach is a difficult fruit to grow, as the pruning and training methods are more involved than with most fruits. They can be affected by a variety of problems, which will need attention throughout the year. That said, they are a very juicy fruit which, if thinned correctly, should produce a bumper crop for up to 30 years.

DATES

Flowering time April

Harvesting July–September

Cropping age 4 years

SITE AND SOIL

Site Free-draining, moisture-retentive soil in full sun.

pH 6.5–7.0

Fertilizer For the first four years, feed in early spring with pelleted chicken manure. Then apply an annual mulch of well-rotted manure or garden compost.

Water Do not allow to dry out during the growing season.

DIMENSIONS

Height of tree
Fan-trained 2–2.4 m (6–8 ft)
Bush and Pyramid 2–2.4 m (6–8 ft)

Spread of tree
Fan-trained 3.3–4.5 m (11–15 ft)
Bush and Pyramid 1.5–2 m (5–6 ft)

ROOTSTOCKS

St Julien A (Semi-vigorous) Suitable for bushes, pyramids or fan-trained plants.

Brompton (Semi-vigorous) Suitable for fan-trained plants.

Montclaire (Medium vigour) Suitable for bushes, pyramids or fan-trained plants.

Pixy (Dwarfing) Suitable for container-grown plants.

AFTER CARE

Hand-pollinate flowers using a camel-hair brush, taking pollen from one flower and passing it to another.

PRUNING

It is important to prune peaches once the sap has started to rise and they have just started into growth, as this will minimize the risk of infection by silver leaf and bacterial canker. Peaches fruit on the young wood formed during the previous season, producing two distinct types of bud, the rounded fruiting bud and the much more pointed growth bud. When pruning it is important to cut to a growing bud, as this will then grow out to produce the following year's crop. Bushes and pyramids are very easy to prune as this only really involves cutting out dead, diseased or crossing branches. However, fan-trained trees are a little more complex in their pruning. Each summer it is necessary to let the side-shoots grow until they have achieved four-to-six leaves, and a new shoot is growing at the base. At this point, the growing tip is removed. In order to channel all the trees efforts into producing fruit, it is important to pinch out any other new growth. In late summer, once all the fruit has been picked, cut out the shoots that have borne all the fruit and tie in the replacement shoots ready for fruiting the following year.

HARVESTING AND STORAGE

Peaches are ripe when they can be removed easily from the tree with a gentle twist; do not squeeze them. The fruits do not store for more than a few days, unless they are bottled.

PESTS

Aphids, red spider mite and scale insect.

DISEASES

Peach leaf curl, bacterial canker, silver leaf and brown rot.

SPECIAL TIP

To prevent the tree succumbing badly to peach leaf curl and looking unsightly, attach a thin polythene cover that can be rolled down during wet weather and rolled up when no rain is forecast.

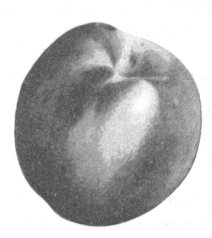

SELECTED VARIETIES

Peaches

Duke of York Reliable, early cropper. Green fruit with white flesh. Harvest in mid-July.

Francis Late flowering. Red flush over a white skin, white flesh. Some resistance to leaf curl. Harvest in early September.

Garden Lady Dwarf. Protect in greenhouse or conservatory during winter. Fruit with yellow flesh. Harvest in August.

Oriane Flat peach. Yellow flesh. Fruits well in its early years. Harvest in August.

Peregrine Light green and crimson skin, white flesh. Harvest in August and September.

Red Haven Orange skin, red flush with yellow flesh. Harvest in August

Rochester Excellent in cooler climates. Large, golden and crimson-skinned fruit, yellow flesh. Harvest in August.

Sirius Very early. White flesh. Harvest in late July and early August.

Nectarines

Early Rivers Pale yellow flesh. Harvest in August.

Fantasia Crimson skin, yellow flesh. Harvest in late August.

Jalousia Flat-fruited. Yellow-skinned. Harvest in early September.

Pineapple Yellow flesh, flavour reminiscent of pineapple. Harvest in September.

PEARS
Pyrus communis

Rosaceae

A fruit that is found in most gardens and no
wonder, as it must be the best-tasting tree
fruit there is. However, it does require more
mollycoddling than apples to achieve a good crop.
It flowers early, so the flowers are very susceptible to
frost damage, which could impact on the final yield. It
also require more sunlight and warmth than apples, so
planting in a sheltered sunny area or next to a south or west
facing wall would improve the yield. Pears are closely allied to
apples, in that their pollination requirements are similar. The
fruit is ready at the same time of year and pruning methods are
identical, as are their training and storage methods. As with
apples, they are very tolerant of poor soils, although
incorporating plenty of organic matter will reap rewards. The
tree will require protection from the wind. Unlike apples, most
pear varieties will need a period of time to ripen fully after
being harvested from the tree; usually about two to three
weeks. Depending on the variety, pears will usually begin to
fruit after two years and will continue providing a good crop
for up to 40 years, if maintained correctly.

DATES

Flowering time March–April

Harvesting August–October

Cropping age 2 years

SITE AND SOIL

Site Warm, sheltered sunny site out of the wind. Can be grown under glass. They prefer a rich, fertile soil that is well-drained. The ideal time to plant pear trees is in the autumn, when they are dormant and the soil is still warm and moist.

pH 6.0–6.5

Fertilizer When planting, apply a good handful of bone meal to the hole. Once growing, apply blood, fish and bone or pelleted chicken manure in the spring. Apply in a wide band where you think the root tips are, and not around the tree stem. Once established, feeding should no longer be required.

Water Pears are not tolerant of a lack of water so they need to be kept moist, particularly during the growing season.

ROOTSTOCKS

Quince C (Dwarfing) Use for all growing methods.

Quince A (Semi-dwarfing) Used by growers for orchard trees. Can be used for bush types and trained forms on poor soils.

DIMENSIONS

Height of tree
Quince C 2.4–3 m (8–10 ft)
Quince A 3.6–4.5 m (12–15 ft)

SPECIAL TIP

When choosing your tree it is worth bearing in mind that the form, rootstock and cultivar will determine the crop yield. For example, a bush tree grown on Quince A will produce a high yield, while one grown as a cordon on Quince C will produce the lowest yield.

AFTER CARE

Keep watering, particularly in dry weather. Each year the trees will require pruning, either in summer or winter, to maintain their shape and to keep them under control. As they are not as vigorous as apples, pears can be pruned harder if necessary, without stimulating too much growth. Thin fruits to one fruit per cluster, on normal soils and two fruits per cluster on poorer soils. Pears are somewhat heavier than apples, so you might need to support some of the branches in good fruiting years.

PRUNING

This is almost identical to the methods used for apples (see pages 39–40) and, as most pears are spur bearers, an established tree is pruned in mid-summer to create more fruiting spurs. As with apples, crossing, diseased and dead branches should be removed.

TREE FORMS

Pears can generally be grown using the same methods as for apples: bush, half-standard, pyramid, espalier, fan, stepover, cordon, festooned and double-"U" cordon.

HARVESTING AND STORAGE

The method of twisting and lifting, as for apples (see pages 41–2), also applies to pears. This is usually carried out while they are still firm and not fully ripe, as they will ripen off the tree. Early maturing varieties will require about two to three weeks before they are fully ripe, after which they will begin to turn mushy. The later season pears can be stored beyond Christmas by using the same method as for apples.

PESTS

Sawfly, aphids, winter moth, codling moth, pear leaf blister mite, apple and pear sucker, birds and wasps.

DISEASES

Canker, brown rot, scab and fireblight.

SELECTED VARIETIES

Beth Upright, so ideal for small gardens. Late season flowering. Pale yellow fruits. Harvest in August and September. Store until September. Pollinate with Catillac, Doyenne du Comice or Onward.

Beurre Hardy Large, russet-brown fruits. Spectacular scarlet autumn leaf colour. Mid-season flowerer. Harvest in September. Store until October. Pollinate with Concorde, Conference and Williams bon Chretien.

Catillac Late season flowerer. Large and hard fruits. Ideal for cooking. Harvest in September and October. Store until March or April. Pollinate with Beth, Doyenne du Comice or Onward.

Concorde Late-season flowerer. Excellent pollinator. Pale green fruits, rosy flush. Harvest in October. Store until November. Pollinate with Beurre Hardy, Conference and Williams bon Chretien.

Conference Mid-season flowerer. Long and narrow, pale green, firm fruit. Harvest in September and October. Store until November. Self-fertile. Better if cross-pollinated with Beurre Hardy, Concorde and Williams bon Chretien.

Doyenne du Comice Late flowerer. Red flushed, green fruits that turn yellow when ripe. Harvest in September and October. Store until November. Pollinate with Beth, Catillac or Onward

Emile d'Heyst Early flowering. Yellow-green fruit. Harvest in October and November. Store until the end of November. Pollinate with Louise Bonne of Jersey.

Louise Bonne of Jersey Early flowering. Pale green fruits, red flush. Harvest in September and October. Store until the end of October. Pollinate with Emile d'Heyst.

Onward Mid-season flowering. Red flushed, yellow-green fruits. Harvest in September. Store until November. Pollinate with Beth, Catillac or Doyenne du Comice.

Williams Bon Chretien Mid-season flowering. Red-spotted, yellow-skinned fruit. Harvest in September. Store until October. Pollinate with Beurre Hardy, Concorde and Conference.

PLUMS, GAGES AND DAMSONS
Prunus domestica and *Prunus insititia*

Rosaceae

An extremely worthwhile crop to grow in areas that do not suffer from late spring frosts, as these early flowering stone fruits are very susceptible to the cold. Plums, gages and damsons are all cultivated in the same way, with plums and gages producing earlier and damsons continuing the season with a later crop. Damsons are often grown as untrained trees, hedges or even windbreaks. Plums, gages and damsons can be trained into several forms (although not as many as can be used for apples and pears). There are a lot of very worthy varieties that are self-fertile and others that require a pollinator. Although there are four differing types of rootstock, trees are generally found on one of two rootstocks. Great care and good timing is paramount with any pruning or work that involves cutting, to prevent the trees being infected with the debilitating and often fatal silver-leaf disease. Many varieties will produce an even crop in most years, with the determining factor being the weather conditions. However, some varieties, such as Victoria, will behave as a biennial, producing a bumper crop one year and then only 10 or 20 fruits the next before another bumper crop in the following year.

DATES

Flowering time Early March–April

Harvesting July–October

Cropping age 3–5 years

SITE AND SOIL

Site Sunny and sheltered site with well-drained soil, although clay or deep loam is preferred.

pH 6.0–6.5

Fertilizer As for apples (see page 38).

Water As for apples (see page 38).

ROOTSTOCKS

Pixy (Dwarfing) Suitable for growing all types of tree, except the more vigorous varieties grown as cordons.

Ferlenian (Semi-dwarfing) Similar to Pixy, but produces better-sized fruit. It is prone to suckering and is therefore the least common of the three main rootstock types.

St Julien A (Semi-vigorous) Predominantly used on bush, half-standard, pyramid and fan types.

Brompton (Vigorous) Rarely seen, as it produces trees that are too big for most modern gardens.

DIMENSIONS

Height of tree
Pixy 2–2.2 m (6–7 ft)
Ferlenian 2–2.4 m (6–8 ft)
St Julien A 2.2–2.7 m (7–9 ft)
Brompton 5.5 m + (18 ft +)

Planting distances
Pixy 2.4–3.6 m (8–12 ft)
Ferlenian 2.4–3.6 m (8–12 ft)
St Julien A 3.6–4.5 m (8–15 ft)
Brompton 5.5–6.5 m (18–22 ft)

AFTER CARE

In bumper years, there will be a certain amount of natural fruit thinning, with the tree dropping fruit in early summer. However, to get the best fruit and protect the tree, it is also important to thin again, just after the fruit drop, so that fruits are about 5–8 cm (2–3 in) apart. This will ensure decent-sized fruit and will prevent branches breaking under the weight of a bumper crop.

PRUNING

Due to the potentially devastating effects of the silver-leaf disease, all pruning must be carried out while the tree is active – from bud break in early spring until early autumn. Pruning of established trees involves thinning to allow light and air into the tree and removal of badly placed, diseased or damaged branches.

SPECIAL TIP

To prevent unnecessary silver-leaf contamination from one tree to the next, always disinfect secateurs and saws after pruning has been completed on each tree.

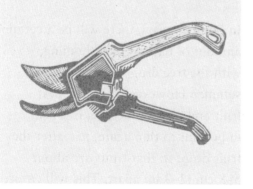

TREE FORMS

Standard, half-standard, bush, pyramid, cordon and fan.

HARVESTING AND STORAGE

If picking for bottling or making jam, the fruits can be picked as soon as the bloom appears on the fruit. If you want them fresh, fruits can be harvested as soon as they are soft to the touch and come away from the tree easily. Their colour will be full, but varied, depending on the variety grown. They can be kept in the fridge for a few days.

PESTS

Aphids, sawfly, wasps and red spider mite.

DISEASES

Silver leaf, bacterial canker and rust.

SELECTED VARIETIES

Cambridge Gage Very prolific. Culinary and dessert. Mid-season flowerer. Harvest in August and September. Pollinate with Victoria.

Coe's Golden Drop Early flowering. Yellow gages. Grow as a fan to maximize ripening. Harvest in October. Pollinate with Cambridge Gage or Victoria.

Czar Self-fertile. Mid-season flowerer. Culinary. Blue-black plums with a yellow-green flesh. Harvest in August.

Dennistons Superb Self-fertile gage. Mid-season flowering. Yellow-green fruits, darker streaks. Harvest in August and September.

Early Laxton Small tree. Mid-season flowering. Yellow fruits, red flush. Harvest in late July and early August. Culinary plum, but a reasonable eater.

King of Damsons Mid-season damson. Large, blue-black fruits. Harvest in September and October. Self-fertile.

Marjorie's Seedling Late-flowering. Self-fertile. Culinary. Large purple fruit. Harvest in September and October.

Merryweather Damson Vigorous. Mid-season flowering. Large, blue-black damsons. Self-fertile. Harvest in September and October.

Opal Self-fertile plum. Mid-season flowering. Early, reddish-purple fruits. Harvest in July and August.

Rivers's Early Prolific Mid-season flowering. Pollinate with Victoria. Small, juicy purple fruits. Harvest in August.

Victoria Popular for eating and cooking. Large reddish-purple fruits. Mid-season flowering. Self-fertile. Harvest in August and September.

RASPBERRIES
Rubus idaeus

Rosaceae

Probably the most popular cane fruit, due to its ease of growth in temperate climates, coupled with the large yield obtained from a relatively small amount of canes. There are two types: the maincrop summer varieties and the autumn-fruiting types. The summer raspberry varieties crop on the canes that grew during the previous year, while the autumn-fruiting ones will crop on the canes grown in the current year. Traditionally, the summer-fruiting types are grown in rows, and are tied to wires supported on posts. However, there is no need to do this if you only have a small garden, as you can always find room for a group of three to five plants. Autumn-fruiting raspberries are often grown in a bed with supports around the outside to stop the outer canes from falling over, but these can also be grown in small groups where necessary. The summer-fruiting varieties will follow the strawberry crop and precede the autumn raspberry crop, so soft fruit should always be available from June until October.

DATES

Flowering time May–June

Harvesting July–September

Cropping age 1 year

SITE AND SOIL

Site Fertile and moisture retentive, but well-drained. Full sun, but will tolerate some semi-shade.

pH 5.5–6.0

Fertilizer Mulch each winter with well-rotted farmyard manure or compost. Apply liquid seaweed to combat iron deficiency. Pelleted chicken manure every other year, in spring.

Water Water as the fruits begin to change colour. Do not water overhead, as this can have disease implications for the fruit.

DIMENSIONS

Planting distances
45 cm (18 in)
180 cm (6 ft) rows

AFTER CARE

On soils that have a pH of over 7.0, raspberries are likely to suffer from iron deficiency which shows as yellowing between the leaf veins. This can be easily remedied with liquid seaweed (as a summer foliar feed, and a dressing of seaweed meal in the spring). Keep hoeing off the new canes that are appearing through the ground, beyond the area allocated to them, leaving canes close to the wire supports to grow on. Once the summer canes have fruited, cut them down and tie in the new canes so that there is approximately 10–15 cm (4–6 in) between each cane along the row.

PRUNING

Summer fruiting varieties are pruned after fruiting, with the old fruiting canes cut out first. These can be cut to ground level. Then, the weak and diseased canes are removed before the strongest new canes are selected to be tied in. As autumn-fruiting raspberries fruit on the canes produced that year, pruning is much simpler and involves cutting all the canes down to the ground. In the spring, the fruit-bearing canes will emerge from below ground level.

HARVESTING AND STORAGE

The fruits are ready when they have turned a lovely deep colour, whether a red or yellow variety, and they can then be carefully removed from the canes leaving the central core behind. Raspberries can be frozen, cooked or kept in the fridge for a couple of days, but cannot be stored in any other way.

PESTS

Birds, aphids and raspberry beetle.

DISEASES

Botrytis and spur blight.

SELECTED VARIETIES

All Gold Yellow fruits. Harvest in September.

Autumn Bliss Good-sized red fruits. Harvest in September.

Glen Ample Very large red fruit. Spineless canes. Harvest from late June until early August.

Glen Magna Large, deep red fruits. Good disease resistance. Harvest in August.

Joan J Red fruits. Spineless canes. Harvest from early August until early November.

Leo Vigorous. Red fruits. Harvest in August.

Malling Jewel Reliable. Red fruits. Harvest in June.

REDCURRANTS
AND
WHITECURRANTS
Ribes sativum

Grossulariaceae

Although similar to blackcurrants (in that they are of the same family and the fruits are the same, except for the colour) redcurrants are cultivated in a different way. Redcurrants are a beautiful ornamental plant in their own right. The hanging strigs of bright red berries look truly stunning. Both redcurrants and whitecurrants are treated in the same way when it comes to cultivation, and can be grown either as bushes or on walls, fences and wires, as single, double or triple-stem cordons. Usually produced in abundance, they have the advantage of freezing very well, which is an added bonus to their summer uses as an essential ingredient of summer fruit dishes, as well as making tasty wine and jam. They are both excellent temperate-climate crops that will fruit well in less fertile soils and even in positions with fewer hours of sunlight than is required for blackcurrants. Also, unlike blackcurrants, they produce their fruit at the bases of short spurs, requiring a totally different pruning method. They are spineless and have excellent disease resistance.

DATES

Flowering time March–April

Harvesting June–August

Cropping age 1–2 years

SITE AND SOIL

Site Avoid planting in frost pockets. Redcurrants do not require a very fertile soil but a good application of well-rotted organic matter, dug in prior to planting, will be beneficial. They dislike waterlogging, so if this is a problem improve the soil before planting.

pH 6.5

Fertilizer Apply rock potash in late winter or early spring. Mulch with well-rotted organic matter each spring. Do not over-fertilize.

Water Water regularly as fruits start to swell and show colour.

DIMENSIONS

Planting distances

Bushes 1.5 m (5 ft);1.8 m (6 ft) rows

Single cordons 30 cm (12 in)
Double cordons 60 cm (24 in)
Triple cordons 90 cm (36 in)
Fans 1.8m (6 ft)

The "arms" of cordons should be spaced 30 cm (12 in) apart.

AFTER CARE

Remove suckers as they appear. Mulch each spring to conserve moisture and suppress weeds. If frosts are forecast in the spring, cover the plants with fleece to protect the flowers. In early summer, before the fruits begin to colour, protect these fruits from attack by birds with netting.

PRUNING

Prune red or whitecurrants in late winter or early spring, as this allows the removal of any winter damage. If grown as a bush, it can be spur-pruned to encourage fruiting spurs to be formed and thus a bigger crop. The aim is to create an open, goblet-shaped bush by removing all the crossing, weak and congested older branches, cutting the remaining sideshoots back to two or three buds. For cordons in

SPECIAL TIP

Most varieties of redcurrant and whitecurrant are thin skinned, so removal of individual fruits is very difficult. Therefore, once the strig has been removed from the plant and taken indoors remove the berries in a bowl by running a fork down the strig.

late winter or early spring, remove all weak spur systems, diseased and congested branches. The rest of the pruning is done in summer to restrict the plants growth and improve air circulation. This minimizes disease and removes a lot of the pests on the shoot tips, when all sideshoots are cut back to five leaves. For fans, once the shape has been formed, winter prune the spurs as for a bush.

HARVESTING AND STORAGE

Remove strigs as soon as all berries are ripe. They do not store well, except when frozen.

PESTS

Aphids, capsid bug, sawfly and birds.

DISEASES

Botrytis, mildew and leaf spot.

SELECTED VARIETIES

Blanka Very high-yielding whitecurrant. Large fruits. Harvest in July and August.

Jonkheer van Tets Early flowering. Full strigs of bright red berries. Harvest in early July.

Junifer Earliest redcurrant. Strigs of bright red berries. Harvest in late June and early July. Good disease resistance.

Red Lake Heavy yield. Long strigs of red berries. Harvest in mid-July.

Rovada Heavy crops. Large red berries. Harvest in early August. Good disease resistance.

White Grape Translucent white berries. Harvest in mid-July. Upright plant.

White Versailles Reliable whitecurrant. Large white fruit. Harvest in early July.

STRAWBERRIES
Fragaria x ananassa

Roseaceae

A very popular fruit, that does particularly well in temperate climates, where it can be grown as a perennial plant with a fruiting life of about four years. In warmer climates, strawberries are very much treated as annuals and will produce a large crop in one year, to be replaced for the following year's crop. With the use of cold stored runners it is possible to obtain a crop within four months of planting. If space allows, and using the correct varieties, strawberries can be harvested from May until September, with the ever-bearing varieties cropping over a much longer period than the maincrop types. Early crops can also be forced to grow under protection, but they do seem to lose some of their flavour if grown in this way. They also make excellent container plants and can be grown in pots, wall troughs or hanging baskets. It is advisable to grow them where you can, because most plants give an average crop. Due to the problems associated with various viruses it is paramount that you buy the initial plants from a reputable source who can supply you with certified stock.

DATES

Flowering time April–May

Harvesting May–October

Cropping age *Cold-stored plants*
4–5 months
Runners 8–12 months

SITE AND SOIL

Site Sunny position in well-drained, but moisture-retentive soil. To counter disease problems, strawberries should, if possible, be grown on a site that has good air movement. When planting, the crown of the plant (where the roots meet the leaves) should be at soil level; any lower and the crown will rot; any higher and the plants will dry out and may push themselves out of the ground. They can also be planted through black polythene, which will help in a number of ways. It conserves moisture, eliminates weed problems, warms the soil and helps to protect the fruit from soil splash when it is ripening, as well as eliminating the rotting problems associated with fruits touching the soil.

pH 5.5–7.5

Fertilizer Sprinkle rock potash around the plants once harvesting has finished.

Water Water in dry weather, particularly when the fruits begin to swell.

DIMENSIONS

Planting distances
60 cm (24 in)
45 cm (18 in) rows

AFTER CARE

If not growing through black plastic, then mulch the strawberries with straw once the fruits start to swell. Lift the fruit trusses and push the straw underneath, and then let the fruits gently back down onto it. The straw will prevent soil splash and will help to prevent slugs getting to the fruits. Remove runners that form through the summer, unless they are to be used for forcing. If you want to force strawberries in a greenhouse or tunnel in early spring of the following year, pin down some runners into 8cm (3 in) pots filled with compost and once rooted, cut the stem attaching it to the main plant. These runners can then be put under cover for early strawberries next year. Do not use these runners to replace old plants as they can spread viruses. As the fruits start to ripen, cover the plants with netting to protect against bird damage.

PRUNING

Once the crop has been harvested cut back all the old leaves to within 2.5 cm (1 in) from the crown, and remove the straw mulch.

HARVESTING AND STORAGE

Harvest the fruits once they are red all over and remove the fruit and the stalk complete. Strawberries do not keep for more than a couple of days in the fridge and will not freeze very successfully, so enjoy them fresh from the plants or turn them into jam.

PESTS

Aphids, slugs and red spider mite.

DISEASES

Botrytis, verticillium wilt and powdery mildew.

SELECTED VARIETIES

Aromel Late-season flowering. Perpetual cropper. Harvest from June to October. Can pick in November, if the plants are protected.

Cambridge Favourite Medium-sized fruit. Harvest in June and July. Resistant to botrytis, powdery mildew and verticilium wilt.

Elvira Early flowering variety. Heavy cropper. Firm, large fruits. Harvest in June. Can be grown under cover for earlier crops. Partial resistance to powdery mildew.

Flamenco Perpetual variety. Medium-to-large firm fruits. Harvest from June to October.

Florence Late-season flowering. Large, bright red fruits. Harvest in June and July.

Hapil High-yielding. Susceptible to verticillium wilt and red spider mite. Large, firm, bright red fruits. Harvest in June.

Mae Exceptionally early. Harvest from early June if grown outside and mid-May if grown under protection. Large, deep red fruits.

Malling Opal Perpetual variety. Large, sweet red fruits. Harvest from June to October.

Pegasus Large, glossy red fruits. Harvest in June and July. Resistant to verticilium wilt, with some resistance to botrytis and mildew.

Totem Sweet red fruit. Harvest in June and July. Holds its colour and texture well when frozen. Good disease resistance.

SPECIAL TIP

Ideally, strawberries should only be grown for three years before the plants need to be replaced because, by that time, fruit production will start to dwindle. Do not replant in the same place, as this can have implications with soil-borne diseases such as verticillium wilt. Always replant with certified stock.

plant organic
VEGETABLES

Artichoke, Globe • Artichoke, Jerusalem • Asparagus
• Aubergine • Beans – Runner and French • Beetroot
• Broad Beans • Broccoli and Calabrese • Brussels Sprouts
• Cabbage • Carrot • Cauliflower • Celeriac • Celery
• Chicory • Cucumber and Gherkin • Endive
• Florence Fennel • Kohl Rabi • Leaf Beet • Leeks
• Lettuce • Marrow and Courgette • Melon
• Onions and Garlic • Parsnip and Hamburg Parsley
• Peas • Peppers • Potato • Radish • Swede
• Sweetcorn • Tomato

ARTICHOKE, GLOBE
Cynara scolymus

Asteraceae

A sought-after plant that can be grown either as an annual or a perennial. It is easy to grow but will produce a relatively small crop for the amount of space the plant takes up. However, if there is no room in the vegetable plot it is ornamental enough to be grown in the flower border. The large, spiky flower buds are the part of the plant that is eaten, but if left to flower they produce beautiful, large blue, thistle-like flowers which, combined with the lovely large, grey-green leaves, makes for a stately display. They can be grown from seed or planted-out as offsets from another plant in April. Growing them as annuals seems to produce a better harvest.

DATES

Sowing February

Harvesting July–September

SOWING METHOD

Sow into 8 cm (3 in) pots, harden off before planting out. Divide or obtain offsets (divisions) in April and plant out immediately.

MINIMUM TEMPERATURE

For germination 18°C (65°F)

For growing on 13°C (55°F)

SITE AND SOIL

Site Sunny and sheltered. Avoid heavy or overly wet sites where the plants may rot in the winter.

pH 6.5–7.0

Fertilizer Dig in well-rotted manure or compost prior to planting and apply a balanced fertilizer, such as blood, fish and bone meal or pelleted chicken manure.

Water They require plenty of water, so never allow to dry out.

DIMENSIONS

Planting depth Plant offsets to their original depth and seed raised plants to the top of the rootball.

Space between plants 1 x 1 m (3 x 3 ft)

SPECIAL TIP

Grow globe artichokes as annuals in raised beds, where the drainage is better. They can be planted at a spacing of 45 x 45 cm (18 x 18 in) giving twice the crop for the space taken.

AFTER CARE

Mulch with well-rotted manure or compost to conserve water. During winter, cover the crown of perennial plants with straw, to protect them from the frost.

COMPANION PLANTS

If grown as a perennial, it is grown with other permanent crops such as rhubarb, asparagus, Jerusalem artichoke, seakale and a wide range of herbs.

If grown as an annual, it can be grown with cabbages, Chinese cabbage, Brussels sprouts, cauliflowers, calabrese, broccoli, kale, swede, turnip, radish and kohl rabi.

HARVESTING

Weeks to maturity: 28 weeks

Cut the heads while they are plump, but still tightly shut, when they will be tender. Once all the heads have been harvested, cut the plants down to within 30 cm (12 in) of the ground to stimulate new leaf production. These leaves, when 60cm (2 ft) high, can be tied together and, like celery, earthed up to blanch them. After several weeks the soil can be pulled back and the leaves cut, cooked and eaten.

HEALTH BENEFITS

A good source of fibre and protein.

STORAGE

They do not store well.

PESTS

Aphids, slugs and snails.

DISEASES

No real disease problems.

SELECTED VARIETIES

Green Globe Very reliable and easy to grow. Produces a tender and delicious crop.

Emerald Heads have a nutty flavour. Needs to be sown early to ensure a crop in its first year.

Romanesco Tight, purple heads produced late. Excellent flavour.

Violetta di Chioggia Very early variety harvested in May, with a second crop later in the year. Small, deep purplish heads. Suitable for growing in the ornamental garden.

ARTICHOKE, JERUSALEM

Helianthus tuberosus

Asteraceae

A hardy perennial related to the sunflower that can require a large area in which to grow. It is a vigorous perennial that, if not kept in check, can take over a vegetable plot. Grown for its winter crop of tubers, it has all the flavour associated with globe artichokes but is much easier to grow. As the top growth can reach up to 3m (10 ft) it can provide an excellent windbreak hedge, as well as a home for various birds and beneficial wildlife among the sturdy stems and large leaves. Another benefit of this crop is that most weeds will not grow among the stems, as they are crowded out. The knobbly tubers are usually peeled and cooked like a potato, but can also be eaten raw. They can be baked, boiled, steamed, fried or stewed and if cleaned thoroughly, they don't really need to be peeled.

DATES

Sowing/Planting February

Harvesting October–April

SOWING/PLANTING METHOD

As soon as it is possible to plant in February, the tubers can go into a pre-prepared trench. Dig out a trench 60 cm (24 in) wide and 30 cm (12 in) deep and fork over the bottom to break it up. Refill the trench, adding plenty of well-rotted organic matter.

MINIMUM TEMPERATURE

For germination: Not applicable

SITE AND SOIL

Site Sun or shade, in any type of soil.

pH Below 6.5

Fertilizer Well-rotted organic matter and a balanced fertilizer, such as blood, fish and bone meal or pelleted chicken manure.

Water Only necessary in dry weather.

DIMENSIONS

Planting depth 15 cm (6 in)

Space between plants 30 cm (12 in)

AFTER CARE

Erect stout stakes or canes in summer and put string around the stems to help support them. Keep the weeds around the edges of the plants at bay and earth up the stems by about 10 cm (4 in) during early summer, to support the stems. Remove any flower buds and mulch the plants annually in early spring, and apply fertilizer. Once the foliage has turned yellow it can be cut down to about 15 cm (6 in) from the ground.

COMPANION PLANTS

Rhubarb, asparagus, globe artichoke, seakale and a wide range of herbs.

HARVESTING

Weeks to maturity 16–20 weeks

They are perfectly happy in the ground and can be lifted as and when they are required.

HEALTH BENEFITS

High in iron, potassium and thiamine, Jerusalem artichokes are recommended as a potato substitute for diabetics since they are filling, but not absorbed by the body.

STORAGE

Jerusalem artichokes do not keep well but, if necessary, they can be stored raw in a cool, dry, well-ventilated area away from direct sunlight for up to three weeks.

PESTS

Slugs and wireworms.

DISEASES

No disease problems.

SELECTED VARIETIES

Dwarf Sunray Only grows to 1.5–2 m (5–6 ft) producing crisp and tender tubers. No peeling of the outer skin is necessary. Flowers freely.

Fuseau Long, smooth-skinned variety with an excellent flavour.

Gerrard Almost round tuber; smooth, purple-red skin.

Long Red Large tubers free from knobs, so easy to clean and peel.

Stampede High-yielding variety, large, white-skinned tubers. Tops only grow to 2 m (6 ft) tall.

SPECIAL TIP

If space is limited, or you're worried that this crop will take over your vegetable plot, grow them in containers. Containers will restrict the spread of the crop and also allow easy harvesting, even when the ground is frozen. To prevent the containers blowing over, they can be sunk into the ground where the tops can then also be used as a windbreak.

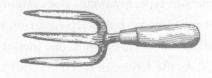

ASPARAGUS
Asparagus officinalis

Asparagaceae

This plant is primarily grown for its delicious spears, produced from April to June, although the ferns it produces once harvesting has ended are beautiful in themselves. Asparagus can be raised from seed, but it will take five years from sowing until it is possible to start harvesting, so the best way to start is by ordering a one-year-old crown from a seed company. These crowns will then produce spears in their second season after planting (a small amount of which can be harvested) and a full crop when they are four years old, which will be their third year after planting. Although female crowns produce more succulent spears, they are not as prolific as male crowns because they put quite a bit of effort into producing unwanted seed. Male plants do not put this effort in, so they produce more slender spears; most crowns available will be F1 male cultivars. It is a perennial plant that takes up a lot of space for the amount of crop harvested, but, due to its unique flavour and crop value, it is definitely worth growing. If cared for in the correct manner, a crown will produce for up to 20 years. Although not too fussed about soil type, asparagus does required a well-drained position that can cope with its deep root run, so heavy clay soils are not ideal. If the soil is not suitable, then it can be grown in raised beds. As the ferns can reach 90 cm (3 ft) in height, it is advisable not to grow asparagus on too windy a site.

DATES

Sowing *Inside* February
Outside March

Harvesting April–June

SOWING METHOD

As a high-value crop, it is better to sow inside rather than out. Sow under cover into large modules or 8 cm (3 ins) pots. When 10–15 cm (4–6 ins) tall, harden off and plant out in June.

Plant crowns in April, which is usually the time of year they arrive from the seed companies. Dig a trench 15 cm (6 ins) deep and 30 cm (12 ins) wide, putting a ridge in the centre of the trench 5 cm (2 ins) high. Place the crowns on the top of the ridge and the fragile, fleshy roots carefully spread out. Refill the trench carefully, covering the crowns with 10 cm (4 ins) of soil.

MINIMUM TEMPERATURE

For germination 10°C (50°F)

SITE AND SOIL

Site Sunny and sheltered.

SPECIAL TIP

When planting crowns, it is advisable to soak them for about an hour before planting out, as they may have dried in transit and this will aid establishment.

pH *6.5–7.5*

Fertilizer Work in well-rotted manure or compost in the autumn prior to planting. Apply blood, fish and bone meal or pelleted chicken manure at planting and repeat each spring.

Water Keep well-watered in their first year, and then water during dry spells.

DIMENSIONS

Planting depth *Seeds* – sow outside at a depth of 2.5 cm (1 in).
Crowns – plant so the top of the crown is 10 cm (4 in) below soil level.

Space between plants 30 x 30 cm (12 x 12 in)

AFTER CARE

In cold springs, protect the young spears with horticultural fleece. Keep weed-free. Always hand-weed as hoeing may damage the crowns. Once harvesting has finished in mid-June, leave the remaining spears to become the ferns that will feed the crowns. This will ensure a good crop the following year. When these ferns begin to turn yellow in the autumn, it important to cut them close to the ground and remove them swiftly, as asparagus beetles can overwinter on old stems. In the autumn, spread well-rotted manure or compost around the plants.

COMPANION PLANTS

Rhubarb, globe artichoke, Jerusalem artichoke, seakale and herbs.

HARVESTING

Weeks to maturity:
From seed 260 weeks
Crowns 156 weeks

Harvest spears when 15 cm (6 in) long, cutting 2.5–5 cm (1–2 in) below ground level. Cut all spears produced to keep the supply, but from mid-June stop harvesting and leave all spears to grow up into ferns.

HEALTH BENEFITS

Good source of vitamins C and E.

STORAGE

Best served fresh, asparagus will only keep for three to four days in the fridge.

PESTS

Asparagus beetle and slugs.

DISEASES

Violet root rot, foot rot, root rot and asparagus rust.

SELECTED VARIETIES

Cito F1 Medium-sized, green spears.

Dariana F1 Consistently high-yielding. Large, straight, green spears.

Jacq ma Pourpre Improved, early purple variety. Cut the dark-purple spears when 20 cm (8 in) long. Purple spears grow up into green ferns.

Jersey Knight Improved All male variety, with thick, green spears.

AUBERGINE
Solanum melongena

Solanaceae

Also known as the "Eggplant", this tender, tropical, slightly
spiky plant is suited to both indoor and outdoor cropping.
If the climate is unpredictable, it is best grown as a tender
annual in a greenhouse or polythene tunnel. However, in
warmer areas it can be grown outside as a perennial, although
it is best to start the seed in a greenhouse or on the windowsill.
When initially put out, cover with a cloche for extra protection
and to ensure good early growth. The fruits produced can
vary in shape as well as colour, with various shades of purple,
black, red and yellow available as well as white fruits (the latter
being the instigator of their common name). They are a
relatively easy plant to grow, as they will naturally branch into
generally compact and bushy plants, making them ideal for
growing in containers.

DATES

Sowing/Planting January–March

Harvesting August–October

SOWING/PLANTING METHOD

Sow thinly into a seed tray and once germinated, when the leaves are big enough to handle – about 5 cm (2 in) tall, prick them out into 8 cm (3 in) pots. Keep at a constant temperature of 16–18°C (60–64°F) and pot on when necessary. If they are to be planted outside, there is no need to pot on further than a 2–3 litre (6–7 in) pot, but if being grown in the greenhouse then a final pot size of 7.5–10 litre (9–10 in) is ideal.

MINIMUM TEMPERATURE

For germination 21–30°C (70–86°F)

SITE AND SOIL

Site Full sun and sheltered, in a greenhouse or polythene tunnel.

pH 6.5

Fertilizer Feed every 10–14 days with a liquid, animal fertiliser or high-potash, seaweed liquid feed from the setting of the first fruits until harvesting begins.

Water Keep well-watered.

DIMENSIONS

Planting depth To top of rootball.

Space between plants
In greenhouse 60–75 cm (24–30 ins)
Outside 40–45 cm (16–18 ins) in staggered rows

AFTER CARE

Only plant out once the danger of frost has passed. Branching should naturally occur, but if it doesn't, then pinch out the growing tip when the plants reach 30 cm (12 in) high. Only allow four to six fruits to set on each plant. If growing outside, cane the plants and mulch around each to help conserve water.

COMPANION PLANTS

Cucumber, squash, pumpkin, melon, potato, tomato, carrot, beetroot, parsnip, scorzonera, salsify, Hamburg parsley, celeriac, onion, shallot, leek, garlic, celery, Florence fennel, marrow, courgette and pepper.

HARVESTING

Weeks to maturity: 16–24 weeks

Harvest only when the required size has been achieved, and always before the skin starts to lose its shine. Cut through the stem at about 2.5 cm (1 in) from the top of the fruit.

SPECIAL TIP

If the plant does not branch very well once the main tip has been removed, remove the tips from the shoots produced and, if necessary, keep doing this until a nice bushy plant has been achieved.

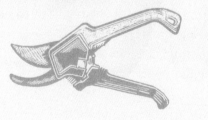

HEALTH BENEFITS

Vitamins E and K; also high in potassium, folate, magnesium and fibre.

STORAGE

They do not store well.

PESTS

Whitefly, aphid and red spider mite.

DISEASES

Botrytis and verticillium wilt.

SELECTED VARIETIES

Black Beauty Large, purple-black, pear-shaped fruits; earlier than most.

Black Enorma F1 Largest fruit. Early, pear-shaped, purple-black fruit.

Bonica F1 High-yielding, compact, purple variety; ideal for containers.

Kermit F1 Small, round, green and white fruits about 5 cm (2 in) in size on compact plants.

Mini Fingers Baby aubergine, 15 cm (6 in) long, dark purple fruits in clusters of three to six fruits.

Mohican F1 Compact, white-fruited variety; perfect for containers.

Moneymaker F1 Early variety. Good crop of uniform fruits.

Rotunda Very fleshy variety. Large, white, round fruit with a hint of purple.

BEANS – RUNNER AND FRENCH

Phaseolus coocineus and *Phaseolus vulgaris*

Papilionaceae

These beans are quite prolific and will produce an excellent crop throughout the summer. Runner beans and the climbing varieties of French bean will require supports to grow up, whereas French beans are a self-supporting bush. They all help with the fertility of the plot and assist in the crop rotation, as their roots fix nitrogen in the soil. These beans all come in a range of sizes and colours of flowers, as well as pods to make the vegetable area look very interesting. They are all frost-tender, so need to be planted out once all risk of frost has passed. The climbing varieties are usually grown up wigwams or on frames made from bamboo canes, although they are perfectly happy growing up a pergola with ornamental climbers.

DATES

Sowing/Planting April–July

Harvesting
Runner beans July–October
French beans June–November

SOWING/PLANTING METHOD

Start the earliest varieties in the green-house. Sow one seed per 8 cm (3 in) pot, deep module or biodegradable tube. Harden off and plant out. Successional sowings can be made to prevent the entire crop being ready all at once. When sowing outside, warm the soil with a cloche or plastic sheet and put one seed at each required spacing. Directly sow or plant out runner beans over a bean trench to ensure adequate moisture at the roots for the duration of the crop. The bean trench is a trench that is dug out a spade's depth at

SPECIAL TIP

When sowing, always sow a few extra beans at the end of a row or in a vacant spot to allow for the odd seed that does not germinate. These extra plants can then be used to fill the gaps.

60–90 cm (2–3 ft) wide. It then needs to be filled with compostable material, such as well-rotted manure or compost that will hold moisture. The soil is then replaced on the top a week or two before sowing or planting.

MINIMUM TEMPERATURE

For germination 12°C (54°F)

SITE AND SOIL

Site Sunny and sheltered position, with a moisture retentive soil.

pH 6.5–7.5

Fertilizer None required in a well-managed plot. If no organic matter was added before the previous crop, then add some before sowing or planting.

Water Once the flower buds appear keep the plants moist.

DIMENSIONS

Planting depth 5 cm (2 in)

Space between plants
Runner beans 45–60cm (18–24 in);

60 cm (24 in) rows
French beans 20 cm (8 in);
30 cm (12 in) rows

AFTER CARE

Mulch plants to help conserve moisture and keep weeds at bay. Water regularly. Protect from slugs and snails immediately after planting.

COMPANION PLANTS

Peas, broad beans, Lima beans, sweetcorn, okra, globe artichokes, lettuce, endive, chicory, cress, spinach, spinach beet and chard.

HARVESTING

Weeks to maturity: 12–16 weeks

Harvest regularly to encourage more beans to be produced. Do not allow beans to get too big, as they will become stringy and unpalatable.

HEALTH BENEFITS

Good source of vitamins A, C and E, folate and iron, as well as protein and fibre.

STORAGE

They can be frozen or dried.

PESTS

Pea and bean weevil, mice, aphids, slugs and snails.

DISEASES

Chocolate spot, rust, foot and root rots.

SELECTED VARIETIES

Runner beans

Celebration Early. Salmon-pink flowers. Long, green pods. Harvest from July.

Enorma Heavy yields. Very long, green pods. Harvest from July.

Galaxy Long, narrow, stringless pods. Red flowers. Harvest from July.

Heista Early. Dwarf version of Painted Lady. Stringless, green pods. Red and white flowers. Harvest from July.

Matilda Early. Long, round, dark-green pods. Harvest from July.

Mergoles Stringless beans. White flowers. Freezes well. Harvest from July.

Painted Lady Stringless, green pods. Red and white flowers. Harvest from July.

Yard Long Narrow, dark-green pods can grow up to 90 cm (36 in).

Dwarf French Beans

Borlotto Firetongue Grow as a green bean when young and tender or grow on to maturity when beans have red flecks. Seeds can be dried and have red streaks and spots on a creamy yellow bean. Harvest from June.

Golden Teepee Golden-yellow, rounded beans. Pods produced above leaves. Harvest from June.

Masterpiece Early. Very prolific. Flat, green beans. Harvest from June.

Purple Queen Heavy-yielding. Attractive purple, stringless beans. Beans turn green when cooked. Harvest from June to July.

Sprite Round, stringless, dark green beans. Harvest from June.

Purple Teepee Early. Round, stringless beans. Beans turn green when cooked. Harvest from June.

Slenderette Dark green, stringless beans. High-yielding. Freezes well. Harvest from June to September.

Speedy Very early. Rounded, green beans. Harvest from mid-June.

Climbing French Beans

Algarve Flat, mid-green, stringless beans, 25–28 cm (10–11 in) long. Harvest from July.

Blauhilde High-yielding. Purple, stringless beans. Turn green when cooked. Harvest from July.

Blue Lake Round, stringless beans. Beans can be dried and used as haricots. Harvest from July.

Cobra Dark green, stringless beans. Harvest from July.

BEETROOT
Beta vulgaris subsp. *vulgaris*

Chenopodiaceae

An excellent crop that is not only quick and easy to grow, but also one that should be available for the table every week of the year. They come in various shapes and colours, from the more common round, to oval, through to long, carrot-like roots. They range in colour from the classic purple to deep red, yellow and white. The inner flesh can also be variable, with varieties producing colours ranging from purple, red, orange-yellow to white and even white with pink-red rings. Even after cooking, these colours will remain. The swollen roots can be harvested from early summer until late in the autumn, when the remainder are stored to last right through the winter, although bolt-resistant varieties need to be used for the early sowings. The seeds are multi-germ, which means that each seed will produce several seedlings, although mono-germ seeds have now been bred that will only produce one seedling per seed. It is important to identify which type is being sown, so that the required amounts of seed can be calculated. They are very versatile and will fill gaps in the garden readily when grown as catch crops, with multi-sown beetroot being an excellent method. Most varieties can be harvested when they are golf-ball size and they can be eaten small and sweet. Alternatively, they can be left and grown on into a maincrop of much larger roots. The rounder varieties are ideal for growing in containers and even the tops can be eaten, by treating them in the same way as spinach. This is a salt-tolerant plant, so it can be grown close to the coast.

111

DATES

Sowing/Planting
Inside February
Outside March

Harvesting May–November

SOWING/PLANTING METHOD

Before sowing it is important to wash the seeds as they may contain a chemical on their outer coating which could inhibit germination, so washing them under a tap will ensure rapid and even germination.

For earliest crops multi-sow round rooted varieties into modules which will be planted out under cloches and picked when about golf-ball size.

Outside sow into drills 2.5 cm (1 in) deep and place one or two seed clusters about 8 cm (3 in) apart.

SPECIAL TIP

Sow every three weeks and mix the sowings with maincrop and faster-maturing varieties to ensure a succession of beetroot from May to November.

MINIMUM TEMPERATURE

For germination 7°C (45°F)

SITE AND SOIL

Site Open, sunny site and a deep, rich soil that is not too heavy.

pH 6.5–7.0

Fertilizer Well-rotted manure applied the autumn prior to planting. Pelleted chicken manure or blood, fish and bone meal prior to sowing or planting.

Water Do not allow to dry out, so water regularly. Irregular watering may create a lot of leafy growth and no root growth.

112

DIMENSIONS

Planting depth Sow into drills 2.5 cm (1 in) deep.

Space between plants
Early and mini-veg varieties 1–5 cm (^{1}/2–2 in);
15 cm (6 in) rows
Multi-sown crops 22 cm (9 in);
22 cm (9 in) rows
Maincrop varieties 8 cm (3 in);
30 cm (12 in) rows

AFTER CARE

Protect any early sowings or plantings not placed under a cloche with horticultural fleece. In order to prevent bolting through lack of water it is important to mulch between the plants and rows with well-rotted manure, garden compost, etc. Keep the weeds suppressed with regular hoeing, taking care not to touch the crop as the plants will "bleed" if the skin is broken.

COMPANION PLANTS

Cucumber, squash, pumpkin, melon, potato, tomato, marrow, courgette, carrot, parsnip, scorzonera, salsify, Hamburg parsley, celeriac, onion, shallot, leek, garlic, celery, Florence fennel, aubergine and pepper.

HARVESTING

Weeks to maturity 7–13 weeks

Harvest mini-veg or multi-sown plants at golf ball size. Round-rooted varieties grown as maincrops can be pulled when tennis ball size. Long, cylindrical varieties are ideal for storage, therefore sow late and harvest for storage. Never let them swell too much as this will only result in woody, inedible roots.

HEALTH BENEFITS

Some vitamin C, but also high in potassium and folate. Boiling can increase the nutrient value, whereas pickling decreases it. Also known to boost the body's immune system. The tops are rich in beta carotene, calcium and iron.

STORAGE

Lift roots carefully and put to one side any that have begun "bleeding", due to broken skin, as these will have to be eaten immediately. Clean the roots and twist off the tops, leaving approximately 2.5 cm (1 in) of top still attached to the root. The roots can then be stored in moist sharp sand, vermiculite, bark, peat, coir or sawdust contained within a box or large pot. Place in a cool, dark, frost-free place where they can be used as required.

PESTS

Aphids and cutworms.

DISEASES

Powdery mildew, fungal leaf spot and damping off. They are also sensitive to boron and manganese deficiencies.

SELECTED VARIETIES

Blakoma Tender and sweet, conical roots are pure white outside and purple inside.

Boltardy One of the best. Resistant to bolting so ideal for early sowings. Smooth, round roots with excellent colour and superb flavour. Grow as "baby beet" or maincrop.

Bull's Blood Deep crimson-red leaves; really tasty variety. Round roots, best harvested young.

Burpee's Golden Golden flesh tasting just like any traditional variety.

Choggia Barabietola Orange roots. Inside, the flesh is made up of rings that alternate between white and pink-red. Mild beetroot flavour.

Cylindrica Does not readily bolt and stores very well. Dark crimson, cylindrical roots have flavour and good disease resistance.

Early Wonder For early sowings or as a maincrop, with excellent resistance to bolting. Good sized, round crimson roots.

Egyptian Turnip Rooted Excellent colour and flavour, both cooked and raw. Early variety matures very quickly, so it's ideal for growing on poor soils, as well as under cover.

Forono Maincrop. Best picked young and tender. Long cylindrical roots with excellent colour and flavour.

Kestrel F1 Best grown as "baby beet", although the round roots do make for an excellent maincrop. Good tolerance to powdery mildew and fungal leaf spot.

Moneta Monogerm type, avoiding the need to thin. Early variety, resistant to bolting.

Pablo F1 Uniform, round roots with a red-purple flesh. Good for exhibition use, as a maincrop or pulled as "baby beets". Stands well in the ground.

Pronto "Baby beet" variety for early crops, as well as successional crops. Harvest from May to October. Small, round roots can be grown on the bed systems as close as 3 cm (1¼ in) apart. Excellent bolting resistance.

Red Ace Primary beetroot grown in the United States and resistant to bolting, so ideal for early sowing. Round variety with deep red flesh. Suited to growing in drier areas.

BROAD BEANS
Vicia faba

Papilionaceae

A cold-climate vegetable that is a hardy and reliable cropper, at its best when grown outside from late autumn. It can be kept in the ground until late summer, giving a very respectable three-month harvesting period. There is nothing to gain from later sowings, as the plants will stop growing well at temperatures above 15°C (69°F). The beans produced are of a unique flavour, especially when harvested younger, and add variety to early-season meal times. With the range of varieties available, it is possible to grow them on the allotment as well as in the ornamental garden. They are scented and loved by bees, and some varieties have gorgeous, coloured flowers. However, their great asset in the vegetable garden is that they are nitrogen-fixing plants, which means that they have tiny nodules on their roots that extract non-available nitrogen from the soil and convert it into nitrogen of a form that can be easily taken up by the plants that follow the crop. It is important, therefore, when the crop has finished and is removed, to cut the top growth and leave the roots to rot in the soil, so that the nitrogen fixed on the roots is available for the following crop. Some varieties of this bean can grow at lower temperatures, so it is an excellent green manure that can be grown at times when there is nothing else in the ground for weeks. If growing in rows, sow the seeds into double rows, which makes them easier to support later.

DATES

Sowing
Early varieties:
OUTSIDE November–January
Main crops:
OUTSIDE February–March
INSIDE December–February

Harvesting June–August

SOWING METHOD

Inside Sow into modules of about
5 cm (2 in) diameter or sow two seeds
into 8 cm (3 in) pots and remove the
weaker seedling.

MINIMUM TEMPERATURE

For germination
Inside 15°C (59°F)
Outside 5°C (41°F)

SITE AND SOIL

Site Sunny position, sheltered if
growing winter varieties.

pH 6.0–7.0

Fertilizer Low-fertility soil improver.

Water Water when dry.

DIMENSIONS

Planting depth 5 cm (2 in)

Space between plants:
In beds 20–30 cm (8–12 in)
In rows 10 cm (4 in);
90 cm (36 in) rows

AFTER CARE

Protect autumn-sown varieties with
cloches or fleece, which can be
removed once the plants have reached
the top of the cloche (or 20 cm [8 in] if
being grown under fleece). Pinch out
growing tip once the bottom cluster of
flowers have opened to deter black
bean aphids; earlier sowings will be
attacked less. Support taller varieties
and all those in exposed conditions
with four corner posts and twine.

SPECIAL TIP

Do not discard the soft tips of broad beans
when they have been pinched out, because
these can be lightly steamed and served.

COMPANION PLANTS

Peas, French beans, climbing French beans, runner beans, Lima beans, sweetcorn, okra, globe artichokes, lettuce, endive, chicory, cress, spinach, spinach beet and chard.

HARVESTING

Weeks to maturity 12–16 weeks

Harvest when young and fresh.

HEALTH BENEFITS

Source of protein, fibre and A, C and E.

STORAGE

They freeze very well. Dry beans in the sun and store them in sealed bottles.

PESTS

Black bean aphid, pea and bean weevil and mice.

DISEASES

Chocolate spot, broad bean rust, foot and root rots.

SELECTED VARIETIES

Aquadulce Claudia Early variety with pods 23 cm (9 in) long. Autumn or spring sowing.

Crimson Flowered Heritage variety. Chocolate-spot tolerant. Ornamental crimson flowers; medium-sized, green pods of excellent flavour.

Express Early variety. Long pods, containing five or six plump seeds. Suitable for freezing.

Imperial Green Longpod Pods grow to 38 cm (15 in) long, containing up to nine large seeds.

Martock Heritage variety dating back to the 14th century. Medium height with small pods.

The Sutton Ideal for small gardens and successional sowings. Autumn- or spring-sowing.

Witkeim Manita Autumn- or spring-sowing. Long pods, plants grow fast.

BROCCOLI AND CALABRESE

Brassica oleracea Italica
Group

Brassicacaceae

These two types of brassica are relatively easy to grow and have been classed together, as calabrese is quite literally a summer-maturing broccoli. Both are in the ground for a long time, taking up valuable growing space. This makes them ideal subjects for intercropping with a catch crop that will mature before the tops get too big and shade the crop below. They produce spears that can be purple, white or green in colour and are harvested over a large proportion of the year, with broccoli being available from the garden when freshly harvested vegetables are in short supply. Broccoli is hardy and produces smaller spears that often are only instigated after a period of cold, whist calabrese produces larger heads and matures faster, but will not stand the colder weather. As they are a member of the brassica family they are heavy feeders, so will require plenty of fertilizer, but if harvested on a regular basis they will produce more than enough spears for most families. If not harvested regularly then both types will quickly run up to flower and ultimately seed, although these flowering shoots can be cut out and composted without any harmful effect to the plant.

119

DATES

Sowing/Planting

Broccoli

INSIDE April

OUTSIDE April–May

SPRING CROP August

Calabrese

INSIDE March

OUTSIDE April–August

Harvesting

Broccoli December–May

Calabrese June–November

SOWING/PLANTING METHOD

Sow inside into modules or they can be sown outside into shallow drills in a seed bed. Once they are of manageable size they can be carefully lifted and transplanted into their final positions. Calabrese does not like root disturbance, so station sow, where two or three seeds are sown into each spot and after germination two seedlings are removed. Calabrese is well suited to early and late cropping if grown under cover, but do not plant out if the

weather is too hot as this will encourage small heads to be produced.

MINIMUM TEMPERATURE

For germination

Broccoli 7°C (45°F)

Calabrese 5°C (41°F)

SITE AND SOIL

Site Sunny, open position protected from strong winds as the plants can be quite top-heavy and will readily blow over. They can cope with a less fertile soil than most brassicas, but firm them in well on planting.

pH 6.0–7.5

Fertilizer Plenty of well-rotted organic matter and pelleted chicken manure or blood, fish and bone meal before planting or sowing.

Water Water broccoli in dry weather, but calabrese will need to be kept moist right through the growing and harvesting season. Mulch once the first crop of heads has been removed.

DIMENSIONS

Planting depth 2 cm (¾ in)

Plant module or transplant so that the bottom set of leaves are just resting on the surface to minimize the problems of cabbage root fly.

Space between plants
Broccoli 60 cm (24 in);
60 cm (24 in) rows
Calabrese (smaller) 15 cm (6 in);
30 cm (12 ins) rows
(larger) 20 cm (8 in);
45 cm (18 ins) rows

Closer spacing of calabrese plants will encourage smaller heads to be produced, but a more plentiful crop. If fewer but larger heads are required, then use the wider spacing.

AFTER CARE

Protect plants against attack from cabbage root fly after planting. Also protect from the cabbage white butterfly with netting for the length of the crop. Keep plants weed-free by hoeing regularly or mulching with organic matter. Stake broccoli over the winter months, although earthing up around the base of the stems will encourage extra rooting and aid in supporting them. Only water broccoli in dry weather because, if watered too frequently, the plants may become too "soft" to survive the winter temperatures, whereas calabrese will need to be watered regularly to prevent the plants running to seed.

COMPANION PLANTS

Cabbage, Chinese cabbage, Brussels sprouts, cauliflower, kale, swede, turnip, radish and kohl rabi and catch crops such as lettuce, spring onions, rocket and spinach.

HARVESTING

Weeks to maturity
Broccoli 10–40 weeks
Calabrese 11–16 weeks

Cut heads when ready and keep harvesting spears to encourage more to be produced.

HEALTH BENEFITS

High in vitamins A and C, as well as being a good source of iron and an antioxidant.

STORAGE

They do not store well.

PESTS

Cabbage root fly, cabbage white butterfly caterpillar, aphids, flea beetle, birds, whitefly and, to a lesser degree, slugs, snails and cutworms.

DISEASES

Downy mildew (calabrese only) and clubroot.

SELECTED VARIETIES

Broccoli

Bordeaux Purple spears produced without cold. Can be ready in 10–15 weeks. Sow from March to June for harvest between June and November. Not tolerant of frost.

Claret F1 Vigorous. Performs well on poorer soils. Large quantities of bigger-than-usual, purple spears. Harvest from March to May.

Nine Star Perennial Very unusual, tall perennial variety which can last two to three years. Small, creamy-white heads have to be harvested regularly to prevent this plant from running to seed and dying out. Allow at least 90 cm (36 in) between plants.

Purple Sprouting Hardy and very prolific variety with delicious, purple side shoots during March and April.

Red Arrow F1 Early maturing purple variety. Cut from late February.

Rudolph Start cropping it in September from an early sowing, but usually from

December. With successional sowing, it is possible to crop plants until February.

White Eye The white spears are of good quality and can be cut from February.

Calabrese:

Arcadia F1 Green heads from June to September that hold well on the plant. Grows in a wide range of soils.

Autumn Spear An excellent variety for extending the season. Dark-green spears. Harvest, September to November.

Chevalier F1 Produces many sideshoots, once the main head has been cut, that are well-suited to freezing.

Crown and Sceptres One main head of rich green, followed by sideshoots that have an asparagus flavour.

Hydra F1 Once the main head has been cut in July the plant continues to produce sideshoots well into November.

Kabuki F1 Ready in nine weeks. Suited to the bed system and growing under cloches.

Marathon Excellent disease resistance and tolerance to cold. Blue-green heads cropped into November.

Romanesco Known as Italian Broccoli. Pale-green, pyramid-shaped heads. Almost unbeatable in flavour.

Trixie Compact variety. Dark-green central head, followed by many sideshoots. Good tolerance of clubroot.

BRUSSELS SPROUTS
Brassica oleracea Gemmifera Group

Brassicaceae

An extremely cold-tolerant plant that will produce a crop from late autumn until late winter, when freshly picked vegetables are at a premium. It is a long-term crop that is sown in the spring and with most modern-day cultivars being F1 hybrids, they will produce a uniform and high-yielding group of plants that can be harvested over a long period. Due to this crop's necessity for a wide spacing between the plants, there is the possibility of growing catch crops between the rows, such as radish, spring onions, and lettuce. The small, button-sized sprouts freeze well and, in fact, the sprouts picked fresh from the stem will be improved after being subjected to a good, hard frost. It is a crop that offers more than just sprouts, as the cabbage-like, leafy top can also be eaten; although small, it is very tasty. It is now also possible to incorporate Brussels sprouts into the ornamental garden, with the colour range extending to incorporate not just green but also purple-red varieties. The only other point to bear in mind when deciding on which types to grow is to choose varieties that will mature at different times, giving the longest harvesting period possible.

124

DATES

Sowing/Planting
Inside February
Outside Early March–late April

Harvesting October–February

SOWING/PLANTING METHOD

Sow the earliest varieties into large modules or directly into the ground in drills and cover with a cloche or cold frame. Plant out when the seedlings are about 5–8 cm (2–3 in) tall. Sow maincrop varieties in modules or directly into a seed bed and plant out during midsummer into their final positions. Before the seeds in the seedbed germinate, it is important that they are covered with netting to keep off birds, as they will rapidly strip the plants.

MINIMUM TEMPERATURE

For germination 7°C (45°F)

SITE AND SOIL

Site Open sunny site with a fertile, but firm, soil. Avoid windy sites.

pH 6.5–8.0

Fertilizer Plenty of well-rotted organic matter and pelleted chicken manure or blood, fish and bone meal before planting or sowing. If plants are not growing well, a fertilizer application can be made during the second half of July.

Water Keep seedlings well-watered and water transplants well just after planting, but then leave for a week to encourage the roots to grow out, before watering when required.

DIMENSIONS

Planting depth 2 cm (¾ in) in seed bed drill, rows 15 cm (6 in) apart.

Plant as for broccoli (see page 121). Firm around the plant well, as they like very firm ground.

Space between plants:
Eating fresh 1 m (3 ft) square
For freezing 50 cm (20 in) square
In rows 45–60 cm (18–24 in);
75 cm (30 in) rows

AFTER CARE

Protect against cabbage root fly, birds and the cabbage white butterfly. Keep plants weed free and if a catch crop hasn't been grown, or it has been harvested, then the soil can be mulched with well-rotted manure, garden compost or even lawn clippings to help retain the moisture. If applying a summer feed to the crop, then water after application, although too much fertilizer can produce sprouts that are "soft" and less likely to survive a harsh winter. Do not excessively firm Brussels sprouts grown in beds, instead secure them with a cane for extra support. Water in dry weather. Stake Brussels sprouts to support the laden stems and earth up around the base of the stems to encourage extra rooting to aid support. Pick off all yellowing leaves in the autumn and put onto the compost heap.

COMPANION PLANTS

Cabbage, Chinese cabbage, broccoli, calabrese, cauliflower, kale, swede, turnip, radish, kohl rabi and catch crops such as lettuce, spring onions, rocket and spinach.

HARVESTING

Weeks to maturity: 30–36 weeks

Begin harvesting when the sprouts are 2–3 cm (¾–1¼ in) in diameter. Harvest from the bottom of the stem upwards.

HEALTH BENEFITS

High in vitamins A and C. A good source of calcium and iron, as well as being an antioxidant.

STORAGE

The whole stems can be pulled out of the ground and put into a bucket of water that just covers the roots. This should stand for about a week in a cool spot before the sprouts begin to yellow. Will freeze well.

PESTS

Cabbage root fly, cabbage white butterfly caterpillar, aphids, flea beetle, birds, cabbage moth, whitefly and to a lesser degree slugs, snails and cutworms.

DISEASES

Clubroot, brassica white blister and downy mildew.

SELECTED VARIETIES

Bedford Fillbasket Large, solid sprouts from October to December.

Bosworth F1 Excellent holding capacity. Well-spaced, dark-green sprouts during November and December. Good downy mildew resistance.

Braveheart F1 Sweet, dark-green sprouts from November to January. Excellent disease resistance.

Breeze F1 Good on less fertile soils with excellent disease resistance. Harvest from October to December.

Brigitte F1 Dark-green sprouts from October to mid-December. Excellent resistance to disease.

Falstaff Purple-red sprouts with unusual nutty flavour. Colour intensifies after hard frost. Steam or microwave.

Icarus F1 Large sprouts for harvest from October to February. Frost- and disease-resistant plants.

Red Bull Red variety with the colour intensifying after hard frost. Harvest from October to December.

Romulus F1 Dark-green, smooth-skinned, tight sprouts, harvested from August to January. Holds well in the ground and has good disease resistance.

Trafalgar F1 Heavy crop of the sweet sprouts. Harvest from December to March. Good holding capacity.

Wellington F1 Resistance to cold. Harvest from December to March. Dark-green sprouts.

SPECIAL TIP

For faster composting once harvested, put the stems through a shredder or smash them up using a hammer, before putting them onto the compost heap.

CABBAGE
Brassica oleracea Capitata Group

Brassicaceae

An outstanding vegetable that can be harvested every week of the year. It has a variety of conical and round shapes, combined with a range of colours from green through to grey-blue and red; combined with the range of flavours available, this is a vegetable that has to be part of every gardener's plot. They can be grown using the usual row method or in the deep-bed system and, although they like a firm soil, growing on deep beds in uncompacted soil seems to have no detrimental effect on the crop – as long as the right varieties are used. The earliest cabbages can be picked as spring greens, while the hearts are still leafy and have not firmed up. The remainder of the crop can then be left to heart up and can be cut until mid-summer. These are then followed by the summer- and autumn-maturing varieties that are harvested as soon as the hearts feel firm. Early summer cabbages tend to have pointed heads, while the late summer- and autumn-maturing varieties are rounded. With winter cabbages, the savoy types tend to stand the cold much better and will stand in the ground for a long time, until ready for harvest (when the heads become solid). All these types of cabbages are heavy feeders, so ample fertiliser is required to keep the crops growing to their maximum potential.

SUMMER-/AUTUMN-MATURING

DATES

Sowing/Planting February–May

Harvesting See individual varieties, as this can be anytime between June and November.

SOWING/PLANTING METHOD

Start early crops off in a greenhouse, coldframe or on a windowsill. Place them in seed trays, prick out into large modules and harden off before planting out under a cloche. At the same time, some of the hardened off plants can be set outside unprotected, so that they mature later and continue the crop succession. It is important to harden off this type of cabbage well, otherwise they have a tendency to bolt, although covering with fleece will help to prevent this happening. Sow in shallow drills in a seed bed, before transplanting when they are big enough to handle, about 5–8 cm (2–3 in). Water the seedlings well the night before you intend to transplant them and then lift them very carefully. Pull out a shallow and narrow trench that is then filled with water. The bunches of newly lifted cabbages can then be placed in this water and left for a couple of minutes, so that the roots become coated with muddy water; this will ensure the seedlings do not dry out after planting. Make a hole with a dibber at a depth of about 15 cm (6 in) and firm the plant into it, so that the bottom leaves rest on the soil surface. Water them in well.

MINIMUM TEMPERATURE

For germination 7°C (45°F)

SITE AND SOIL

Site Sunny, open site with a fertile, firm soil. Cabbages will tolerate exposed positions.

pH 6.5–8.0

Fertilizer Well-rotted organic matter and pelleted chicken manure or blood, fish and bone meal before planting or sowing.

Water Water during dry spells.

DIMENSIONS

Planting depth

2 cm (¾ in) in seed bed drill

15 cm (6 in) rows

Plant as for broccoli (see page 121). Firm around the plant well.

Space between plants

35–45 cm (14–18 in);

35–45 cm (14–18 in) rows

AFTER CARE

Protect against cabbage root fly, birds and cabbage white butterfly. Once the leaves from one row to the next are almost touching, the plants can be top-dressed with dried blood. Keep the weeds at bay and regularly remove any dead leaves.

COMPANION PLANTS

Brussels sprouts, Chinese cabbage, broccoli, calabrese, cauliflower, kale, swede, turnip, radish, kohl rabi and catch crops such as lettuce, spring onions, rocket and spinach.

HARVESTING

Weeks to maturity 17–26 weeks

Harvest when the heads feel firm and cut as required. Cut just below the head.

HEALTH BENEFITS

Good source of vitamins A and C; also an antioxidant.

STORAGE

They do not store well, but the late autumn varieties can be harvested and hung in a net in a cool dry place for a few days.

PESTS

Cabbage root fly, cabbage white butterfly caterpillar, aphids, flea beetle, birds, cabbage moth, whitefly and – to a lesser degree – slugs and snails and cutworms.

DISEASES

Clubroot, brassica white blister, downy mildew and fusarium wilt.

SELECTED VARIETIES

Advantage F1 Can also be used as spring greens. Pointed heads. Harvest from June to November.

Brigadier F1 Harvest in autumn but will also stand well and continue to be available for harvest during winter. Enormous heads can reach 6.5 kg (14 lb). Good resistance to fusarium wilt.

Duncan F1 Dark-green pointed heads. Harvest from June to November. Can also can be sown in the autumn and harvested as a spring cabbage.

Derby Day Round head variety. Excellent resistance to bolting. Harvest in June and July.

Golden Acre Primo Small variety suited to deep beds, with firm round heads. Harvest from June to August.

Greyhound Pointed heads and suited to growing on deep beds. Harvest in June.

Guardian F1 Blue-green leaves; round-headed. Very resistant to bolting. Harvest from June to October.

Hispi F1 Sow in February, under protection. Harvest from June onwards. Ideal for growing on deep beds. Pointed heads.

Huzaro F1 Uniform solid, dark-red heads having few outer leaves, so ideal for closer planting.

Minicole F1 Compact, round, Dutch white cabbage. Harvest, early autumn from an April sowing. Stands for a long time.

Redcap F1 Small variety ideally suited to deep beds. Superb, deep-red heads about the size of a hand, with few outer leaves. Stands very well. Harvest from July to November from a March-to-May sowing.

Red Drumhead Ideal for pickling. Tight deep-red heads have solid hearts and can reach up to 2 kg (4.5 lb) in weight. Stands well.

Red Jewel F1 Large crisp, ruby-red hearts; delicious raw, cooked or pickled. Stands and stores well.

Stonehead F1 Firm heads stand well. Harvest, from July to September. Can be closely planted. Some resistance to mildew and will store.

Winnigstadt Firm, pointed heads have a superb sweet flavour. Harvest from August to October.

SPECIAL TIP

Once the cabbage has been picked, you can cut a cross in the top of the remaining stalk to encourage a couple of smaller cabbages to develop.

SPRING-MATURING CABBAGES

DATES

Sowing/Planting July–August

Harvesting April–May

Some can be harvested before the hearts have formed as spring greens, with the remainder being cut once the hearts have become firm.

SOWING/PLANTING METHOD

Sow into a seed bed and transplant when they are 5–8 cm (2–3 in) tall. Soak the plants well the night before and stand in a water-filled trench, as with summer/autumn maturing cabbage, prior to planting with a dibber. The plants should be buried up to the bottom set of leaves to help prevent attack from cabbage root fly. Once planted, they must be watered in well.

MINIMUM TEMPERATURE

For germination 7°C (45°F)

SITE AND SOIL

Site Sunny, open site with a fertile, firm soil. Cabbages will tolerate exposed positions.

pH 6.5–8.0

Fertilizer Well-rotted organic matter and pelleted chicken manure or blood, fish and bone meal before planting or sowing. Top dress with dried blood or any other high-nitrogen feed in spring to boost the crop if necessary.

Water Water until established, then only in long, dry spells.

DIMENSIONS

Planting depth
2 cm (^{3}/4 in) in seed bed
15 cm (6 in) rows

Space between plants
15 cm (6 in) for spring greens
25 cm (10 in) for hearted cabbages
30 cm (12 in) rows

AFTER CARE

Protect against cabbage root fly, birds and cabbage white butterfly. Keep the weeds at bay. Regularly remove dead leaves. Apply dried blood in spring.

COMPANION PLANTS

Brussels sprouts, Chinese cabbage, broccoli, calabrese, cauliflower, kale, swede, turnip, radish and kohl rabi. You can also try catch crops such as lettuce, spring onions, rocket and spinach.

HARVESTING

Weeks to maturity 36 weeks

Cut heads as required.

HEALTH BENEFITS

Good source of vitamins A and C and an antioxidant.

STORAGE

They cannot be stored.

PESTS

Cabbage root fly, cabbage white butterfly caterpillar, aphids, flea beetle, birds, cabbage moth, whitefly and – to a lesser degree – slugs and snails and cutworms.

DISEASES

Clubroot, brassica white blister and downy mildew.

SELECTED VARIETIES

April Dark-green, pointed, crisp hearts. Harvest in April and May from a July or August sowing or from September to November from a June or July sowing.

Avon Crest Very early variety. Large, dark-green heads. Very resistant to bolting.

Durham Early Dark green and hardy. Use as spring greens or leave for large, pointed heads in the spring.

Durham Elf Crunchy hearts. Stands well over winter. Can be used as spring greens. Harvest in April and May.

Offenham 2, Flower of Spring Large and solid pointed heads ready April or May. Can be cut throughout the winter as spring greens.

Pixie Small, pointed heads ideal for beds. Harvest in April and May, but can use as spring greens before this.

Precoce de Louviers French variety. Big, conical green heads. Harvest from mid-January to end of March. Harvest in autumn from a spring sowing.

Spitfire Fresh green, pointed heads. Harvest in April.

Spring Hero F1 Round-headed type. Harvest in July. Stands well.

Wheelers Imperial Can be grown for harvest in April and early May or sown in spring for harvest in the autumn. Dark-green compact heads. Ideal in beds or rows.

Wintergreen Hardy variety. Use as spring greens or leave until April or May.

SPECIAL TIP

When protecting the crop against cabbage white butterflies, make sure the netting is held well above the cabbages or the butterflies will still be able to lay their eggs on the leaves.

WINTER-MATURING CABBAGES

DATES

Sowing/Planting May–June

Harvesting November–March

SOWING/PLANTING METHOD

Sow into a seed bed during May and June and transplant during June and July when 5–8 cm (2–3 in) tall. Soak the plants well the night before and stand in a water-filled trench, as with summer/autumn maturing cabbage, prior to planting with a dibber. The plants should be buried up to the bottom set of leaves to help prevent attack from cabbage root fly. Once planted, they must be watered in well.

MINIMUM TEMPERATURE

For germination 7°C (45°F)

SITE AND SOIL

Site Sunny and open, with fertile, firm soil. They will tolerate exposed sites.

pH 6.5–8.0

Fertilizer Well-rotted organic matter and pelleted chicken manure or blood, fish and bone meal before planting or sowing.

Water Water until established, then only in long dry spells.

DIMENSIONS

Planting depth
2 cm (3/4 in) in seed bed
15 cm (6 in) rows

Space between plants 45 cm (18 in); 45 cm (18 in) rows

AFTER CARE

Protect against cabbage root fly, birds and cabbage white butterfly. Earth up around the base of the plants and firm in well during late autumn/early winter. Regularly remove any dead leaves. Keep the weeds at bay.

COMPANION PLANTS

Brussels sprouts, Chinese cabbage, broccoli, calabrese, cauliflower, kale,

SPECIAL TIP

Do not overfeed winter-maturing cabbages, as the plants will put on too much lush growth and will be less likely to survive the winter undamaged.

swede, turnip, radish, kohl rabi and catch crops such as lettuce, spring onions, rocket and spinach.

HARVESTING

Weeks to maturity 28–36 weeks

Cut heads, as required, at the top of the stalk.

HEALTH BENEFITS

Good source of vitamins A and C and an antioxidant.

STORAGE

There is only need to store them if there is a glut, as they stand in the ground so well. Some varieties can be lifted complete with stalk and roots and hung upside down in a cool shed, where they can hang for up to two months during the winter.

PESTS

Cabbage root fly, cabbage white butterfly caterpillar, aphids, flea beetle, birds, cabbage moth, whitefly and – to a lesser degree – slugs, snails and cutworms.

DISEASES

Clubroot, brassica white blister and downy mildew.

SELECTED VARIETIES

Best of All Large, rounded heads. Harvest in October and November. Stands well for several weeks.

Capriccio F1 Matures late autumn. Delicious, dark-green heads that can weigh up to 2 kg (4 lb) each.

Celtic F1 Uniform, very firm, dark-green round heads. Harvest, from December and will stand in the ground until February.

Christmas Drumhead Dwarf variety. Large, round blue-green heads. Harvest late October to end of December.

Holland Late Winter White cabbage. Large, solid heads stand well without splitting. Harvest from October to February. Good for coleslaw.

January King 3 One of the hardiest varieties there is. Red-tinged, rounded heads ready for harvest from November through to January.

Marner Lagerrot Round-headed red variety. Stores very well. Plant at the standard distance or closer for smaller heads. At standard spacing, each head could reach 4.5 kg (10 lb) in weight. Harvest in October and November.

Marner Lagerweiss The green variety of the above, which also stores well and can be harvested from October through to December if sown during April and May.

Protovoy F1 Savoy type. Tennis ball-sized, conical heads can be grown at a close spacing. Harvest from August to the end of November. Stands well.

Quintal de Alsace French "drumhead" type. Very large, round heads of blue-grey leaves. Harvest from early September to end of December.

Roulette F1 Cross between January King and Dutch White. Medium-sized heads. Harvest from December to February.

Savoy King F1 Can sow to harvest at any time, but it makes an excellent winter cabbage. Savoy type. Large, green heads. Good in cooler conditions. Harvest from mid-October.

Savoy Siberia F1 Winter-hardy. Large dark, blue-green heads. Stands well. Harvest from September.

Tarvoy F1 Dense, dark-green heads. Stands well. Harvest from December to April.

Traviata F1 Savoy cabbage. Dark green, round heads with crinkled leaves. Stands well. Good tolerance to disease. Harvest from November to February.

Tundra F1 Winter hardy. Medium-to-large-sized heads. Harvest from November to February.

Vertus Winter-hardy savoy type. Dark-green heads with crinkled leaves. Harvest from December to February.

CARROT
Daucus carota

Apiaceae

Carrots are not easy to grow perfectly on all soils, but with the correct soil improvements and careful selection of variety, they are a crop that can be available all year round. With most root crops, the best soil type is a light soil that does not contain many obstructions, such as stones; this will give the root an easy passage downwards. On heavier, less-suitable soils, digging in organic matter each year will help, as will the addition of sharp sand.

Carrots like an open, sunny position and can be grown in rows, where the younger more tender and sweet roots are pulled to give space to the main crop (while producing early carrots for the table), or at a much closer spacing in the bed system. They can be grown in short rows and treated in the same way, multi-sown in modules or sown into biodegradable tubes, before planting out. If space is limited, then the shorter varieties can be grown successfully in containers. With such a wide choice of varieties, it is possible to have carrots available for any type of meal, as well as unusual coloured varieties to suit different moods or needs. If the soil is right, they are a relatively straightforward crop to grow, as they are not affected by many pests or diseases and are an excellent source of vitamins and fibre. They have a rare attribute, whereby the longer they are cooked, the more nutrients become available. The harvesting season can be extended at both ends by growing the correct varieties under cover.

DATES

Sowing *Inside* February–August
Outside February–July

Harvesting April–November

SOWING METHOD

Outside Sow thinly into shallow drills. Thin as they become large enough to use.

Inside Use modules or tubes. Multi-sow into modules, a method suitable for the salad varieties or maincrop types that are being grown to be picked young and tender. For longer roots, sow two to three seeds into biodegradable tubes. Thin to leave one seedling. Once the roots have established, both types can be planted out – under protection, if early or out into the open for later crops.

MINIMUM TEMPERATURE

For germination 7°C (45°F)

SITE AND SOIL

Site Sunny position.

pH over 6.5

Fertilizer Dig in well-rotted manure in the autumn, before the crop is to be sown or planted out. Do not over fertilise or roots will fork.

Water Water in dry weather.

DIMENSIONS

Planting depth
Sow into 2 cm ($3/4$ in) drills.
Plant to bury rootball.

Space between plants
8 cm (3 in)
23 cm (9 in) rows for salad varieties.
30 cm (12 in) rows for maincrop varieties.

AFTER CARE

Hoe regularly between rows to keep down weeds. Pull soil over the shoulders of the developing crop to prevent them going green and to limit the damage caused by carrot root fly. Later sowings can be left in the ground and pulled as required during winter, although in colder areas it will be necessary to protect them with a good layer of straw. If left in the ground for too long they may split, becoming more attractive to slugs.

COMPANION PLANTS

Cucumber, squash, pumpkin, melon, potato, tomato, marrow, courgette, beetroot, parsnip, scorzonera, salsify, Hamburg parsley, celeriac, onion, shallot, leek, garlic, celery, Florence fennel, aubergine and pepper.

HARVESTING

Weeks to maturity
Early varieties 9 weeks
Maincrop varieties 20 weeks

HEALTH BENEFITS

High in vitamins A and C, Beta-carotene and fibre.

STORAGE

During October and November, lift and clean undamaged carrots. Store in a box, tray or large pot and pack with moist sharp sand, peat, coir, sawdust or vermiculite. Place in a cool, dark place where they can be used as required.

PESTS

Carrot fly, slugs.

DISEASES

Violet root rot, downy mildew, cavity spot, alternaria and powdery mildew.

SELECTED VARIETIES

Adelaide F1 Grow under protection for a really early crop.

Amsterdam Forcing 3 Small, succulent roots. Ideal for early sowings under protection or outside. Excellent for successional sowings.

Autumn King 2 Long, large roots can be left in the ground all winter without them splitting. Stores very well.

Bangor F1 Maincrop. Long, cylindrical roots. Stores well. Resistant to shoulder-greening and internal cracking.

Chantenay Red Cored 2 Maincrop variety. Stores very well.

Early Nantes 5 Short, early variety. Excellent for growing under protection or successional sowings.

Flyaway F1 Sweet variety. Resistant to carrot fly.

Ideal Baby variety, ideal for beds or multi-sowing. Rich orange roots.

Kingston F1 Maincrop. Large, cylindrical roots, ideal for storing.

Maestro F1 Carrot-fly resistant and tolerant to alternaria and cavity spot. Cylindrical roots.

Nelson F1 Pull when young and sweet, or leave as maincrop. Smooth-skinned, cylindrical roots. Resistant to shoulder-greening and internal cracking.

Parmex Round, early maturing variety. Ideally suited to multi-sowing or growing in containers.

Purple Haze F1 Purple-skinned, maincrop with deep, orange flesh. Colour becomes less intense when cooked.

Resistafly F1 Early, sweet carrots or as maincrop. Long, well-coloured roots. Carrot fly resistant.

Samurai Red-skinned with pink flesh. Holds its colour well, even after cooking.

St. Valery Maincrop variety. Can be grown for showing. Stores well.

Sytan Good carrot-fly resistance. Long, coreless, rich orange roots.

Yellowstone Yellow variety. High in vitamin A and C as well as Beta-carotene.

> **SPECIAL TIP**
>
> In order to guarantee carrots being available every week of the year, it is important to sow every three weeks, which will give a succession from April to November.

CAULIFLOWER
Brassica oleracea Botrytis Group

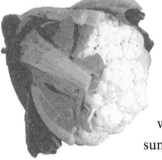

Brassicaceae

This wonderful vegetable has six definite growing groups that will give a harvest of cauliflowers every week of the year, starting with early summer cauliflowers, followed by summer, autumn, winter, spring and finally mini-veg varieties. Having such a diverse and extensive harvesting period they vary in growing times, with the largest winter cauliflowers being in the ground for almost a year and the much quicker mini-veg varieties only occupying their spot for up to four months. To avoid any transplant shock – which seems to be more apparent with cauliflowers than other brassicas – it is best to raise them in modules, as opposed to a seed bed. However, if modules are not an option, then a seed bed will suffice. The classic cauliflower look is that of a white or cream curd, but recent innovations have meant that there is now more variety, with yellowish, green, orange and even purple curds available. They are a difficult crop to grow, as they need constant moisture. With the longer-term crops, this is not usually supplied by natural rainfall, so supplementary watering will be required. Although usually grown in rows, the smaller varieties are well-suited to the bed system, where a large crop is possible with minimal growing space taken up.

142

DATES

Sowing/Planting

Spring maturing May
Early summer maturing October–January
Summer maturing March–April
Autumn maturing April–May
Winter maturing May
Mini-veg April–July

Harvesting

Spring-maturing March–June
Early summer-maturing June–July
Summer-maturing August–September
Autumn-maturing September–November
Winter-maturing December–March
Mini-veg August–November

SOWING/PLANTING METHOD

Summer-maturing Sow into a seed tray and when the seedlings are large enough prick out into modules, or sow directly into modules. The module method can be used for all types, but is essential for the earliest sowings, which will begin in late autumn, with these being planted out into their final positions under a cloche or cold frame.

Autumn-maturing If not raised in modules, these can be sown into a seed bed in April and May and transplanted during June and July, when the seedlings are no more than 8 cm (3 in) high.

Winter- and spring-maturing Either to be raised in modules or in a seed bed and sown during May, these can be transplanted into their final positions during August at about 8 cm (3 in) high.

Early summer-maturing Sow from October to January into a seed tray or modules and transplant outside under cloches or a cold frame during March.

Mini-veg varieties Sow in succession in a seed tray or modules from April to July, and transplant during June and July.

MINIMUM TEMPERATURE

For germination 7°C (45°F)

SITE AND SOIL

Site Open sunny site with a fertile but firm, moisture-retentive soil. Avoid frost pockets.

143

pH 6.5–8.0

Fertilizer Double dig, adding plenty of well-rotted organic matter and pelleted chicken manure or blood, fish and bone meal before planting or sowing.

Water Cauliflowers will quickly run to seed if not kept moist, and a single day of dryness can cause this. It is therefore vital to supplement rainfall with regular watering, especially on warmer, windy days.

DIMENSIONS

Planting depth Plant at the depth the plants were initially grown at. For modules, this is the top of the module and for seed-bed-raised plants, it is at the level of the soil in which they were raised.

Space between plants

In seed bed 15 cm (6 in) rows
Early summer-maturing 45 cm (18 in); 60 cm (24 in) rows
Summer-maturing 45 cm (18 in); 60 cm (24 in) rows
Autumn-maturing 60 cm (24 in); 60 cm (24 in) rows
Winter- and spring-maturing 70–75 cm (28–30 in); 70–75 cm (28–30 in) rows
Mini-veg 15 cm (6 ins); 15 cm (6 ins) rows

AFTER CARE

Protect against cabbage root fly, birds and cabbage white butterfly. Cauliflower curds need to be kept protected from severe frost and direct sunlight. The easiest way to do this is to bend one of the large outer leaves over the curd. Another method, particularly suited to winter- and spring-maturing cauliflowers, is to bend the plants to face the north in late autumn, so that after a frosty night the rising sun does not hit the curds until the frost has melted. If the heads did suffer rapid thawing, this may discolour them and even taint the taste of the curd. Support autumn-maturing cauliflowers by drawing soil around the stem and firming it well with the heel of your boot. Keep weeds at bay. Mulch around the plants with well-rotted manure, garden compost, paper or black polythene to conserve moisture.

COMPANION PLANTS

Brussels sprouts, Chinese cabbage, broccoli, calabrese, cabbage, kale, swede, turnip, radish, kohl rabi and catch crops such as lettuce, spring onions, rocket and spinach.

HARVESTING

Weeks to maturity: *Early summer, summer and autumn* 16–20 weeks
Winter and spring 40 weeks
Mini-veg 15 weeks

Cut heads as required.

HEALTH BENEFITS

Excellent source of vitamin C. Good for slimmers, as cauliflowers are very low in calories.

STORAGE

If there is an over abundance of the early summer, summer and autumn crop they can be lifted, stem, root and all and hung upside down in a shed or on a fence in a cool, shady place. If regularly sprayed with water these will hang for several weeks, although the storage period will be less in very hot weather.

PESTS

Cabbage root fly, cabbage white butterfly caterpillar, aphids, flea beetle, birds, cabbage moth, whitefly and – to a lesser degree – slugs and snails and cutworms.

DISEASES

Clubroot, brassica white blister and downy mildew.

SELECTED VARIETIES

Spring

Aalsmeer Pure white curds. Very winter hardy. Harvest in April and May.

Galleon Dense, creamy-white heads. Overwinters very well. Harvest in April and May.

Medallion F1 Roscoff type. Compact and uniform, firm white curds. Harvest in February to March. Needs a sheltered part of the garden.

Prestige Hardy type. White heads. Harvest in April and May.

Purple Cape Rich purple heads. Harvest from late March to early April.

Walcheren Winter 3 Armado Pure white curds. Very hardy. Harvest in March and April from an April/May sowing.

Walcheren Winter Pilgrim Heavy-cropping cauliflower. Winter hardy, deep creamy white, compact curds. Harvest in May.

Early Summer

Evita White curds. Harvest in May and June. Excellent frost resistance.

Rapido F1 Pure white curds. Good in both cool and very warm conditions. Leaves wrap around curd to protect it from frost and sun. Harvest from May.

Snowball Suited to the beds. Very compact white heads. Harvest in June from October sowing or sow March–April for a late-summer/autumn harvest.

Summer

All-the-Year-Round Can be grown for harvest during any of the four seasons. White curds well-protected by the outer leaves.

Avalanche F1 Can be grown as mini-veg at a closer spacing, or for larger heads at a wider spacing. Snow-white curds, well-protected by the leaves. Stands well. Harvest from mid-May.

Candid Charm The long harvesting period makes this variety a must, with the deep white heads being available from July to November.

Cheddar F1 Unusual. Buttermilk-orange curd, resembling the colour of cheddar cheese. Turns brighter orange when lightly cooked. Harvest, June to September from a March–June sowing.

Early Romanesco Alternative to standard cauliflower. Unusual lime-green florets forming a conical shape. Harvest from September.

Green Harmony F1 A cauliflower and broccoli hybrid. Curds look like cauliflowers, but have a broccoli taste.

Harvest from June to October from a March–May sowing.

Gypsy F1 Excellent for growing on less fertile soils. White, round curds. Harvest from June to August.

Idol Ideal on beds. Small white heads. Harvest from June until end of July.

Igloo Excellent for successional sowing. Large and firm snow white curds. Leaves protect curds. Harvest from July to November.

Lateman Medium-sized, white heads. Harvest from July to October.

Mayflower F1 Earliest summer variety. Pure white curds in May from a January sowing.

Purple Graffiti F1 Purple curds. Harvest from July to October. If boiled, the purple will be held better if lemon juice is added to the water.

Snowball Medium-sized white heads. Large leaves protect curds. Stands well. Can be grown as an early summer-maturing cauliflower if sown in autumn. Harvest from June to September.

Snow Crown Pure white curds. Leaves protects curds from the sun. Harvest in July and August.

Autumn

Andes Large, blue-green leaves protect creamy-white curds from sun. Harvest in September and October.

Astral F1 Very late autumn variety. Harvest in October and November. Pure white heads, well-protected by outer leaves.

Autumn Giant 3 Large, pure white heads from October to end of December.

Pavillion F1 Pure white, well-protected curds. Harvest from mid-September to end of October.

Red Lion Purple heads. Harvest in autumn.

Sunset F1 Orange curds. Harvest in September and October from May/June sowing.

Sydney F1 Dense, pure-white curds from September to October.

Trevi F1 Light-green curds. Harvest in September and October.

Violet Queen Small, deep-purple heads. Curds turn green during cooking. Harvest from August to October.

Pericles F1 Very deep, white curds. Harvest during October.

Winter

Deakin F1 Dense, firm white curds are well-protected by the wrapped leaves. Harvest from late October to January from a spring sowing.

Castlegrant Ivory-white heads. Harvest from late October to December. Wrap around leaves.

Optimist F1 Hardy, with good disease resistance. Performs well in cold, wet conditions. Sow May to June. Harvest in November and December.

White Dove F1 Large white heads can weigh up to 1 kg (2 lb). Harvest from February to March.

Triomphant F1 White, well-protected curds. Harvest from December to January.

SPECIAL TIP

Before planting out cauliflower seedlings, check each one to make sure it is not "blind". A "blind" cauliflower is one that has no growing tip and will therefore come to nothing, taking up the space occupied by a cauliflower that would potentially produce an excellent curd.

CELERIAC
Apium graveolens var *rapaceum*

Apiaceae

Although most people see this as a root – and in most cases it is
grouped with the root vegetables – it is actually a swollen stem
and a close relative of celery, which is why it has a celery-like
flavour. The knobbly, swollen "bulb" will grow to a good size
and can be used either cooked or raw in winter salads. It is a
good vegetable to grow, as it is fairly hardy, down to
temperatures of -10°C (14°F), when protected by straw, and
stores very well, so it is a useful winter substitute for celery.
Celeriac is a relatively easy vegetable to grow, although it does
occupy the ground for a fairly lengthy period and requires
totally unchecked growth to produce a good crop.

149

DATES

Sowing/Planting March–April

Harvesting August–April

SOWING/PLANTING METHOD

As celeriac needs a continuous period of uninterrupted growth to produce its best crop, sowing directly into modules is the preferred method, although it can be sown into seed trays and pricked out into modules when it is at the first, true, leaf stage. There is no advantage in trying to get an early harvest by sowing earlier, as they will surely run to seed. The seedlings need to be kept at a temperature of no less than 10°C (50°F), until they are ready to harden off during late spring. Try not to leave it too late when planting out, as it is beneficial to the crop to get established before the hot and dry weather; planting in April and May is better than June.

MINIMUM TEMPERATURE

For germination 15–18°C (59–65°F)

SITE AND SOIL

Site Sunny position, although tolerates some shade, in a soil that is moisture-retentive and contains plenty of organic matter.

pH 6.0–7.5

Fertilizer Organic matter prior to planting and double dig the plot if possible. High-nitrogen fertilizer such as blood, fish and bone meal or pelleted chicken manure prior to planting out.

Water Water regularly to avoid drying out, as it will quickly run to seed.

SPECIAL TIP

There is no advantage in planting celeriac too close together, as this will only result in smaller roots and therefore a reduced crop.

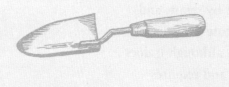

150

DIMENSIONS

Planting depth Plant out so that the swollen stem sits on the surface of the soil.

Space between plants 30 cm (12 in); 37 cm (15 in) rows

AFTER CARE

Mulch the crop with organic matter to conserve moisture and, in dry spells, water twice a week. From mid-summer onwards, remove any yellowing leaves that are coming away from the crown, as this will help to produce less knobbly stems that are easier to peel. In early autumn, draw soil around the swollen stems to blanch them. If the crop is being left in the ground for the winter, and harvested as required, you should cover it with a layer of straw or bracken to protect the crop from severe frost.

COMPANION PLANTS

Potatoes, carrots, salsify, scorzonera, beetroot, parsnip, tomatoes, leeks, garlic, onions, courgette, marrow, pumpkin, celery, cucumber, aubergine, Florence fennel, peppers and Hamburg parsley.

HARVESTING

Weeks to maturity 26 weeks

Celeriac is always at its best when harvested straight from the ground, so once the swollen stems have reached about 8–13 cm (3–5 in) in diameter, harvesting can begin. Leaves can be used in soup, and the swollen stems should be peeled before use.

HEALTH BENEFITS

A good source of vitamin C, as well as being an excellent supply of dietary, fat-free fibre.

STORAGE

Store in boxes packed with moist sharp sand, compost or bark.

PESTS

Carrot fly, leaf miner, slugs and snails.

DISEASES

Celery leaf spot, crown rot and violet rot.

SELECTED VARIETIES

Alabaster Bolt-resistant. High yields of smooth, round roots with a strong celery flavour.

Brilliant Smooth-skinned, so easier to peel. White flesh.

Claudia Probably the least knobbly of all the varieties.

Giant Prague Excellent inner quality and superb smooth skin.

Globus Larger than normal roots. Slow to mature.

Iram Medium-sized variety. Remains very white when cooked.

Jose Fast-maturing, uniform variety.

Marble Ball Medium-sized stem, strong celery flavour. Excellent when stored.

Monarch Smooth-skinned variety. Large and firm roots with white flesh.

Prinz Resistant to bolting, so ideal for the early sowing. More knobbly skin, but nice white flesh.

Snow White Delicate flavour. White, fleshed roots.

Tellus Smooth-skinned, quick-growing variety. White flesh.

CELERY
Apium graveolens var *dulce*

Apiaceae

Grown for its crisp and crunchy, succulent stems, this vegetable comes in two types: trench celery and self-blanching celery. Self-blanching celery is easier to grow, but it does not have the flavour or the texture of trench celery. It is becoming increasingly difficult for the organic gardener to find and buy celery seed that has not been coated or treated with a fungicide. The stems of self-blanching celery range from an off-white, creamy colour to green and they are less hardy than the trench types, which have green stems that are blanched to produce white, pink or red stems. This is done by growing them in a trench that is gradually filled in, or by growing them on the surface of the soil and covering the stems with a collar to eliminate the light, thus blanching the stems.

153

DATES

Sowing/Planting March–April

Harvesting
Self-blanching July–October
Trench celery November–December

SOWING/PLANTING METHOD

Sow into seed trays on the surface of the compost. Do not cover the seed as it needs light and moisture to germinate. Once it has reached the one true leaf stage, it can be pricked out into modules and grown on at a temperature that falls no lower than 10°C (50°F), to avoid possible bolting. During late spring, at about the four true leaf stage, the seedlings can be hardened off. From late spring/early

SPECIAL TIP

If growing trench celery, you could wrap newspaper around the stalks of each plant, totally enclosing them, and tie it on with string. When the soil is replaced into the trench it does not then fall in between the stalks, keeping them nice and clean for harvest time.

summer they can be planted out into their final positions. Self-blanching celery needs to be planted out in blocks, so that the plants will shade each other and help with the blanching process. Trench celery should either be planted at the bottom of a prepared trench or on the flat, if collars are to be used for blanching. If a trench is to be used for blanching, it should be dug out to a spade's depth, approximately 45 cm (18 in) wide and the soil heaped on either side. A layer of well-rotted manure can then be spread over the bottom at a depth of about 5 cm (2 in) and covered with about a 2.5 cm (1 in) layer of soil, before the module-raised seedlings are planted out.

MINIMUM TEMPERATURE

For germination 15–18°C (59–65°F)

SITE AND SOIL

Site Sunny, open position in a soil that is moisture-retentive and contains plenty of organic matter.

pH 6.5

Fertilizer Add organic matter prior to

planting and double dig the plot if possible. Add an application of a high-nitrogen fertilizer such as blood, fish and bone meal or pelleted chicken manure prior to planting out.

Water Water regularly, as it will quickly run to seed if it dries.

DIMENSIONS

Planting depth Plant out so that the crown of the plant sits on the surface of the soil.

Space between plants
Self-blanching 25 cm (10 in);
25 cm (10 in) rows
Trench celery 30 cm (12 in);
30 cm (12 in) rows

AFTER CARE

To avoid stringiness, celery must be grown with constant moisture at the root, so watering is essential. Mulching with organic matter will not only help to retain the moisture but will also add available nutrients to the soil. In mid-summer, when the plants are about half their final size, give them an application of liquid animal feed or another high-nitrogen alternative, and repeat a month later. Keep weed free. In mid-summer, remove any suckers that may have appeared at the base of trench celery and then refill the trench until the soil is level with the base of the leaves. If growing trench celery on the flat, then the stalks need to be wrapped in newspaper, corrugated cardboard or brown paper, and tied on with string, to eliminate the light for blanching.

COMPANION PLANTS

Potatoes, carrots, salsify, scorzonera, beetroot, parsnip, tomatoes, leeks, garlic, onions, courgette, marrow, pumpkin, celeriac, cucumber, aubergine, Florence fennel, peppers and Hamburg parsley.

HARVESTING

Weeks to maturity
Self-blanching 18 weeks
Trench celery 30 weeks

Self-blanching celery needs to be harvested before the frosts begin as it is not frost hardy, but the trenched celery can be dug up as required, re-covering the rest until they are needed.

HEALTH BENEFITS

Source of potassium, low in calories and has anti-inflammatory properties.

STORAGE

Trench celery can be stored by covering the plants with soil in situ and digging them out as required.

PESTS

Carrot fly, leaf miner, slugs and snails.

DISEASES

Celery leaf spot, crown rot and violet root rot.

SELECTED VARIETIES

Brydon's Prize Red Hardy trench variety. Stands well. Thick, fleshy stalks, tinged red turn a more intense colour when blanched.

Giant Pascal Trench variety. Long, succulent and crisp stems.

Gaint Red Reddish-green stems. Leaves can be used like Italian parsley.

Golden Self-Blanching 3 Very early maturing. White stems ready August.

Golden Spartan Self-blanching. Pale green stems. Excellent bolting resistance.

Lathom Self-Blanching Galaxy Tolerates an early sowing, without running to seed. Thick, crunchy stems.

Loretta Self-blanching, vigorous variety. Smooth, succulent white stalks.

Solid Pink Hardy trench variety. Stays red even after cooking. Harvest in November and December.

Solid White Trench variety. Crisp stems. Harvest in November.

Tall Utah Trench variety. Good disease resistance. Long, crisp stalks.

Tango F1 Long, apple-green stems. Self-blanching.

Victoria F1 Bolt-resistant, self-blanching variety. Very upright, apple-green, crispy stalks; white at the base.

CHICORY
Cichorium intybus

Asteraceae

There are three types of chicory. One is a white blanched "chicon" called witloof chicory, which is grown primarily as a rosette of leaves, with a deep root, that is harvested and forced to produce a second blanched bud, which can be cooked or used in winter salads. The second is red chicory, also known as radicchio, which has red or variegated leaves and finally there is sugarloaf chicory, which resembles a large, green cos lettuce when mature. Both the red and sugarloaf chicories do not need blanching, as their leaves are not as bitter as the witloof type, and they can be harvested in autumn to be used like lettuce in salads. Although not completely hardy, sugarloaf chicory will withstand more frost than the red chicory.

DATES

Sowing/Planting
Witloof mid-June–early July
Red late April–August
Sugarloaf June–September

Harvesting
Witloof November–March
Red July–November
Sugarloaf September–November

SOWING/PLANTING METHOD

Don't try to get an advanced crop by sowing early, as this will only result in the plants running to seed. Sow red chicory into modules in the greenhouse before transplanting outside under a cloche or fleece. Witloof and sugarloaf chicory can be directly sown outside into shallow drills and thinned.

MINIMUM TEMPERATURE

For germination 10°C (50°F)

SITE AND SOIL

Site Sunny and open spot, but will tolerate some shade. Rich and moisture-retentive soil, although it will grow adequately on poorer soils.

pH 6.5–7.5

Fertilizer No extra fertilizer, if soil was improved for previous crop. If blood, fish and bone meal or pelleted chicken have not been added, use manure two to three weeks before sowing.

Water Water during dry weather, until established.

DIMENSIONS

Planting depth Sow into drills 1 cm (1/2 in) deep.

Space between plants:
Witloof 23 cm (9 in);
30 cm (12 in) rows
Red 30 cm (12 in);
30 cm (12 in) rows
Sugarloaf 30 cm (12 in);
30 cm (12 in) rows

In deep beds, witloof varieties can be spaced in blocks at 20 cm (8 in), with the other types grown at 25cm (10 in).

AFTER CARE

Water plants during establishment. They may need to be covered with fleece or a cloche, if frost is forecast. Weed between the plants as necessary. If the growth of the red and sugarloaf chicory is disappointing, feed with a high-nitrogen liquid or an application of dried blood. In the autumn lift the roots of the witloof varieties for forcing. Trim the top leaves to within 1 cm (1/2 in) of the root and lay them in a box of moist compost or sand, where they will be kept cool until needed for forcing. In order to keep a continuity of "chicons" it is necessary to plunge roots for forcing every three to four weeks. Position them upright in a deep container of moist compost, or peat substitute, which is firmly packed around the roots. Then cover the roots with another 23 cm (9 in) of compost, or peat substitute, also firmed well. Put a lid on top to block out the light. Leave the box in a warm dark place for the "chicons" to be produced. After about four to five weeks, the "chicons" will have grown about 15–20 cm (6–8 in) and will be ready for harvest. Lift out the complete root and cut the "chicons" away from the roots about 1 cm (1/2 in) from the top of the root. These roots can then be used to force another crop. The chicory tops can be harvested in summer and used in salads, although without blanching they have a rather bitter taste.

SPECIAL TIP

Once cut, the stumps of both red and sugarloaf chicory can be covered with a cloche for another crop of leaves. The sugarloaf can be cropped throughout the winter this way.

COMPANION PLANTS

Peas, French beans, climbing French beans, runner beans, Lima beans, sweetcorn, okra, globe artichokes, lettuce, endive, broad beans, cress, spinach, and chard.

HARVESTING

Weeks to maturity
Witloof 32 weeks
Red 14–16 weeks
Sugarloaf 16 weeks

HEALTH BENEFITS

High in vitamin A and potassium.

STORAGE

They do not store.

PESTS

Slugs and caterpillars.

DISEASES

Tip burn may be a problem on light soils, caused by a calcium deficiency.

SELECTED VARIETIES

Witloof Zoom F1 Forcing variety. Tightly packed hearts. Harvest all winter.

Pain de Sucre Look like well grown cos lettuce. Harvest from October onwards from a June/July sowing.

Palla Rossa Bella Radicchio type. Firm, red-green hearts with prominent white veins. Harvest from September. Extend season by covering with a cloche or fleece.

Rosso Treviso Radicchio type. Can be forced. Non-hearting variety. Head of loose, white-veined green leaves, which turn red as the weather gets colder. Harvest through winter.

Lightning High-yielding witloof variety. Long, smooth "chicons", yellow at the top and white below. Harvest from January.

Brussels Witloof Crisp "chicons". Harvest in winter.

Grumolo Verde Tall, narrow leaves. Radicchio type. After summer harvest, leave alone and the plant will produce green rosettes that will stand the winter for use in the spring.

Witloef Alba Witloof type. Solid hearts for winter harvest.

Late Rossa di Chioggia Very resistant to frost. Large and heavy heads up to 400 g (1 lb) in weight. Large, white-veined, deep-red leaves.

Cesare Radicchio type. Dark-red leaves, tangy taste. Harvest September to February.

Zuckerhut Sugarloaf type. Dark-green outer leaves, well-blanched inner hearts. Harvest from September to November.

CUCUMBER AND GHERKIN

Cucumis sativus

Cucurbitaceae

With greatly improved new varieties now readily available, these annual and tender plants are worth space in anybody's cropping plan. Cucumbers are generally grown under protection, although the outdoor varieties are productive and very flavoursome, if there is no greenhouse available. Gherkins are much shorter and harvested earlier, when they are usually pickled. Cucumbers are naturally trailing plants, so they would need to be grown up supports in the greenhouse, whereas outside they can be left to spread across the ground or trained up wigwams, trellis or wires. The varieties suitable for greenhouse culture have smoother and longer fruits than the outdoor types, which are smaller, rougher and tougher-skinned but with just as good a flavour. The modern greenhouse varieties of cucumber have been bred to be all female, which dispenses with the need to pollinate and makes growing them just that little bit easier. They need to be grown at a minimum temperature of 15–18°C (60–65°F), which makes them an expensive crop to produce, but grown correctly they should produce more than enough fruits to compensate.

161

DATES

Sowing/Planting March–June

Harvesting June–October

SOWING/PLANTING METHOD

Sow into 8 cm (3 in) pots in a heated greenhouse at a temperature of at least 20°C (68°F) putting two seeds per pot. If both seeds germinate, then remove the weaker one. For outdoor cucumbers, grow on until the risk of frost has passed and then plant them out. To minimize waste of space, it is best to grow them upwards, so a wigwam is an excellent and aesthetically pleasing way to train them (although growing them up a trellis, wire or strings is just as good). As for the greenhouse varieties, they can be grown in several ways. Firstly, they can be potted on into successively larger pots until they finish up in a 10 litre (10 in) pot, which will be their final size, or they can be planted straight from the 8 cm (3 in) pot into grow bags. Alternatively, you can plant them out from their 8 cm (3 in) pot into the border soil of the greenhouse.

MINIMUM TEMPERATURE

For germination 20°C (68°F)

SITE AND SOIL

Site Warm, sunny and sheltered situation that has a well-manured, moisture-retentive, but well-drained soil.

pH 6.0

Fertilizer Well-rotted manure or garden compost before planting and an application of blood, fish and bone meal or pelleted chicken manure.

Water Like plenty of water, so never let the plants dry out. Be careful not to overwater the greenhouse varieties.

SPECIAL TIP

At least two weeks before planting outdoor cucumbers, spread a sheet of polythene over the area so that the soil is warmed, which will increase the amount of cucumbers harvested.

DIMENSIONS

Planting depth Sow into pots at a depth of 2.5 cm (1 in).

Space between plants
Outside If growing up supports 60 cm (24 in)
If growing on the flat 90 cm (36 in)
Inside 60 cm (24 in)

AFTER CARE

Greenhouse cucumbers have an optimum growing temperature of 28°C (82°F) combined with a minimum night-time temperature of 20°C (68°F), although they will grow perfectly well at an average daytime temperature of 18–24°C (65–75°F). They like a humid atmosphere, so damp down pathways and benching at least twice a day and ventilate on hotter days. For outdoor and greenhouse cucumbers being grown up supports, tie in regularly and remove the first three sideshoots completely, to prevent the fruits from touching the ground as they would inevitably spoil or cause potential disease problems. The next three sideshoots can be cut back to one leaf with all subsequent sideshoots cut back to two leaves. This will prevent overloading any part of the plant and give good, even-sized fruits over a long period. Once the plants reach the tops of the supports, pinch out the growing tip. For plants grown on the flat, regularly pinch out the growing tips at five or six leaves, to encourage more bushy growth. Mulch the ground with straw to keep the fruits clean and prevent rotting when in contact with the soil. Water all types regularly and feed with an animal or seaweed-based balanced fertilizer from mid-summer at fortnightly intervals, until harvesting begins. If any male flowers appear on the greenhouse varieties, remove immediately, but do not remove male flowers from gherkins or outdoor cucumbers, as these are required for pollination.

COMPANION PLANTS

Carrot, squash, pumpkin, melon, potato, tomato, marrow, courgette, beetroot, parsnip, scorzonera, salsify, Hamburg parsley, celeriac, onion, shallot, leek, garlic, celery, Florence fennel, aubergine and pepper.

HARVESTING

Weeks to maturity 12 weeks

Regularly harvest fruits from outdoor and greenhouse cucumbers as well as gherkins, to encourage more fruit. With outdoor varieties and gherkins, cut the fruit when it is young and still has the flower attached.

HEALTH BENEFITS

Low in calories.

STORAGE

Will store for a long time in the fridge or wrap the fruit in cling film and store in a cool room.

PESTS

Slugs and snails, whitefly, red spider mite and aphids.

DISEASES

Cucumber mosaic virus, powdery mildew, botrytis and stem rots.

SELECTED VARIETIES

Greenhouse

African Horned Unusual fruit that can be eaten by halving, adding some salt and lemon and then scooping out the very juicy flesh. Harvest from September.

Armenian Cucumber Huge fruit, with light-green, heavily ribbed skin. Can reach 60–90 cm (24–36 in) long, with a diameter of 8 cm (3 in).

Bella F1 Vigorous, all-female variety. Heavy yield of long, slightly ribbed dark green fruits. Resistant to powdery mildew.

Carmen F1 Dark-green fruits, 50 to 100 per plant. All-female variety. Resistant to powdery mildew. Day-length sensitive, therefore sow after 1st March.

Cumlaude RZ F1 Good in an unheated greenhouse. High-yielding variety. Mildew resistant plants. Harvest from June to September.

Flamingo F1 Tolerant of low light levels, so good for early and late cropping. High yields of dark-green fruits. Tolerant of powdery mildew.

Hana F1 Short-fruited, all-female variety. Crops prolifically throughout the season. Grow in a heated or cold greenhouse/tunnel. Harvest from July to October.

Palermo F1 High yields of dark-green fruits in a heated or unheated greenhouse. High tolerance to powdery mildew.

Passandra F1 Small, dark-green, lightly ribbed fruits about 15 cm (6 in) long. Grow in a heated or unheated greenhouse. Tolerant of powdery mildew and cucumber mosaic virus.

Pepinex 69 F1 All female variety. Mid-green, long fruits with no sign of bitterness.

Prima Top F1 Small, 23 cm (9 in), mid-green, slightly ridged and spiky fruits. Grow inside and out.

Stimora F1 Can harvest young and treat as gherkins or leave for cucumbers.

Sunsweet Yellow F1 Looks more like a lemon than a cucumber. Oval yellow fruits produced in bunches of two or three at each leaf joint. Harvest yellow to eat raw or leave to turn orange, when they can be treated like a courgette.

Suprami F1 Grows at lower temperatures. All-female variety. Good tolerance to powdery mildew.

Tiffany F1 Vigorous, all-female variety. Grow in a hot or cold greenhouse. Dark-green fruits over 30 cm (12 in) long.

Outside

Burplees Tasty Green F1 Best outdoor variety. Dark-green fruits, best picked at 23 cm (9 in) long. Tolerant of summer heat and resistant to powdery mildew.

Crystal Apple Round, yellow fruits. Pick when 8–10 cm (3–4 in) in diameter.

Diamant F1 Early gherkin, ideal pickled or in salads. Harvest from June to October.

Klaro F1 Dark-green fruit, up to 25 cm (10 in) long and 6 cm (2½ in) in diameter. Harvest from June to October. Ideal for pickling when picked immature.

Long White Thin, tender, white skin. Distinct flavour.

Marketmore Reliable variety. Dark-green fruits from July onwards.

Masterpiece Slightly spiny, dark-green fruits. Best picked at 20 cm (8 in) long.

Natsuhikari F1 Long, dark-green fruits. Can trail along the ground or be trained up supports.

Venlo Pickling Crops well all summer. Best picked young for pickling.

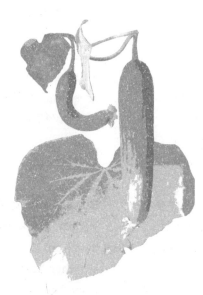

166

ENDIVE
Cichorium endivia

Asteraceae

An invaluable crop for all those who enjoy salads and miss that
delight through the winter, as it is similar to lettuce. However,
it is related to both the dandelion and chicory, with the same
bitter flavour, although if grown correctly, the bitterness is kept
to a minimum. Ready for harvest from late summer and
available through the autumn and winter the crop is not totally
hardy and will require some sort of protection from the worst
of the winter. It is also well suited to container growing, so can
be brought inside for winter and grown on the kitchen
windowsill, as it can take lower light levels than lettuce. The
curled-leaf types are also very ornamental, particularly when
there is less to look at in the garden, although there are also
broad-leaved varieties, with the latter being much hardier and
therefore more suited to winter cropping, while the curled-leaf
varieties cope better with the summer heat.

167

DATES

Sowing/Planting April–September

Harvesting All year round

SOWING/PLANTING METHOD

For planting out under cover, sow in April into modules, which can then be planted out during early summer under a cloche. If planting directly outside with no protection, then it is better to wait until May for sowing into modules in a greenhouse. All other sowings can be made directly into shallow seed drills outside, making sure that there will be enough space to erect a cloche later. For winter crops, sow under cover and in the open, dependent on variety, although both will ultimately need the protection of a cloche.

SPECIAL TIP

It is also possible to grow endive as a cut-and-come-again lettuce crop from mid-spring until late summer under the protection of a cloche, tunnel or greenhouse.

MINIMUM TEMPERATURE

For germination 4.5°C (40°F)
If the temperature falls below this for any length of time during the seedling stage, then there is a risk that these seedlings will bolt.

SITE AND SOIL

Site For mid-summer crops, a semi-shaded position is best, otherwise they may become bitter and run to seed. Winter crops prefer a sunny, open spot with a soil that is fertile and moisture-retentive, although well-drained.

pH 6.5–7.5

Fertilizer Do not add any fertilizer or organic matter if some was applied for the previous crop. If not, then apply well rotted garden compost.

Water Water during dry weather.

DIMENSIONS

Planting depth Sow into drills 2 cm ($^3/4$ in) deep.

Transplant modules so that the top of

the module is level with the soil surface.

Space between plants
30 cm (12 in);
30 cm (12 in) rows
In beds, plant in blocks at 23 cm (9 in) spacing.

AFTER CARE

Weed and water when necessary. The later sowings will need to be covered with a cloche to protect them from the frosts. Blanch the leaves about three months after sowing by covering them with a flower pot that has had all the holes blocked to exclude the light or a bucket. This will remove most of the bitterness. Alternatively, just tie the plants up into a bunch, with twine, to exclude the light to the inner leaves.

COMPANION PLANTS

Peas, French beans, climbing French beans, runner beans, Lima beans, sweetcorn, okra, globe artichokes, lettuce, broad beans, chicory, cress, spinach, and chard.

HARVESTING

Weeks to maturity 7–13 weeks

With the summer-leaf types, cut them as required. If the plants have been prepared for blanching then leave them for 10 days in summer or 20 days in winter before harvesting. It is important that they are harvested after this time, because if you leave them any longer they will start to regain their bitterness.

HEALTH BENEFITS

High in vitamin C and iron.

STORAGE

Endive can be lifted in autumn and winter, the leaves tied up as before and replanted in a box of compost and put into a frost-free, cool place where they can be harvested two to three weeks later.

PESTS

Slugs, aphids, and caterpillars.

DISEASES

Basal rot can be a problem in winter on poorly drained soils.

SELECTED VARIETIES

Batavian Broad Leaved Escarole Good winter variety. Broad, slightly twisted lettuce-like leaves in rounded head. Needs some winter protection.

Blond Full Heart Large heads of green and white leaves, curled at the edges. Blanch before eating. Harvest from August to October. Can bolt during sudden spells of hot weather.

Bubikopf 2 Large, semi-erect heads have creamy-white hearts. Harvest from autumn into winter.

Fine de Louvier Non-hearting variety. Long, toothed leaves. Harvest from August to October. One of the best varieties.

Kentucky Curly leaved type with good tangy flavour.

Moss Curled Dark-green, curly leaves. Blanch before eating.

Pancalieri Curly leaf variety. Self-blanching. Better cut as young salad leaves. Dark-green, very serrated outer leaves, creamy-white hearts and rose-tinted white mid-ribs. Harvest throughout the year.

Wallone Traditional French type. Heads of very tightly packed leaves. Self-blanching. Harvest through winter from an August/September sowing.

FLORENCE FENNEL
Foeniculum vulgare var. azoricum

Apiaceae

A very versatile vegetable that is much desired for the unique aniseed flavour of its swollen stem and the fact that it can be eaten raw or cooked. An attractive plant to grow on the vegetable plot, but not the easiest from which to get a good return, as it is quick to bolt. The swollen stem is the main edible part of this plant and has become much sought after in recent years, although the fine, feathery leaves and stalks are also very tasty.

171

DATES

Sowing/Planting March–August

Harvesting June–November

SOWING/PLANTING METHOD

As the plants dislike their roots being disturbed, sowing early crops into modules or biodegradable pots is the answer. Sow during March and April and plant them out when they have no more than four true leaves, being careful not to disturb the roots. Cover them with fleece or a cloche until the weather improves. Later sowings from April through to August can either be made in modules or directly outside into shallow drills. For sowings made

SPECIAL TIP

Florence fennel can be used as a seedling crop where it is directly sown with a few seeds put in at 5 cm (2 in) intervals in rows 30 cm (12 in) apart. It is important not to thin them. They can then be harvested as seedlings for use in salads and stir fries.

prior to mid-June, it is important to use only bolt-resistant varieties. If sowing directly outside, once germinated, the seedlings will need to be thinned. Sow the crop little and often, so that the plants mature in succession as opposed to vast quantities all being ready at once, as they do not store well. To extend the harvesting season, this crop can be grown in a cool polythene tunnel or greenhouse for earlier and later crops.

MINIMUM TEMPERATURE

For germination 15°C (60°F)

SITE AND SOIL

Site Warm, sunny position in a moisture-retentive, but well-drained soil that contains plenty of organic matter.

pH 6.5–7.5

Fertilizer Organic matter, if none dug in for the previous crop.

Water Water regularly.

172

DIMENSIONS

Planting depth Sow into drills 2.5 cm (1 in) deep.

Plant out module or pot-raised plants so that the base of the swelling stem is on the soil surface.

Ensure that the seeds sown or seedlings planted out are at the correct depth. If they are too shallow, they will rock in the wind and may snap off at the root.

Space between plants
20–30 cm (8–12 in);
30 cm (12 in) rows

AFTER CARE

Once planted, it is advisable to mulch with compost or any low-fertility material, in order to conserve the soil moisture and stop the plants bolting. Keep weed free. Rake up the soil around the swelling once they are beginning to show a bulbous shape. This will keep the bulbs sweet and tender, as well as holding the white colour. They will be ready for harvest about two to three weeks later.

COMPANION PLANTS

Cucumber, squash, pumpkin, melon, potato, tomato, marrow, courgette, beetroot, parsnip, scorzonera, salsify, Hamburg parsley, celeriac, onion, shallot, leek, garlic, celery, carrot, aubergine and pepper.

HARVESTING

Weeks to maturity 10–15 weeks

Cut the bulbs once they have reached the size of a tennis ball. Often, if left in the ground, the cut stems will re-shoot, producing another crop of leaves for use in salads.

HEALTH BENEFITS

Rich in potassium and folic acid.

STORAGE

Once cut, the bulbs will last for a maximum of two weeks in the fridge.

PESTS

Slugs.

DISEASES

Rhizoctonia can be a problem, both with seedlings and mature bulbs, but with a good crop rotation there should be no sign of it.

SELECTED VARIETIES

Amigo F1 Suited to early sowing. Excellent resistance to bolting. Slightly flattened bulbs. Harvest from June to November. Use tops as a replacement for herb fennel.

Fennel Di Firenze Mild flavour from the large, crisp white bulbs. Harvest from July to October. Use the tops as a substitute for the herb fennel.

Pronto F1 Ready in June from an April sowing. Roundest and earliest of all varieties. Harvest from June to September.

Romanesco Very large and round, pure-white bulbs. Good resistance to bolting. Harvest from September. Use tops from June as a replacement for the herb fennel.

Rudy F1 Rounded, white bulbs very resistant to bolting. Harvest from July to October.

Zefa Fino Nicely rounded, flat bulbs. High resistance to bolting. Harvest from June to September..

KOHLRABI
Brassica oleracea Gongylodes Group

Brassicaceae

An unusual vegetable that looks like a turnip, is eaten like a turnip but tastes like a cabbage. It is a fast-growing vegetable with a tennis-ball-sized swollen root, which sits on the surface of the soil; this is the edible part. There are two types of kohlrabi and they are differentiated by colour: one green and one purple. The green varieties tend to be quicker growers and are usually used as the main summer crop, while the purple varieties, being slower to mature, are harvested later. The roots are crisp and white inside and can be used raw in salads or cooked, having a distinctive cabbage flavour, with a hint of turnip. As the green varieties are quick to mature, they make ideal catch crops, which can be used between slower-maturing brassica crops, such as Brussels sprouts or cabbages. Also, because of their interesting and unusual appearance, they make ideal subjects for the ornamental garden or growing in containers. They can be sown and produced almost all the year round and are a very easy crop grow.

175

DATES

Sowing/Planting March–August (bolt-resistant varieties can be started as early as January).

Harvesting March–December

SOWING/PLANTING METHOD

To ensure a good supply, it is important to sow a little of this crop every couple of weeks to avoid a glut. Sow the early crops in shallow drills in a seed bed, and transplant them into their final positions before they reach over 5 cm (2 in) in height, to minimize the problems of bolting. Kohlrabi does not like to be transplanted in hot weather, so make sure that all the future sowings are in situ and the seedlings thinned. Sow the seed fairly sparsely. There is no advantage in trying to get a crop too early, as any seedlings sown at a temperature below 10°C (50°F) will bolt. They can also be multi-sown in modules in the greenhouse for use in beds and harvested when they are golf-ball size.

SPECIAL TIP

Sow a variety that produces a good crop of top leaves, as these tops can be harvested and used as greens.

MINIMUM TEMPERATURE

For germination 10°C (50°F)

SITE AND SOIL

Site Open site in a wide range of soils. For heavy soils, grow in slightly raised beds.

pH 6.5–7.0

Fertilizer Not a heavy feeding crop like the other brassicas. If on light, sandy soil, then dig in organic matter a few weeks before sowing.

Water Water regularly until established.

DIMENSIONS

Planting depth Sow in drills 2cm (3/4 in) deep.
Transplant to same depth as soil level

in seed bed. Plant out so that the top of the module is at soil level.

Space between plants 23 cm (9 in); 30 cm (12 in) rows.

AFTER CARE

It is essential that the crop does not dry out, as this will encourage bolting and cause the flesh to become woody and inedible. Keep weed free.

COMPANION PLANTS

Brussels sprouts, Chinese cabbage, broccoli, calabrese, cabbage, kale, swede, turnip, radish and cauliflower.

HARVESTING

Weeks to maturity 5–12 weeks

Harvest when the plants are tennis-ball size by lifting the whole root. Pull multi-sown kohlrabi when it is golf-ball size.

HEALTH BENEFITS

High in vitamin C, potassium and fibre.

STORAGE

If the winter weather becomes severe, then the crop in the ground needs to be lifted and stored. They can be placed in a box of moist sharp sand, peat-free compost or vermiculite and placed in a cool, dark place where they will be happy for up to two months.

PESTS

Cabbage root fly, cabbage white butterfly caterpillar, aphids, flea beetle, birds, whitefly and – to a lesser degree – slugs, snails and cutworms.

DISEASES

Clubroot can be severe, brassica white blister and downy mildew.

SELECTED VARIETIES

Azur Star Purple-blue skins. Mildly flavoured white flesh. Hardy type, suitable for late cropping.

Blusta Intense purple roots. White flesh with distinct nutty flavour. Stands well.

Lanro F1 White roots. As good raw as they are cooked.

Logo Bolt resistant. Start sowing in February under cover. Pale green roots.

Olivia F1 Bolt resistant, large roots. Very white and crisp flesh. Stands well.

Purple Danube F1 Purple-skinned. Sweet, white flesh. Stands well.

Purple Delicacy Later to mature. Purple skin and white flesh.

Quickstar F1 Sow under cover as early as January, to harvest in March. Light-green roots. Stands well. Good as multi-sown, mini-veg.

White Delicacy Earlier than the purple form. Flattened, globular roots. Crisp, white flesh.

LEAF BEET
Spinacia oleracea and *Beta vulgaris Cicla* Group

Chenopodiaceae

These two types of leaf beet are invaluable in the organic
vegetable garden, not only as a supply of food but also for their
ornamental value. The two groups covered under this heading
are spinach and chard; both of which are cultivated for their
edible stems and leaves which are available for harvest right
through the year. Spinach, in particular, is best when grown in
cooler temperatures, as it has the tendency to run to seed if it
gets too hot. Early crops can be achieved by sowing and planting
out under cloches. They taste better when harvested young, so
each crop requires regular harvesting. The stems of chard can be
cooked separately and served independently of the leaves.

DATES

Sowing/Planting
Spinach January–September
Chard April–August

Harvesting
Spinach All year round
Chard July to February

SOWING/PLANTING METHOD

Early crops of spinach can be taken from modules sown in the greenhouse, after which they can be directly sown into shallow drills. Sow successional crops so that one is sown as the other germinates, usually at monthly intervals. Chard is sown directly into shallow drills in the spring and then again in mid-summer, for winter cropping. Both types are thinned to the required spacing.

MINIMUM TEMPERATURE

For germination 7°C (35°F)

SITE AND SOIL

Site Semi-shade in summer and full sun for the rest of the year. A moisture-retentive soil, with plenty of organic matter.

pH 6.5–7.5

Fertilizer Plenty of well-rotted organic matter prior to sowing or planting.

Water Water in dry weather.

DIMENSIONS

Planting depth Sow into drills 1 cm (1/2 in) deep.

Space between plants
Spinach 10–15cm (4–6 in); 30 cm (12 in) rows
Chard 23–30 cm (9–12 in); 35 cm (14 in) rows

AFTER CARE

Mulch chard to retain moisture. Keep weed free. Place cloches or fleece over plants in very cold weather.

COMPANION PLANTS

Peas, French beans, climbing French beans, runner beans, Lima beans, sweetcorn, okra, globe artichokes, broad beans, endive, chicory, cress and lettuce.

HARVESTING

Weeks to maturity
Spinach 4–14 weeks
Chard 10–12 weeks
Harvest regularly to encourage new growth.

HEALTH BENEFITS

High in fibre, vitamins A and C.

STORAGE

Does not store.

PESTS

Birds.

DISEASES

Mildew.

SELECTED VARIETIES

Bordeaux F1 Green-leaf spinach with red stems and leaf veins. Harvest from June to September.

Bright Lights Green-leaved chard. Stems are red, white, pink, yellow and orange in colour. Very ornamental. Harvest from July to February.

Galaxy F1 A baby-leaf spinach. Dark-green leaves. Mildew resistant. Harvest from June to September.

Lucullus Prolific chard. Green leaves, bright-white stem. Harvest from July to February.

Perpetual Spinach Hardy and very prolific. Biennial. Green leaves and stems. Good on dry ground, as rarely runs to seed. Harvest all year round.

Rhubarb Chard Scarlet stems. Dark-green leaves, with underlying scarlet colouring. Harvest from July to February.

Scenic F1 Spinach. Green leaves. Mildew resistant. Harvest from June to September.

LEEKS
Allium porrum

Alliaceae

An easy-to-grow, hardy crop that will not take up much space in the vegetable plot and will be available for harvest right through the autumn and winter months when the requirement for a variety of good fresh vegetables is at its premium. They are grown for their blanched, white stems that will stand well in the ground for a long time during the colder months, although they can also be sown for harvesting during late summer and autumn. Generally, the lighter-foliage varieties, producing the longer white stems are the late-summer and autumn-maturing varieties, while the winter- and spring-maturing varieties have darker foliage and shorter, stumpier white stems. Leeks are an ideal crop for multi-sowing and tender young leeks can be produced in a relatively short space of time, increasing the harvesting period dramatically. They are a must for any gardener to grow, not just because of all the attributes mentioned above, but because their strong root systems will help to improve the soil structure of any plot. This is another crop that is best sown in succession, although they do store well if necessary.

182

DATES

Sowing/Planting January–April

Harvesting August–April

SOWING/PLANTING METHOD

The earliest crops can be multi-sown into modules in January at a temperature of 10°C (50°F), hardened off and planted out in blocks in beds. Alternatively, they can be sown into seed trays and transplanted individually into modules when large enough to handle, but this is a rather labour-intensive operation. The other main method of raising seeds is to sow them directly into a prepared seed bed from March to May in shallow drills. When the seedlings reach about 20 cm (8 in) in height, they are ready for transplanting into their final positions. Make a hole about 15 cm (6 in) deep using a dibber, and trim the roots of each plant by about two thirds and the leaves by about half before dropping them into the hole, roots first. At this stage, do not refill the hole with soil, as this may inhibit the growth of the leeks. Instead, fill the hole with water

from a watering can, which will draw down enough soil to cover the roots and get the plants growing. The trimming of the roots encourages the leeks to root faster than if they are not trimmed, while the leaf height is reduced to balance the fact that you have just cut off most of the roots. Some gardeners prefer to grow their leeks in a trench, which is a perfectly acceptable method. A trench is dug out about 20–30 cm (8–12 in) deep and the leeks are planted down the centre. They are not planted as deeply as mentioned above, but at the soil level they were at in the seed bed. As the leeks mature, the trench is gradually

SPECIAL TIP

For larger leeks, plant out at a slightly wider spacing of 20–23 cm (8–9 in) to give them more room to produce wider stems.

filled in with the soil that had been piled at the sides, blanching the stems in the process.

MINIMUM TEMPERATURE

For germination 7°C (45°F)

SITE AND SOIL

Site Sunny, open site with a fertile soil rich in organic matter.

pH 6.5–7.5

Fertilizer Organic matter prior to planting and blood, fish and bone meal or pelleted chicken manure.

Water Water regularly until established.

DIMENSIONS

Planting depth Sow into 2.5 cm (1 in) drills.
Transplant 15 cm (6 in) deep.
For trench cultivation plant 2.5 cm (1 in) deep.

Space between plants 15 cm (6 in); 30 cm (12 in) rows.
Multi-sown 23 cm (9 in) square.
In bed, plant in staggered rows 15 cm (6 in) between plants in all directions.

AFTER CARE

Hoe regularly to keep the weeds under control and, as the leeks mature, pull a little soil around the leek stems to blanch them. Be careful with this operation, as the vigorous pulling of soil will result in soil getting down between the leaves, which will cause headaches in the kitchen at a later date.

COMPANION PLANTS

Cucumber, squash, pumpkin, melon, potato, tomato, marrow, courgette, beetroot, parsnip, scorzonera, salsify, Hamburg parsley, celeriac, onion, shallot, carrots, garlic, celery, Florence fennel, aubergine and pepper.

HARVESTING

Weeks to maturity 16–32 weeks

Leeks are very hardy and will stand in the ground right through winter until required. Multi-sown leeks can be harvested when young, tender and sweet at 1–2 cm in diameter.

HEALTH BENEFITS

High in vitamin A, potassium and folic acid.

STORAGE

If the weather turns severe during winter, then lift a few leeks at a time and heel them in, in a trench, to be pulled when required. It is a lot easier to lift leeks that are lying in a trench with only loose soil covering them, than trying to dig out a crop that is 15–20 cm (6–8 in) below ground level with the soil frozen solid.

PESTS

Onion fly, onion thrips and cutworms.

DISEASES

Leek rust and fusarium.

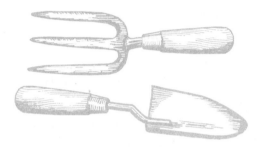

SELECTED VARIETIES

Ardea Resistant to leek rust. Pure-white stems. Harvest in September and October.

Autumn Poristo Medium-sized, uniform stems. Stands well. Harvest from November to April. Tolerant of rust.

Bulgarian Giant Quick to mature. Greenish-white stems.

185

Carentan Winter variety. Large, thick, white stems with blue-green leaves. Stands well. Harvest from October to early January.

Carlton F1 Long, white stems, almost no bulbing. Multi-sow early. Harvest maincrop in September and November.

Hannibal Harvest in January. Long thick, white stem. Does not bulb.

Imperial Summer F1 Early variety. Ideal for multi-sowing and growing as mini-veg or as a maincrop. Long white stem, almost no bulbing. Harvest in September.

King Richard Mini-veg variety. Ideal for multi-sowing or sown thinly in shallow drills and harvested as a less pungent alternative to salad onions.

Lyon Prizetaker Long white and thick stems. Harvest from September to November.

Musselburgh Traditional, very hardy Scottish variety. Excellent white stems. Stands very well. Harvest from December to April.

Natan Very late variety. Long, white stems, with blue-green leaves. Harvest from January to April.

Pancho Long white stems. Matures early, but stands until well into the winter.

Porvite High-yielding. White, bulb-free stems. Resistant to bolting and stands well. Harvest from September to January.

Tadorna Medium-sized white stems, dark-green foliage. Stands well during winter. Harvest from January to May.

Varna Grow as multi-sown, mini-veg or directly sow as an alternative to salad onions.

Winter Giant 3 Medium-sized white stems. Harvest through the winter.

Zermatt Early variety. Use as multi-sown, mini-veg or grow into long-stemmed leeks. Harvest from September to November.

LETTUCE
Lactuca sativa

Asteraceae

This vegetable has to be considered as essential for every vegetable plot, being the main ingredient of salads and available for harvest all year round. Although there has been a dramatic increase in the types and varieties of lettuce, there are still only two main groups, lettuces that form a heart and those that do not. They come in all shapes, sizes and colours including: iceberg, cos, butterhead, salad bowl, crisphead, small hearted, loose-leaved, mixed salad leaves, frilly-leaved, oak-leaved, green and burgundy. There now seems to be not only a lettuce for every season and salad type, but also one to fit the décor of every gardeners home! There is absolutely no excuse for salads to look boring and uninteresting as, unlike some types of vegetables, the more ornamental lettuces have an excellent flavour and texture. Once it is possible to sow outside, then the principle of "little and often" must be adhered to, so a sudden glut of lettuce can be avoided, as they do not stand well when ready and will not store.

DATES

Sowing/Planting January–September. Transplant early, greenhouse-raised plants outside, from March to May. It is also possible to continue sowing in the greenhouse until September and transplant the seedlings out when ready.

Harvesting All year round

SOWING/PLANTING METHOD

Lettuce can be sown into seed trays containing a coir compost, leaf mould or any organic seed-and-cuttings compost, with first sowings being made in January, in a heated greenhouse. Once the seedlings are large enough to handle, they can be pricked out into a module tray and grown on at a temperature of about 10°C (50°F), until they reach a height of 5 cm (2 in), when they can be planted outside under cloches. Lettuce dislike root disturbance, so the preferred method is to sow directly into the module tray, placing two seeds per module and removing the weaker one. Start to sow inside at two weekly

intervals, which will give a continuous supply of lettuce. From early February, they can be sown directly into shallow drills outside under a cloche or cold frame. Sow thinly and thin them as soon as the seedlings are large enough to handle. They do not transplant well, so it is best to avoid using the thinnings as transplants. The directly sown lettuce can also be sown at two weekly intervals, with the inside sowing stopping once it is warm enough to sow the lettuce outside with no protection. For autumn and winter crops, sow in late August and September, either in modules in a cold greenhouse or directly outside as before, and cover with a cloche once the weather starts to deteriorate. Lettuce grown inside for winter harvest needs to be sown in modules and then potted into a 10 cm or 12cm (4 or 5 in) pot.

MINIMUM TEMPERATURE

For germination 5°C (42°F)

At temperatures above 25°C (77°F) lettuce germination becomes inhibited.

SITE AND SOIL

Site Well-drained but moisture-retentive soil. Cool semi-shaded position is beneficial if garden gets hot.

pH 6.5

Fertilizer On poor soils, incorporate garden compost prior to sowing or planting. Blood, fish and bone meal or pelleted chicken manure should be applied a week prior to sowing or planting.

Water Water regularly, until established.

DIMENSIONS

Planting depth Sow into drills 1 cm (3/4 in) deep
Plant out modules so that the top of the module is at soil level

Space between plants
In beds 15 cm (6 in) early sowing/smaller types
23 cm (9 in) later sowing/larger types
In rows 25–35 cm (10–14 in) dependent on variety
30–38 cm (12–15 in) rows

AFTER CARE

Water in dry spells to prevent the leaves becoming tough and bitter, and hoe to keep weeds down. With greenhouse crops, ventilate as much as possible and check winter types regularly for botrytis. Remove any infected or damaged leaves.

COMPANION PLANTS

Peas, French beans, climbing French beans, runner beans, Lima beans, sweetcorn, okra, globe artichokes, broad beans, endive, chicory, cress, spinach and chard.

HARVESTING

Weeks to maturity 4–14 weeks

When the heart of the lettuce feels firm, the whole plant can be pulled out of the ground, with the root cut off and put onto the compost heap. Loose-leaf lettuce varieties can also be harvested in the same way or, if less lettuce is required, outer leaves can be pulled off as needed. With cut-and-come-again lettuce, the tops are cut off flush with the ground and the roots left in situ for another crop of leaves to be grown.

HEALTH BENEFITS

Good source of beta-carotene and vitamin A; also reputedly has a sedative effect.

STORAGE

Iceberg lettuce will store for several days in the fridge.

PESTS

Slugs, snails, millipedes, aphids and cutworms.

DISEASES

Botrytis and downy mildew.

SELECTED VARIETIES

All the Year Round Harvest summer, autumn and spring. Compact and crisp, reliable butterhead type.

Amorina Lollo rossa type. Deep burgundy leaves. Resistant to mildew and bolting. Harvest from May to October.

Aruba Oakleaf variety. Very ornamental, dark-red leaves. Resistant to downy mildew and bolting. Harvest leaves as required in summer.

Belize Bright green oakleaf lettuce. Resistant to aphids, mildew, tipburn and bolting. Harvest from April to October.

Buttercrunch Butterhead variety. Small, dark-green heads with a creamy-yellow heart.

Catalogna Oakleaf variety. Bright green leaves. Slow to bolt. Harvest leaves from April or June, to October for whole plant.

Claremont Large-headed cos variety. Dark-green leaves. Excellent mildew resistance and stands well. Harvest from June to October.

Diana Butterhead type. Dark-green leaves. Excellent mildew resistance. Harvest through summer and autumn.

Dickinson Crisphead type. Round heads. Harvest all summer and autumn.

Embrace Iceberg. Downy mildew resistant. Large, tight and crisp. Harvest from May to October.

Freckles Speckled, green leaf. Cos type with distinct nutty flavour. High-yielding and resistant to bolting.

Fristina Hardy variety. Very frilly, green leaves. Harvest from May to November; longer if protected by cloches or in a cold greenhouse.

Granada Oakleaf type. Leaves green at the base, gradually changing to a deep red at the tips. Harvest from May to October.

Jefferson Iceberg variety. Rich green, crisp leaves form a dense head. Resistant to mildew. Harvest as early

as May and it will continue to crop until October.

Little Gem Ideal for growing in beds or rows and as a catch crop. Closer planting. Green leaves. Semi-cos type. Resistant to root aphid. Harvest from May to October.

Lollo Rossa Dark crimson, frilly leaves. Non-hearting variety. Bolt-resistant. Harvest from April to October.

Lobjoits Green Cos Large, green-leaved, firm-hearted variety. Harvest in April and from June to September.

May King Hardy variety. Early crops under protection. Green leaves slightly tinged red. Oddly not harvested in May, but from March to April.

Milan Butterhead type. Large, green heads. Resistant to downy mildew and tolerant of lettuce root aphid. Harvest from June to October.

Nymans Cherry-red, medium-sized cos variety with a yellow heart. Resistant to mildew and bolting. Harvest from June to October.

Red Fire Very resistant to bolting. Very frilly red leaves. Harvest from June to October.

Red Salad Bowl Long, deeply cut, red-bronze leaves. Harvest from May to October.

Rosetta Medium sized, hardy butterhead variety. Grow under protection. Dark-green leaves. Resistant to downy mildew. Harvest from October to April.

Salad Bowl Long, deeply cut, green leaves. Non-hearting variety. Harvest from May to October.

Saladin One of the best iceberg types. Large, well-wrapped heads of bright green and crisp leaves. Resistant to mildew and stands well. Harvest from June to September.

Sangria Butterhead variety. Outer leaves red and inner leaves pale green. Some resistance to mildew. Harvest from May to September.

Tom Thumb Grow in beds. Very quick to mature. Small, solid heads can be planted much closer. Slow to bolt. Harvest from April to October.

Unrivalled Butterhead type. Medium-sized hearts. Suitable for early sowings under cover. Harvest from April to October.

Webbs Wonderful Large, crisp solid hearts. Resistant to bolting. Harvest from May to October.

Valdor One of the best for winter use. Resistant to the cold weather. Deep green, solid hearts. Grow under protection or potted in a cold greenhouse. Resistant to botrytis. Harvest from December to April.

Warpath Iceberg variety. Compact heads with crunchy, crisp leaves and small hearts. Well-suited to growing in beds. Harvest from May to October.

Winter Density Smaller variety ideal for beds. Sow in autumn for early spring cropping, as well as spring and early summer for cropping before the weather gets too hot. Harvest in March and April.

MARROW AND COURGETTE

Cucurbita pepo

Cucurbitaceae

These two varieties of squash have been grouped together because they have exactly the same growing methods and also because courgettes are really just small marrows. They are classed as two separate vegetables because some will produce much tastier small fruits, while other varieties will form much better large fruits. However, if short of space, as both marrow and courgette plants cover a wide area in the vegetable plot, it might be prudent to grow only courgette varieties and later in the season allow a few courgettes to grow on to marrow size. They are a warm-season crop that won't tolerate frost, which usually means that they are best germinated inside, either in a frost-free greenhouse, conservatory or windowsill, so that when the weather improves they can be planted straight out into the ground. If you cannot grow them inside then it is possible to sow pairs of seeds about two weeks before the last frost and cover them with a cloche or fleece. They are a crop that enjoys moisture at the root, although they will rot if left sitting in water, so a generous helping of well-rotted manure or garden compost at the planting stage will help to give an excellent crop, as will a regular application of water.

193

DATES

Sowing
Inside Mid-February–mid-May
Outside Mid-May

Harvesting July–October

SOWING METHOD

Sow two seeds into an 8 cm (3 in) pot and when germinated remove the weaker seedling, allowing one to develop.

MINIMUM TEMPERATURE

For germination 18–20°C (65–69°F)

SITE AND SOIL

Site Sunny, sheltered position.

pH 5.5–6.8

Fertilizer Blood, fish and bone meal or pelleted chicken manure prior to planting. Well-rotted manure or garden compost added for moisture retention. Then feed every two weeks with a balanced seaweed fertilizer.

Water Every day, when dry.

SPECIAL TIP

Another space-saving method for courgettes and vegetable spaghetti is to grow them up a tripod or on strings attached to the top of a pergola, which are then pinned into the ground with wire pegs. Harvest regularly to prevent overloading. Once the plants have reached the top of their structures, then pinch out the tip.

DIMENSIONS

Planting depth 2.5 cm (1 in)

Space between plants
In beds
BUSH 60–90 cm (24–36 in)
TRAILING 120–180 cm (4–6 ft)

In rows
BUSH 60–90 cm (24–36 in);
90–120 cm (36–48 in) rows
TRAILING 120–180 cm (4–6 ft)
180 cm (6 ft) rows

AFTER CARE

Check three times a week and remove fruits that are ready to ensure good and regular production of courgettes.

COMPANION PLANTS

Cucumber, squash, pumpkin, melon, potato, tomato, carrot, beetroot, parsnip, scorzonera, salsify, Hamburg parsley, celeriac, onion, shallot, leek, garlic, celery, Florence fennel, aubergine and pepper.

HARVESTING

Weeks to maturity
Courgette 12 weeks
Marrow 16 weeks

Cut courgettes when they are 15 cm (6 in) long and marrows when 35 cm (15 in) long.

HEALTH BENEFITS

High in vitamins A, C and E.

STORAGE

Marrows can be ripened at the end of the season by placing a mature fruit onto a brick to raise it from the soil to stop it rotting. They can then be stored in a frost-free place for a few weeks.

PESTS

Slugs, snails and whitefly.

DISEASES

Powdery mildew, foot and root rots and cucumber mosaic virus.

SELECTED VARIETIES

Courgettes

Cavill F1 Can set fruit without being pollinated. Ideal for early cropping, when no pollinating insects. Pale-green fruits.

Defender F1 Compact. Resistant to cucumber mosaic virus. Mid-green fruits.

On Ball F1 Heavy crop of tennis-ball-sized, golden-yellow fruits.

Orelia F1 Vigorous, heavy-cropping variety. Bright-yellow fruits.

Supremo F1 Cucumber mosaic virus-resistant. Very early yields of dark-green fruit.

Tromboncino Long, cream-coloured fruits. Ideal for training up supports.

Zucchini F1 Very early. Deep-green fruits. Excellent for freezing.

Marrows

Badger Cross Bush type. Dark-green fruits, longitudinal pale-green stripes. Resistant to cucumber mosaic virus.

Long Green Trailing variety. Extra-long, deep-green fruits with light stripes. Stores well.

Long Green Bush 2 Improved Early, high-yielding variety. Medium-sized, green, striped fruits.

Tiger Cross F1 Early. Resistant to cucumber mosaic virus. Heavy crop of green, striped fruits.

Tivoli F1 Vegetable spaghetti. Flesh resembles spaghetti after cooking. Ideal for growing up supports.

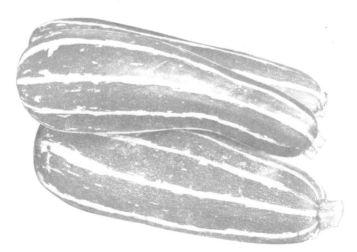

MELON
Cucumis melo

Cucurbitaceae

Sweet melons are tropical, annual plants that do not tolerate any frost. They are better-suited to protected cropping, although there are varieties that will grow and produce a good crop outside. Their natural habit is to trail, which makes them ideal for growing up supports in the greenhouse or leaving them to ramble outside under a cloche. There are three basic types of sweet melon: musk, winter and cantaloupe. The musk and cantaloupe varieties need the highest growing temperatures, so they are best-suited to protected cropping, whereas some cantaloupe varieties can cope with lower, outdoor temperatures. The rest of the varieties are only suitable for greenhouse culture. Musk melons have the smallest fruit of the three and very often have smooth skins, while the winter melons, including the popular honeydew types have a yellow or striped yellow and green skin. Cantaloupe melons, on the other hand, have a thick, rough skin that is generally green or grey-green in colour.

DATES

Sowing/Planting Sow April–June

Harvesting July–October

SOWING/PLANTING METHOD

There is no great advantage in starting the seed off too early, as the light levels after germination will not be high enough for rapid growth. If you're ultimately going to plant the melons outside, they will have to be held back until all the frosts have passed anyway. It is always best to start melons in the greenhouse at a temperature of about 18°C (64°F) and sow them on their sides into 8 cm (3 in) pots. With expensive F1 hybrids, sow one seed per pot, as they are more likely to germinate. With non-F1 hybrids, put two seeds into each pot and remove the weaker one after germination. Once germinated, keep the greenhouse temperature between 13–16°C (55–61°F) and pot on into 13 cm (5 in) pots as soon as the roots hold the compost together; then move on into a 5-litre (8 in) pot before finally potting into a 10-litre (10 in) pot. If growing outside or in growbags in a cold tunnel, the plants may need to be potted from 8 cm (3 in) to 13 cm (5 in) to stop them becoming pot bound, but there will be no need to pot on further than this before planting out.

MINIMUM TEMPERATURE

For germination 18°C (64°F)

SITE AND SOIL

Site Best in a greenhouse. Sunny and sheltered spot with a moisture-retentive soil that is high in organic matter if planting out.

pH 6.0–7.0

Fertilizer Blood, fish and bone meal or pelleted chicken manure prior to planting.

Water Do not let the plants dry out, but also don't over-water, particularly if growing in containers or growbags.

DIMENSIONS

Planting depth Sow to a depth of 2.5 cm (1 in) in the pots.

Plant out with the top of the pot at soil or compost level. Planting too deeply may cause the stem to rot. On heavier soils, it is beneficial to plant onto a slight mound to prevent waterlogging of the plant.

Space between plants

Inside 60–90 cm (24–36 in)
Outside 90 cm (36 in) square

AFTER CARE

Protect outdoor plants from colder nights early in the season with a cloche, cold frame or fleece. Water frequently to ensure the plants do not dry out. Once the weather warms up, protect greenhouse plants with netting or paint-on shading to shade the plants from the strong direct sunlight. Outdoor melons need their tips pinching out on a regular basis to encourage maximum fruit production. Once the main shoot grows away, pinch out the tip after the second leaf to encourage two further shoots to be produced. The sideshoots that are subsequently produced should be stopped after they have reached five leaves. When the fruits start to appear, pinch out all laterals produced to two

SPECIAL TIP

An excellent early crop of melon "Sweetheart", or a similar cold-resistant variety, can be obtained by growing in a hot box. After the new potatoes have been harvested in late April, refill the box with fresh manure, leave for a week and plant the melons, covering the whole bed with a cloche. These melons can be produced at least a week earlier than the greenhouse varieties, with the plants totally unaffected by the night frosts or low daytime temperatures. Once harvesting has begun the cloche can be removed.

leaves beyond this fruit. This will ensure that all the plant's energies are channelled into producing decent-sized fruits that will ripen well, without overloading the plant. As the first fruit to set seems to inhibit the others from forming, it is important to keep a cloche or cold frame over the plants to encourage as many flowers to form simultaneously as possible. The cover can then be removed to allow insects to pollinate. With greenhouse-raised melons, pinch out the growing point after two true leaves, as before, and train them up the supports you have in place. Pinch out the tips of these shoots once they have made about seven leaves. This will encourage more sideshoots to be produced, which will carry the fruit. When the small fruits are visible, the shoot can have its growing tip pinched out two leaves beyond the developing melon, as before. With both outdoor and greenhouse crops, only allow four or five fruits to develop on each plant, otherwise the fruits produced will be small and will not ripen. Once the flower buds start to appear, feed weekly with a high-potash, seaweed liquid feed. If the plants are not looking at their best in mid-summer, a general-purpose seaweed feed can also be applied at weekly intervals.

Ventilate the greenhouse well, to allow insects access in order to pollinate, or pollinate by hand if you prefer. This is done by removing a male flower and pushing them into the female flower to transfer the pollen. Once the fruit has begun maturing on trained plants, it is necessary to support each fruit so that it does not pull the plant down. Place netting around each fruit and tie it onto a supporting wire or something similar.

COMPANION PLANTS

Cucumber, squash, pumpkin, aubergine, potato, tomato, carrot, beetroot, parsnip, scorzonera, salsify, Hamburg parsley, celeriac, onion, shallot, leek, garlic, celery, Florence fennel, marrow, courgette and pepper.

HARVESTING

Weeks to maturity: 12–20 weeks

Cut the fruits as soon as they are ripe, when they smell sweet and the flower end of the fruit is soft when pressed.

HEALTH BENEFITS

High in vitamins A, C and E as well as potassium.

STORAGE

Unripe fruits picked at the end of the season can be placed in a cool place where they will gradually ripen.

PESTS

Slugs and snails, whitefly, red spider mite and aphids.

DISEASES

Cucumber mosaic virus, powdery mildew, botrytis, verticillium wilt, fusarium and sclerotinia.

SELECTED VARIETIES

Ambrosia Aromatic, sweet, orange flesh with superb texture. Quite vigorous plants produce round fruit 14–16 cm (5½–6 in) in diameter, weighing 1.5–2.5kg (3½–5½ lb) and maturing in 80–100 days. Harvest from August to October.

Blenheim Orange Fragrant, scarlet flesh. Harvest, August to October.

Castella Grow in greenhouse or outside. Large melons 1.3–1.6 kg (3–3½ lbs). Resistant to downy mildew and fusarium.

Early Sweet F1 Deep, salmon flesh. Canteloupe variety. Round-fruited variety with yellow skin.

Edonis F1 Pale, orange flesh. Early variety. Resistant to fusarium.

Galia F1 Early variety. Sweet and very juicy, round fruits. Mildew resistant.

Heart of Gold Early cantaloupe variety. Orange flesh with a small seed cavity.

Honeydew Green Flesh Round, smooth, pale skin, with light-green flesh. Harvest from August to October.

Lunabel F1 Greenhouse variety. Round fruits. Resistant to powdery mildew. Harvest in August and September.

Mira F1 Greenhouse melon. Green with stripes and a crisp, sweet inner flesh. Ready for picking within 40 days from sowing.

Ogon Canteloupe variety. Small, rounded fruits. Yellow-green flesh.

Sugar Baby Water melon. Honey-sweet, juicy, red flesh. Grow in a greenhouse or start inside and plant out once the weather improves. Harvest from August to October.

Sweetheart F1 Medium-sized canteloupe melon. Quick to mature. Oval fruits with salmon-pink flesh and a grey-green skin. Very cold tolerant, so suited to growing outside.

ONION AND GARLIC
Allium cepa

Alliaceae

These versatile vegetables can be made available all year round, due to the numerous different varieties and the fact that they store well over a long period. Onions can be divided into two groups: bulbing onions, which can be harvested for four months of the year and stored for the remaining eight months and salad onions, which become ready within only eight weeks after sowing (these do not store well and need to be eaten fresh). Garlic is sometimes classified as a herb, but it is an onion at heart and, strictly speaking, a vegetable. Onions and garlic are easy to grow from sets, cloves or seeds and the bulbing types can be grown from sets, sown into trays, pricked out and grown as individual onions or multi-sown into modules. Salad onions are easy to grow from direct sowings into shallow drills. Bulbing onions do take up space in the vegetable plot for a long period, while salad onions can be used as catch crops and are also well-suited to the bed system of growing. The size of a bulbing onion is usually determined by a combination of variety and planting distance. They come in a range of sizes, as well as skin colours, ranging from white, through to yellow- and red-fleshed. Garlic also takes some time to produce its crop, but takes up much less space than bulbing onions.

DATES

Sowing/Planting

Salad onion March–September

Bulbing onion January–April and
August–October

Garlic October–March

Harvesting

Salad onion All year

Bulbing onion June–October

Garlic May–September

SOWING/PLANTING METHOD

For bulbing onions, there are three definite sowing times. The first is to multi-sow into modules in the greenhouse during January or February, with most varieties being well-suited to this type of growing. This gives a very high yield in a small space, but only produces medium-sized bulbs. For larger bulbs, the seeds can be sown into seed trays and individually pricked out into modules, and then planted out from there. Once the seedlings are about 10 cm (4 in) high they can be hardened off, before being planted out.

Once the soil has warmed sufficiently, usually by the end of March or early April, direct sowing can be started outside. The onion seed can be thinly sown into shallow drills and then thinned, or two or three seeds can be dropped into a shallow drill at 4–10 cm (1¼–4 in) spacings, dependent on the required final bulb size, as the wider the spacing, the larger the bulb. The resulting seedlings are then thinned to leave just one per station. It is important when sowing onion seeds directly into the ground that they are sown into a "stale seedbed", which will prevent them being swamped by weeds as they germinate. The autumn sowing is limited to the winter hardy varieties of Japanese onion.

The final method involves onion sets that need a period of cold to initiate their growth, so these are planted out from either September to November or during March and April. These "mini onion bulbs" need to have any excess brown top growth removed before planting, to prevent birds from pulling the sets out of the ground. It is quite obvious which way up they go into the ground, as the flat bottom end is where the roots will be formed and the pointed upward end is where the top growth will emerge. These sets are pushed into the ground so that the pointed tips are just below the soil surface.

Garlic requires a period of cold to initiate the bulbs into growth, so planting from late autumn to early spring is essential. Break cloves from the bulb and plant them as for sets.

Salad onions can be directly sown into shallow drills, outside, under cloches from February. They can then be sown in succession right through the season, using winter-hardy varieties for the last sowings during October and November. Do not thin, as the larger thinnings can be used as salad onions later.

MINIMUM TEMPERATURE

For germination 5°C (45°F)

SITE AND SOIL

Site Sunny, open site but will tolerate some semi-shade. Well-drained and preferably light soil.

pH 6.5–7.5

Fertilizer Organic matter prior to planting and blood, fish and bone meal or pelleted chicken manure. Before sowing Japanese onions, apply dried blood in autumn and to other over-wintered onions in spring.

Water Keep the crop moist.

DIMENSIONS

Planting depth Sow into 2 cm (^{3}/4 in) drills.
Plant out modules so that the top of the module is level with the soil surface.
Push sets and cloves into the ground so that the growing tip is just below the surface.

Space between plants
Bulbing onions 5–10 cm (2–4 in); 30 cm (12 in) rows

Garlic 15 cm (6 in);
30 cm (12 in) rows

Salad onions 30 cm (12 in) rows

AFTER CARE

Keep weed-free and the soil moist
during development, and then only
water when very dry. Too much water
during growth will result in the bulbs
not storing as well.

COMPANION PLANTS

Cucumber, squash, pumpkin, melon,
potato, tomato, marrow, courgette,
beetroot, parsnip, scorzonera, salsify,
Hamburg parsley, celeriac, leeks,
shallots, carrots, celery, Florence
fennel, aubergine and pepper.

HARVESTING

Weeks to maturity
Bulbing onions spring sown and
spring sets, 18–24 weeks
Autumn sown and autumn sets
36–42 weeks

Garlic 16–36 weeks

Salad onions 8 weeks

Bulbing onions and garlic can be
pulled at any time to be eaten fresh,
once the bulbs have swollen to a
usable size. In late summer, the bulbs
will have stopped growing and the
foliage will naturally fall over and turn
brown. Do not bend over the foliage
of onions early, as this will limit their
storage potential. Once the foliage has
withered and gone brown, gently lift
the bulbs – avoiding bruising them –
and spread them out on a slatted
bench or wire hammock to dry. This
drying of the bulb ripens the skin and
lengthens the storage potential. Once
the skin has dried, the onion and garlic
bulbs can have their tops cut off and

stored. Alternatively, leave the tops on if they are to be tied up in storage. If the weather is wet, and the bulbs are not drying, then they will have to be moved under cover to complete this process.

The strength of flavour of salad onions increases the longer they stand.

HEALTH BENEFITS

Antiseptic, anti-asthmatic, anti-bacterial, lowers blood pressure, and helps to lower cholesterol.

STORAGE

Place into a netted bag or tie up into bunches. Hang in a cool, dark, frost-free place, such as a shed.

PESTS

Onion fly, onion thrips and bulb eelworm.

DISEASES

Onion neck rot, onion white rot, fusarium and downy mildew.

SELECTED VARIETIES

Ailsa Craig Large bulbs, superb colour, shape and flavour. Short-term storage. Harvest from August to October.

Albigensian Wight Garlic. Early variety. White skin and slightly squatter bulbs. Ideal for roasting.

Beacon F1 Perfectly shaped for exhibiting, weighing in at over 2.6 kg (6 lb) each.

Bedfordshire Champion Excellent for storage. Globular bulbs with golden brown skin. Harvest from August to October.

Brown Pickling Sy 300 Pickling onion. Small and solid bulbs. Stores well and does not go soft when pickled.

Brunswick Very reliable, red-skinned variety. Medium-sized, excellent blood-red skin, white flesh, but mild onion flavour. Stores very well.

Centurion F1 Plant as onion sets. Early, heavy crop of globe-shaped bulbs. Excellent for storing.

Crimson Forest Red-stemmed variety. Grow in the ornamental border. Harvest from June to October.

Giant Zittau Globular shape, golden-brown skin and strong flavour. One of the longest storing capabilities of any onion. Harvest from August to October.

Guradsman Vigorous salad onion. Harvest through most of the year. Stands very well through winter. Mild flavour, does not become stronger the longer it stands.

Kamal F1 Red skin and flesh. Stores well. Tolerance to mildew.

Keepwell Lasts four to five months in store, hence its name. Harvest in August and September.

Lancastrian Enormous onions can weigh 1.8 kg (4 lb) if started in January under glass. Smaller bulbs good for storing.

Mammoth Improved Onion Enormous onion, can reach 3 kg (6 lb) in weight and 56 cm (22 in) in circumference. Still has a sweet flavour.

Mammoth Red Onion Largest red onion. Strong flavour and stores well.

Paris Silverskin Used for pickling, but can also be cooked whole. No need to thin.

Purplette Can either be harvested as young salad onions or left to mature into small, purple-red skinned onions. Harvest from June to October.

Red Baron Grow from seed or sets. Red-skinned onions with pink and white flesh. Harvest from August to October.

Red Pearl F1 Red skin and pearly white flesh. Stores well. Mildew tolerant.

Rijnsburger Large, rounded bulbs. Golden skin; crisp, white flesh. Stores very well.

Senshyu Semi-Globe Yellow Japanese bulbing onion. Sow late summer. Harvest in June and August.

Setton Plant as sets. Globe-shaped bulbs. Superb storage capabilities.

Solent Wight Large garlic. Excellent flavour.

Sturon Plant as sets. Large, crisp golden bulbs. Excellent for long-term storage.

Walla Walla Large bulb. Can be stored for up to eight months.

White Lisbon Salad onion. Very quick to mature. Ideal for successional sowing. White and green stalks. Harvest spring, summer and autumn.

White Lisbon Winter Hardy As for the above, but sown from June to October for harvesting July to January.

Winterover Even hardier form of White Lisbon.

Wolf F1 Brown-skinned onion. Resistant to bolting. Can be sown in the autumn for a crop the following year.

PARSNIP AND HAMBURG PARSLEY

Pastinaca sativa and *Petroselinum crispum* var *tuberosum*

Apiaceae

Both have a fine edible root, with Hamburg parsley also having tops that can be used as a substitute to flat-leaf parsley. Their long, white roots have a sweet and distinctive taste, making them a popular and well-used vegetable during the winter. There are two schools of thought on how the sweetness is achieved in these roots, with one side arguing that the faster the growth, the sweeter the root, and the other convinced that the sweetness is gained by freezing during frosty weather. Either way, it is important to keep either type growing well, to maximize the final yield. As they are harvested during the winter months, they have generally been frosted before harvest, so both theories have usually been fulfilled before they are eaten. The seed is normally viable for the year after it has been harvested and becomes more unreliable the longer it is kept, so it is important to use only fresh seed and not to save any leftovers until the following year. The seed is also notoriously slow to germinate, sometimes taking up to three weeks to come through, particularly when sown outside. They have great storage potential, both in and out of the ground, so even when the weather is bad, the crop remains available for use.

209

DATES

Sowing/Planting
Parsnip April–May
Hamburg parsley March–July

Harvesting August–April

SOWING/PLANTING METHOD

Neither parsnips or Hamburg parsley are crops that can be bought on for early crops, as the seed will only germinate at a very slow rate when the temperatures are below 12°C (54°F). The first crops are better sown into shallow drills, when the soil has warmed, placing two or three seedlings at 10–15 cm (4–6 in)

SPECIAL TIP

As the germination of the seeds is very slow, you should ensure that you do not hoe off the emerging seedlings with other weeds. Sow a few radish seeds in the same drill as marker plants. The radishes can be harvested as normal, because they will be ready long before they interfere with the parsnip crop.

intervals. You should then thin as required, once the seedlings have developed two true leaves. Bear in mind that the closer the spacing, the smaller the roots will be, so for exhibition size roots, the wider spacing must be used. To try and speed up the germination, the rows could be covered with cloches or thin polythene. It is also possible to sow in July, in order to get an early crop the following year, as this will extend the harvesting period. It is also possible to grow parsnips to be pulled as young and tender roots. If they are grown in this way, they can be sown thinly in a drill and harvested as required, with no thinning needed. The row spacings can therefore be much narrower than for the maincrop varieties, making them ideal for growing in beds.

MINIMUM TEMPERATURE

For germination
Parsnip 1.5°C (35°F)
Hamburg parsley 7°C (45°F)

SITE AND SOIL

Site Open sunny site, with a light sandy soil, but will also tolerate some shade and needs the soil to have some moisture retention.

pH 6.5–8.0

Fertilizer Apply ample organic matter prior to the previous crop.

Water To prevent the roots from splitting, it is best to apply water little and often as this crop does not have a high water requirement. However, if water is applied after a long dry spell, this could also cause splitting of the roots.

DIMENSIONS

Planting depth Sow into drills 1 cm (¹/2 in) deep

Space between plants
10–15 cm (4–6 in);
20–30 cm (8–12 in) rows

In deep beds, sow in block, so that there are 15 cm (6 in) between the plants.

AFTER CARE

Keep weed free. Apply a mulch to control the weeds, which will also act as a moisture retainer.

COMPANION PLANTS

Cucumber, squash, pumpkin, melon, potato, tomato, marrow, courgette, beetroot, scorzonera, salsify, carrot, celeriac, onion, shallot, leek, garlic, celery, Florence fennel, aubergine and pepper.

HARVESTING

Weeks to maturity
Parsnip 16–36 weeks
Hamburg parsley 30 weeks

The young and tender roots are harvested first, with the maincrop varieties following. They are perfectly hardy, so can be left in the ground and dug up when required.

HEALTH BENEFITS

Vitamin C, iron and potassium.

STORAGE

Wait until after the first frost before lifting any roots for storage. Store as for carrots. Leaves of Hamburg Parsley can be cut as required.

PESTS

Carrot fly.

DISEASES

Parsnip canker.

SELECTED VARIETIES

Albion F1 Resistant to canker. Smooth-skinned variety.

Avonresister Hamburg parsley. Shorter, but uniform white roots. Excellent resistance to canker.

Berliner Hamburg parsley. Long, white roots. Taste is reminiscent of both celeriac and kohl rabi. Harvest from September to January.

Cobham Improved Marrow Tapering white roots. Resistant to canker.

Countess F1 Vigorous variety. White roots. Ideal if your soil is poor. Good disease resistance.

Dagger F1 Mini-veg variety. Smooth-skinned. Ideal for containers or in beds. Excellent canker resistance.

Exhibition Long Very long roots. Excellent quality.

Hamburg Parsley Most common variety available. Long, tapering white roots. Flavour of parsnip, with a hint of celery. Harvest from September onwards.

Hollow Crown Hamburg parsley. Long, tapering white roots. Wide shoulder. Good canker resistance.

Javelin F1 Can be grown as maincrop or mini-veg. Pull young and tender roots for early crop. Leave enough to grow on to maincrop. Long, slim, smooth-skinned white roots.

Lancer Mini-veg variety. Pull when 10–15 cm (4–6 in) long. Smooth white skin. Ideal for beds or containers. Very resistant to canker.

Panache F1 White-skinned roots, cream flesh. Excellent resistance to canker.

Tender and True Very tasty, tapering white roots that have some resistance to canker.

The Student Long, tapering roots, with creamy flesh. Very mild flavours.

White Gem Shorter roots. Can grow on most soils. Resistant to canker.

213

PEAS
Pisum sativum

Papillonaceae

Peas greatly prefer cooler climates and can withstand the cold and lighter frosts outside without any protection. They are an easy crop to grow and, by using the right varieties, they can be harvested fresh from the plant from May right through until October. There is no comparison to the taste of a pea picked freshly from a plant in the garden. The earliest varieties can be sown outside in early winter and protected with cloches for an early spring crop, with the remainder of the maincrop sown at regular intervals to give a good succession of peas for harvest. It is the smoother rounder peas that tend to be used for the earlier crops, as these are the hardier varieties. The wrinkled pea has the better taste, but a weaker constitution. There are now many different varieties to choose from, which will give the desired extended season, as well as varieties with lovely flowers, coloured pods and mange-tout or sugar-snap varieties, where you eat the whole pod. You can also get peas for windy sites that are shorter and therefore do not require as much support as the older, taller varieties, as well as leafless types that consist of only tendrils. The advances of the newer varieties mean that they are now producing two or sometimes three pods per flowering node, as opposed to only one pod in the older varieties, thus enormously increasing the yield for the area used. The added bonus with peas is that their roots fix nitrogen, which helps with soil fertility and increases the need for a good crop rotation.

214

DATES

Sowing/Planting
October–February for early crops
March–July for maincrop varieties

Harvesting May–October

SOWING/PLANTING METHOD

The earliest sowings can be made in autumn or late winter, although if there is a particularly hard winter, this will result in smaller plants and a reduced crop – even with protection. Also, if you have problems with mice in the garden, peas are one of their favourite foods. If it is a hard winter when their food is scarce, they will harvest the crop for you before it has had a chance to germinate. Therefore, it is better to start sowing inside in January and February, either into pots or a length of guttering, so that the plants can get off to a good start and are planted out just as the weather begins to improve. Once the first crop has reached 5 cm (2 in) tall, then it is time to sow a crop to succeed this one. Continue this method with indoor and then outdoor crops throughout the season. Outside, they can be sown into a single or double drill, (depending on the system being used) as soon as the weather improves. Sowing can be moved forward if the soil has been warmed artificially by placing a cloche over the ground two weeks prior to the sowing date. A shallow trench dug out with a spade, with the peas put into it as a double row or thinly scattered at random, is the better method. This produces more pea plants in the given area, which in turn results in a bigger crop. The leafless varieties are well-suited to growing in beds or in containers.

MINIMUM TEMPERATURE

For germination 5°C (41°F)

215

SITE AND SOIL

Site Sunny spot, but will tolerate semi-shade. Moisture-retentive soil, but not waterlogged.

pH 6.5

Fertilizer Organic matter prior to sowing or planting.

Water Water during dry spells, until the first flowers start to open. At this point, keeping the plants moist is vital. Moist roots right through until harvest will greatly increase the yield of the crop. Too much water before flowering will result in plenty of good, green, leaf-growth, but not much yield.

DIMENSIONS

Planting depth
Guttering or pots 1 cm ($^{1}/2$ in) deep.
Trench dig out a trench 5 cm (2 in) deep.
Drill sow into a drill 4–5 cm ($1^{1}/2$–2 in) deep.

Space between plants:
Trench 5 cm (2 in) in all directions.
Drills 5 cm (2 in);

60–90 cm (24–36 in) rows.

The row spacing is usually equivalent to the height of the crop used, so shorter crops can have their rows closer together than taller varieties.

AFTER CARE

Support crops early on using pea sticks, netting, wire mesh or some sort of support material. Leafless varieties tend to be self-supporting, but in windier gardens these may also need some support. Mulch with a well-rotted manure or compost to keep the soil moist and hoe regularly. Water as required.

COMPANION PLANTS

Broad beans, French beans, climbing French beans, runner beans, Lima

SPECIAL TIP

To protect early crops from mice and birds, as well as protecting the crop from the cold, cover the seedbed with fleece that is dug into the ground, providing an impenetrable barrier to the pests.

beans, sweetcorn, okra, globe artichokes, lettuce, endive, chicory, cress, spinach and chard.

HARVESTING

Weeks to maturity 11–14 weeks

Regular harvesting of peas will encourage the crop to produce more; pick them young when they are at their sweetest. Mange-tout varieties are harvested when they are of a good size, but do not allow them to become too large and stringy. First early varieties will start cropping in May from an autumn sowing, followed by the second earlies and maincrop varieties that will crop until October.

HEALTH BENEFITS

Good source of vitamin B1 and folic acid. Mange-tout varieties are a source of vitamins A and C as well as potassium, as the pod is also eaten. They also contain soluble fibre which is useful for removing cholesterol from the body.

STORAGE

Podded and mange-tout varieties can be frozen successfully. Shell peas should be dried on the plants until they rattle inside the pods, when they can be put into airtight jars.

PESTS

Pea moth, aphids, pea thrip, birds, mice, pea and bean weevil.

DISEASES

Powdery mildew and fusarium wilt.

SELECTED VARIETIES

Alderman One of the highest-yielding maincrop varieties. Long pods, up to 11 large peas.

Ambassador Freezes very well. Pods with seven or eight smooth-skinned peas. Good disease resistance.

Asparagus Pea Ideal for the vegetable plot or ornamental border. Beautiful red flowers and small, winged pods. Harvest when they are no more than 3 cm (1$\frac{1}{4}$ in) long. Trailing plant.

Crops for up to nine weeks, if picked and watered regularly.

Balmoral Late variety. Harvest from September and October from a May/June sowing.

Carouby de Maussane Tall mange-tout variety. Purple flowers. Long, wide, green pods. Harvest for two to three weeks.

Cavalier Maincrop variety. Long pods in pairs. Up to 10 peas per pod. Resistant to powdery mildew. Good for successional sowings.

Celebration First early, wrinkled pea. Small, dark-green, petit pois-like peas. Semi-leafless, self-supporting variety.

Delikata Sugar snap. Dark-green pods. Good resistance to mildew and fusarium.

Douce Provence One of the best varieties for over-wintering. Short plants. Rounded peas. Harvest from May to July.

Early Onward Second early. Heavy crop of smooth, rounded peas.

Ezethas Krombek Blauwschok Mange-tout variety. Beautiful violet flowers followed by violet pods containing flat, green peas. Dries well.

Feltham First Vigorous first early. High yield of well-filled pods. Harvest from late May to July from an autumn sowing.

Fortune Early variety. Sow in autumn, but protect with cloches or fleece.

Gradus Heavy-cropping, second early. Dark-green peas. Harvest from late June until September.

Kelvedon Wonder Second early/maincrop. Heavy crop of wrinkled peas. Ideal for successional sowing.

Markana Semi-leafless maincrop variety. Resistant to fusarium wilt and less attractive to birds. Harvest from July to September.

Meteor First early, dwarf variety. Excellent winter hardiness from an autumn sowing. Smooth, round peas.

Ne Plus Ultra Extremely tall-growing, reaching 150–200 cm (5–6½ ft). Long, rounded pods. Some mildew resistance.

Noroli Fibre-free variety of mange-tout. Upright plants.

Onward Maincrop. Early and heavy crop of dark green pods, in pairs. Resistant to fusarium wilt.

Pilot Probably the hardiest of all from an autumn sowing. Harvest from June and July.

Purple Podded Tall variety, easily grown up an obelisk in an ornamental garden. Purple and white flowers followed by purple pods. Green peas. Can also be eaten as mange-tout, if picked early enough.

Starlight Unusual variety producing three pods per leaf node. Dark-green peas. Early maincrop. Resistant to mildew.

Sugar Ann Early, high-yielding sugar snap pea.

Sugar Crystal Semi-leafless sugar snap pea. Heavy yield of twin pods, containing up to eight peas. Resistant to mildew and fusarium wilt.

Sugar Snap Very tall, reaching 180 cm (6 ft). Can be eaten young as sugar snap peas or left to mature.

Twinkle First early. Matures after only 75 days. Sow in February under cloches for harvest in May, or sow in March for picking from June.

Waverex Variety of "petit pois". Sow from March to June. Short pods of small peas. Freezes well.

Zucolla Dwarf, sugar snap pea. High yields of glossy, dark-green pods and peas. Resistant to mildew and fusarium.

PEPPERS

Capsicum annuum Grossom Group (sweet pepper) and *Capsicum annuum Longum* Group (chilli)

Solanaceae

These exotic fruits have become very popular, due to the wide variety available to the amateur grower. These varieties have much more texture, colour and taste than those bought in the shops. They are relatively easy to grow, in both hot and cooler climates. However, to maximize the crop in cooler areas, it is always worthwhile giving them the protection of a greenhouse, tunnel or cloche, if grown outside. Although their cultivation is identical, the colours, shapes and flavours of the two types are quite different, with some varieties that wouldn't look out of place in the ornamental garden. The modern F1 hybrids have been bred to crop well in cooler seasons although, being tropical plants, they still require good light levels to achieve an ample yield. Both crops will require a higher temperature than tomatoes, but are less reliant on the heat than aubergines. Sweet pepper varieties ripen from green to red, with chilli peppers becoming hotter the more mature they become.

DATES

Sowing/Planting February–April

Harvesting July–October

SOWING/PLANTING METHOD

Sowing can start in February, if the greenhouse is heated, but needs to be a month later for unheated greenhouses and windowsills. The seeds of F1 hybrids are expensive, so great care needs to be taken when sowing, pricking out and planting, to ensure that all seedlings survive. Start by sowing them into seed trays on heat if possible. Once big enough to handle, they can be carefully pricked out into 8 cm (3 in) pots. These need to be well-spaced, to give each plant plenty of light and air. For optimum growth, they need to be kept at a minimum temperature of 16–18°C (60–64°F). As they only have a minimal root system, they do not like a lot of cold, wet compost around their roots, so never over-pot them. Once the roots have filled the 8 cm (3 in) pots, they can be potted on into 10–13 cm (4–5 in) pots, spacing well again. From this size pot,

SPECIAL TIP

Chilli peppers are much more prolific than sweet peppers, so there is no need to grow many plants to obtain enough of a harvest to last until the next season.

once the first flowers have appeared, they can either be planted out into growbags or potted on into a final 20 cm (8 in) pot. If they are being planted out into a border or vegetable plot, then this can be done after the last frost, planting them under cloches to acclimatize the plants. Once a regular temperature of 15°C (59°F) has been achieved day and night, the cloche can be removed. However, in cooler areas it will probably have to stay on for the length of the crop. In the greenhouse, plants will begin to suffer if the temperature rises above 30°C (86°F).

MINIMUM TEMPERATURE

For germination 20°C (68°F)

SITE AND SOIL

Site Sunny and sheltered position with a warm soil and in a greenhouse or polythene tunnel.

pH 6.0–6.5

Fertilizer Blood, fish and bone meal or pelleted chicken manure just prior to planting. Feed plants in pots or growbags regularly, with a high-potash, liquid seaweed fertilizer.

Water Water regularly, as required.

DIMENSIONS

Planting depth Plant to bury rootball.

Space between plants
30–45 cm (12–18 in);
60–75 cm (24–30 in) rows

AFTER CARE

Some varieties may require some support if they are laden with fruit, as the weight might cause a stem to snap. They do not need any of the shoot tips pinched out, as they are naturally self-branching, although some varieties do benefit from the main growing tip being removed when they reach about 15 cm (6 in) tall. Water and feed regularly and damp down the greenhouse or polythene tunnel at least once a day in hot weather to maintain humidity.

COMPANION PLANTS

Cucumber, squash, pumpkin, melon, potato, tomato, marrow, courgette, beetroot, parsnip, scorzonera, salsify, Hamburg parsley, celeriac, onion, shallot, leek, garlic, celery, Florence fennel, aubergine and carrot.

HARVESTING

Weeks to maturity 20–28 weeks

Always pick the first fruits of peppers when they are green, as this will encourage the plant to produce more fruit (some of which can be left to ripen into yellow, orange and red fruits). Allowing the fruits to ripen will slow the production of new fruits, reducing the final yield, but it is these brighter-coloured fruits that have the sweeter flavour.

HEALTH BENEFITS

Red and green peppers are both high in vitamin C, while red peppers are also high in vitamin A.

STORAGE

At the end of the season, the sweet pepper plants that are still carrying a crop can be pulled up and hung upside-down in a frost-free shed or garage, until the fruits have ripened. Pick chilli peppers when green or ripened and sun-dry them at any point through the season, before sealing them in an airtight jar, in the dark, or pickling them. At the end of the season, chilli peppers will last longer in store if left to ripen first, before being removed and dried in the sun, in a greenhouse, prior to storing.

PESTS

Aphids, whitefly, red spider mite and slugs.

DISEASES

Botrytis, blossom end rot, tobacco mosaic virus and tomato mosaic virus.

SELECTED VARIETIES

Sweet peppers

Attris F1 Thin-skinned variety. Tapering fruits, 23 cm (9 in) long. Fruits early.

Big Banana F1 Long, tapering fruits to 25 cm (10 in) long and 5 cm (2 in) across. Turn from green to red.

Cubanelle Yellow-green fruits, maturing to red-orange. Suitable for frying.

Diamond White Starts off transluscent white, turning pale yellow, maturing to scarlet red.

Fenix F1 Italian-type pepper. Long, tapering green-to-red fruit, 20 cm (8 in) long.

Golden Californian Wonder Sets fruit non-stop over the season. Starts light green and matures to golden yellow.

Gypsy F1 Crop in a cold greenhouse. Begins a yellowish-green maturing to deep red. Resistant to virus.

Jumbo F1 Enormous fruit, up to 10 cm (4 in) wide and 20 cm (8 in) long. Ideal for stuffing. Green fruits mature to dark red.

Mavras F1 Shiny purple skin, maturing to dark red.

Mohawk F1 Orange-fruited variety. Good in containers.

Purple Beauty Very early variety. Purple fruit. Resistant to tomato mosaic virus.

Redskin F1 Compact variety for growing on the windowsill. Medium-sized green fruits turn red as they mature.

Sweet Chocolate Starts green and matures to a rich, chocolate-brown skin with bright-red inner flesh.

Unicorn F1 Heavy cropper. Turns from dark green to bright red. Tobacco mosaic virus resistance.

Worldbeater Green fruits mature to bright red. Best in a greenhouse.

Yellow Bell F1 Large, bright yellow fruits up to 250 g (½ lb).

Chilli peppers

Anaheim Long, red fruits have thick walls and a medium-hot flavour. Tolerant of tobacco mosaic virus.

Andy F1 High yields of long and slender fruits. Green to bright red. Stores very well.

Apache F1 Grow on windowsill, in conservatory, greenhouse or on a patio. High yield of red fruits.

Birdseye Possibly the hottest of all the chillis. Thin-walled, oval fruits mature from green to red. Very late to ripen.

Habanero Chocolate One of the hottest chillis. Brown, heavily wrinkled, heart-shaped fruits.

Jalapeno Widely used in Mexican food. Ripens from green to red. Very hot.

Joe's Long Cayenne Excellent fresh or dried. Very long and thin, up to 25 cm (10 in). Green to red.

Numex Twilight Ideal for containers or growing in the border. Medium-hot peppers, produced vertically. Rainbow of colours as they change from purple, to yellow, to orange, to red.

Purple Tiger Hot pepper. Very ornamental. Tri-coloured foliage is green, purple and white. Fruits begin purple, becoming tri-coloured on their way to maturity and a final red colour. Large plants can be restricted by growing in a container.

225

POTATOES
Solanum tuberosum

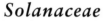

Solanaceae

The potato is a must for almost any vegetable grower, as it can be harvested over a very long period and then stored over the winter, providing a usable crop for 12 months of the year. Potatoes take up a lot of space, so they might not be worth growing if you garden in a small area. Since they are a relatively cheap vegetable to buy anyway, you should use limited space for more expensive and less easily obtainable crops. The only time that you should consider growing them in a small plot is if you don't have a supply of organically grown potatoes nearby. The crop is generally grown from tubers called "seed potatoes", although it is possible to obtain more unusual varieties that have been micro-propagated; these will come as "slips" or small plants. Always buy seed potatoes from a reputable supplier that has been certified as "free from disease". Seed potato tubers are "chitted" before planting to get a better and faster crop. This involves placing the tubers in a tray, or something similar, with one end pointing upwards. The tray can then be put into a light place at a temperature of about 10°C (50°F) – under the greenhouse benching is ideal – where short, stumpy, green shoots will appear. These shoots are the beginnings of the top growth, so the potatoes will be planted out already in growth. As a crop, they are grouped into three different sections, depending on their best time for harvesting. The "first earlies" will mature first and these are

followed by a crop of "second earlies", which will be harvested before the "maincrop" potatoes. It is these maincrop potatoes that will go into storage for use through the winter. Each of the different types of potato will give different flavours and textures, although much of the flavour and success of individual varieties will depend on the area in which they are grown. The only way to discover how well particular varieties will grow in your area, and whether they will produce tubers with flavour, is to see what other gardeners are growing. Alternatively, you could find out by trial and error. Maincrop potatoes will also act as an excellent cleaning crop for any area or garden. This means that they will clean a garden of most weeds and the soil will become well cultivated. The weeds are cleared because the potatoes produce top growth, or haulms, that will make a thick canopy over the soil which excludes light; this prevents most weeds from growing. The soil will become well-cultivated, because the soil will have to be turned three times for initial soil preparation, for planting, and harvest. Therefore, if you're moving into a house with a fairly wild garden that needs to be brought into shape, clear the weeds, cultivate the soil and plant a crop of maincrop potatoes before doing anything else.

DATES

Sowing/Planting

1st early January and March–April
2nd early and maincrop March–May

Harvesting March–October

SOWING/PLANTING METHOD

It is advisable to purchase seed potatoes as early as possible at the beginning of the year, so that they can be put into trays and chitted prior to planting. This ensures that planting is not delayed while you wait for the tubers to start shooting. The first of the first early potatoes can be planted into a hotbox during the middle of January, or once the heat has risen enough to keep out frost. The next crop of first earlies will be harvested from tubers planted into tubs in the greenhouse, followed by first earlies planted into tubs that are moved out into a polythene tunnel during early March.

The first crop to be grown outside can be planted through polythene, during late March, as this will heat the soil, bringing the harvest date of the crop forward. Either black or clear polythene can be used; some growers prefer black and others clear. With black polythene, it is laid out over prepared ground and the edges are dug in or held down with bricks, wood etc. Cross cuts are then made at the planting points and the potatoes tubers are planted through the polythene into the soil. The polythene will eliminate all light, preventing weed growth and warming the soil, with the potato shoots growing up through the holes (although some may need manual direction). With the clear polythene method, the potatoes are planted first and the thin, clear polythene is dug in around the area (as for the black polythene). No holes are cut, keeping all the moisture and warmth in the soil, until the potato shoots are pushing up the polythene. Cross cuts are made at this point, the shoots are teased through and the plants left to grow.

Both of these methods will produce crops at least two weeks earlier than those planted directly into the ground without a polythene cover. The drawbacks of these methods are that with the black polythene some potato shoots will be adversely affected by the lack of light, and with the clear

SPECIAL TIP

If growing very early potatoes using the hot-box method, then a selection of varieties is very important to ensure a small, but steady flow of potatoes from varieties that mature at different times. Start with the earliest first early variety in the hotbox and in a tub followed by two or three different first early varieties which should prevent an early glut.

polythene, weeds can still grow (although they are contained under the polythene, so they do not seed, but they do compete with the crop to a degree).

At the same time the first early potatoes are being planted under the polythene, the rest of the first early varieties can be planted out (as well as the second early and maincrop tubers). If desired, the planting can be staggered to avoid a glut of new potatoes. Planting can be carried out in three ways. The first is to dig a trench at least 8–15 cm (3–6 in) deep and work organic matter into the bottom before placing the potatoes, shoots upwards onto the soil at their correct spacing. The tops of the tubers then need to be covered with at least 8 cm (3 in) of soil. The second method is to prepare the area first, digging in plenty of organic matter and then planting the tubers into a hole dug out with a trowel, to the same depth as before. Finally, potatoes can be grown using the "no dig" method, whereby they are placed at their correct spacing on the ground and then covered with black polythene or a thick layer of straw to eliminate the light.

It is also possible to have fresh new potatoes for Christmas dinner by saving good-quality first early tubers and replanting them in containers or in the ground after harvest. There is no need to use the earliest varieties, as the time factor is not as important at this point in the season. These plants then need to be kept frost free, so move the container into a greenhouse or conservatory and tip out for use. The outdoor crop will probably need covering with a good layer of straw from early November and can be dug up on Christmas Eve.

MINIMUM TEMPERATURE

For germination 10°C (50°F) for chitting.

SITE AND SOIL

Site Sunny, open spot but will tolerate some semi-shade as long as it is not in a frost pocket. They do require a humus rich, preferably acid, moisture-retentive soil for best results, but not one that gets waterlogged.

pH 5.0–6.0

Fertilizer Apply blood, fish and bone meal or pelleted chicken manure prior to planting and dig in plenty of well-rotted manure. Apply another dose of blood, fish and bone meal or pelleted chicken manure once the potato shoots are about 15 cm (6 in) tall.

Water Keep the soil moist for the duration of the crop, but if the crop suffers from lack of water around flowering time, the tubers will not swell. Always water the soil, not the foliage.

DIMENSIONS

Planting depth 8–15 cm (3–6 in)

Space between plants
1st and 2nd earlies 30 cm (12 in);
60 cm (24 in) rows
Maincrop 35 cm (15 in);
75 cm (30 ins) rows

AFTER CARE

If shoots appear before the frosts have passed, then cover with fleece, cloches, straw or newspaper if frost is forecast. Once the potato shoots have reached 15 cm (6 ins) tall and the second application of fertilizer made, they can be "earthed up", which involves pulling soil from between the rows up the potato stems and leaving only a small amount of tip growth showing. A second earthing up can also be carried out two or three weeks later, if desired. This earthing up and the forming of ridges over the potato shoots will not only help to prevent weeds but also covers any exposed tubers and stops them going green. This occurs when they are exposed to the light for a period of time. Water well from flowering.

COMPANION PLANTS

Cucumber, squash, pumpkin, melon, carrot, tomato, marrow, courgette, beetroot, parsnip, scorzonera, salsify,

Hamburg parsley, celeriac, onion, shallot, leek, garlic, celery, Florence fennel, aubergine and pepper.

HARVESTING

Weeks to maturity 16–28 weeks

Both first-early and second-early potatoes are ready for harvest as soon as they begin to flower. Maincrops from September.

HEALTH BENEFITS

A good source of vitamin C, fibre, potassium and protein.

STORAGE

Maincrop varieties can be lifted, and left on the soil surface for a day to dry. Sort the damaged ones for eating straight away and place the perfect potatoes into paper sacks that can be tied at the top and put into a cool, dark and frost-free place, such as a garage or shed.

PESTS

Slugs and wireworms.

DISEASES

Potato blight, scab and potato blackleg.

SELECTED VARIETIES

Anya Second-early, salad variety. Nutty flavour.

Arran Pilot Reliable. First early. Excellent yield and tuber size.

Cara Maincrop. Late variety. Mild flavour. Excellent disease resistance. High-yielding.

Charlotte Second early. High-yielding salad variety. Tubers are blight resistant.

Desiree Maincrop. Early red variety. Excellent all-round potato with good disease resistance.

Estima Second early. Uniform white variety that bakes well.

Highland Burgundy Red Maincrop. An early dark, red-skinned variety. Burgundy red flesh; holds its colour when steamed.

Maris Piper Maincrop. Early white variety. High-yielding with good flavour. Excellent for chips. Prone to scab and slug damage.

Maxine Maincrop. Early red variety. Good all-round culinary potato.

Nadine Second early. White potato. Good for boiling and roasting.

Pink Fir Apple Maincrop. Late, white salad variety. Excellent flavour. Cook whole.

Pomeroy Maincrop. Blight, scab and blackleg resistant. Excellent flavour.

Rocket First early. Mild-flavoured, uniform white variety. Pick early.

Salad Blue Maincrop. Blue-skinned and blue-fleshed. Keeps colour when fried. Excellent for blue chips and crisps!

Swift First early. Mild-flavoured white. One of the earliest. Excellent disease resistance.

Valor Maincrop. High-yielding, late-white variety. Good for all-round culinary uses.

RADISH
Raphanus sativus

Brassicaceae

This easy to grow root crop is well-suited to cool climates and has a very long harvesting season, potentially being available for nine months of the year. It is primarily a salad crop that can be grown in about four weeks to produce roots of various lengths and shapes. They have a crunchy and slightly hot taste. Larger roots can be cooked in the same way as turnips. There are summer and winter varieties that come in various colours, with most summer radishes being red, white and red or white in colour, but the winter varieties can be black, purple, yellow or green-skinned, along with the red and white combinations. An excellent crop for growing in beds or intercropping between longer term crops, such as Brussels sprouts and cabbages. If left to flower, the immature seed pods can also be eaten.

233

DATES

Sowing/Planting
January–September

Harvesting May–January

SOWING/PLANTING METHOD

Sow into shallow drills outside in situ. Can also be scattered onto the surface or into shallow bands. Thin as required, once the thinnings are large enough to use. Early crops can be sown under cloches or fleece.

MINIMUM TEMPERATURE

For germination 5°C (41°F)

SITE AND SOIL

Site Will grow in any soil. Grow summer crops in semi-shade and spring, autumn and winter varieties in full sun.

pH 6.5–7.5

Fertilizer Well-rotted manure incorporated prior to sowing.

Water Water in dry spells.

DIMENSIONS

Planting depth Sow into drills 1 cm (1/2 in) deep.

Space between plants
Summer 2.5 cm (1 in); 10–15 cm (4–6 ins) rows
Winter 20 cm (8 in); 30 cm (12 in) rows

AFTER CARE

Water, if dry, to prevent radishes running to seed, but do not over-water. Keep weed free.

COMPANION PLANTS

Brussels sprouts, Chinese cabbage, broccoli, calabrese, cabbage, kale, swede, turnip, cauliflower, kohl rabi.

HARVESTING

Weeks to maturity
Summer 4–8 weeks
Winter 10–20 weeks
Pull roots as required, using the thinnings first.

HEALTH BENEFITS

High in vitamin C, and potassium.

STORAGE

Summer varieties will only store for one to two days in the fridge. Winter varieties can be stored as for carrots (see page 140).

PESTS

Flea beetle, cabbage root fly, slugs and snails.

DISEASES

Clubroot.

SELECTED VARIETIES

Cherry Belle Excellent early variety. Round, red roots. Harvest from May.

China Rose Winter-cropping. Deep, pink skin; white flesh. Harvest from October to December.

French Breakfast 3 Cylindrical, scarlet root; white ends. Harvest from May to September.

Long White Icicle Cylindrical, white-skinned variety. Harvest from May to September.

Mantanghong Winter variety. White skin; red, nutty flesh. Harvest from September to December.

Munchen Bier Grown for its immature seed pods. The white roots can be used from late summer. Harvest from May to October.

Pink Beauty Pinkish-red skin, white flesh. Globe-shaped roots. Harvest from May to September.

Purple Plum Bright purple skin; white flesh. Stands well without going pithy. Harvest from May to October.

Red Meat Large, round roots. Red tops, white skin and deep-rose, red flesh. Harvest from June to September.

Rougette Large, round, cherry-red roots. Harvest from May to October.

Runder Schwarzer (Black Spanish Round) Winter radish. Round, black-skinned, white flesh. Harvest from October to December.

Sparkler 3 Bright-scarlet, round root with white bottom. Harvest from May to September.

White Breakfast Pure white version of French Breakfast.

SWEDE
Brassica napus Napobrassica Group

Brassicaceae

A tough and hardy root crop that requires significant growing space for a reasonable period of time. It is not an easy crop to grow, but the yellow/orange-fleshed, generally bulbous roots provide a sweet-tasting winter vegetable that will stand out in all weathers. Although they can be stored, the earlier varieties are best left in the ground and harvested as required. The taste and varieties available have moved on considerably in recent years and this crop can no longer be referred to as "cattle fodder".

DATES

Sowing/Planting May–June

Harvesting September–February

SOWING/PLANTING METHOD

Sow directly into shallow drills. There is no advantage in sowing early due to the mildew problems associated with early crops. Thin when big enough to handle. Can also be grown in modules and transplanted.

MINIMUM TEMPERATURE

For germination 5°C (40°F)

SPECIAL TIP

Roots tend to go woody if left in the ground beyond Christmas, so lift and store the later varieties.

SITE AND SOIL

Site Sunny, open spot with well-drained, but moisture-retentive soil. If no organic matter incorporated for previous crop, dig some in.

pH 6.5–7.5

Fertilizer Pelleted chicken manure prior to sowing or planting.

Water Water regularly when dry. Erratic watering can cause roots to split.

DIMENSIONS

Planting depth Sow into drills 2 cm (3/4 in) deep.

Space between plants 23 cm (9 in); 38 cm (15 in) rows.

AFTER CARE

Keep weed free and well-watered.

COMPANION PLANTS

Brussels sprouts, Chinese cabbage, broccoli, calabrese, cabbage, kale, radish, turnip, cauliflower, kohl rabi and catch crops such as lettuce, spring onions, rocket and spinach.

HARVESTING

Weeks to maturity 20–26 weeks

Pull as required.

HEALTH BENEFITS

Source of vitamin C, potassium, calcium and magnesium.

STORAGE

Store as for celeriac (see page 151).

PESTS

Flea beetle, cabbage root fly and aphids.

DISEASES

Clubroot and mildew.

SELECTED VARIETIES

Airlie Red-skinned, yellow flesh. Medium size. Resistant to mildew.

Harvest from September to December.

Angela Purple skin, orange-yellow flesh. Uniform. Some mildew resistance. Harvest from October to February.

Brora Deep, purple skin, yellow flesh. Harvest from September to December.

Joan Medium-sized, uniform roots. Dark purple root tops, cream bottom. Yellow flesh. Some clubroot and mildew resistance. Harvest from September to December.

Magres Purple-topped roots, yellow flesh. Mildew resistant. Harvest from October to February.

Ruby Dark, purple skin, creamy-yellow flesh. Mildew resistant. Harvest from October to February.

Virtue Red skin, yellow flesh. Harvest from October to February.

Willemsburger Green root top, pale orange flesh. Resistant to clubroot. Stores well. Harvest from October to February.

SWEETCORN
Zea mays

Poaceae

A half-hardy crop that can be grown in temperate climates, although in cooler summers the yield will be less successful than in long hot summers. It is far better when home-grown and picked fresh, because as soon as a cob is picked from a plant the sugar in that cob begins to turn to starch. They are a high-value crop, with the taste being incomparable to cobs bought in the shops. Generally, the cobs are cooked whole and the corn is eaten from the cob. They are tall plants and are wind-pollinated, so require to be planted in a block rather than in rows, for the best pollination. The "supersweet" varieties have been bred to have a much sweeter flavour that will last longer once picked.

DATES

Sowing/Planting April–May

Harvesting July–October

SOWING/PLANTING METHOD

The seeds are generally started in the greenhouse, and, as they dislike root disturbance can be sown into deep modules, tubes or 8 cm (3 in) pots. Sow two seeds per container and remove the weaker one once germinated. Harden off before planting out. They can also be directly sown outside in a warm spot, if there is not a greenhouse or windowsill available. Warm the soil a couple of weeks before sowing, using a cloche or plastic sheet, and sow two seeds at their ultimate spacing (thinning to one when they germinate).

MINIMUM TEMPERATURE

For germination 10°C (50°F)

SITE AND SOIL

Site Sunny and sheltered position.

pH 5.5–7.0

Fertilizer Dig in plenty of well-rotted manure or garden compost prior to planting or sowing, as well as an application of blood, fish and bone meal or pelleted chicken manure.

Water When the tassels start to appear, water on a regular basis.

DIMENSIONS

Planting depth 2.5 cm (1 in) in containers and in the ground.

Space between plants 45 x 45cm (18 x 18 ins)

Plant in a block with equidistant spacing between plants.

AFTER CARE

Keep weed free and mulch to conserve water. In more exposed sites, earth up

SPECIAL TIP

Do not grow supersweet varieties close to ordinary ones, as they may cross pollinate and the supersweets will lose their extra sweetness.

around the plants to encourage more roots to be formed.

COMPANION PLANTS

Broad beans, French beans, runner beans, Lima beans, peas, okra, globe artichokes, lettuce, endive, chicory, cress, spinach and chard.

HARVESTING

Weeks to maturity 12–16 weeks

Harvest when tassels turn brown by breaking whole cob from the main stem. Harvest minipop when the tassels first start to show – when the cobs are about 8–15 cm (3–6 in) long.

HEALTH BENEFITS

Good source of vitamin B and fibre. Low in calories and gluten-free.

STORAGE

Can be frozen.

PESTS

Mice, birds, squirrels and slugs.

DISEASES

No real disease problems.

SELECTED VARIETIES

Ambrosia F1 Early. White and bi-coloured cobs. Very sweet variety.

Applause F1 A supersweet variety. Good, long cobs.

Black Aztec Blue-black kernels.

Earlybird F1 Earliest sweet variety.

Indian Summer F1 Multi-coloured kernels in yellow, red, white and purple. Supersweet variety.

Lark F1 Sweet kernels with a less chewy texture. Supersweet variety.

Minipop F1 Ideal for growing in beds. Does not need to be planted in block as it is harvested before pollination.

Sundance F1 Early variety. Good creamy-yellow kernels on lengthy cobs.

Sweet Nugget Supersweet variety. Grows well in cool conditions.

TOMATO
Lycopersicon esculentum

Solanaceae

Generally thought of as a greenhouse or tunnel crop, this half-hardy perennial is grown as an annual and can be grown inside and out, even in temperate climates. That said, some varieties have been bred for greenhouse cultivation, while others will grow adequately both inside and outside. Technically a fruit, they are classed as a fruiting vegetable, which can be eaten raw or cooked, making the tomato a very versatile commodity in the garden and the kitchen. They come in a range of sizes, from tomatoes the size of grapes through to giant beef-steak types, as well as colours that range from white to green, to yellow and almost black, as well as the traditional red. The plants themselves are available as two types. Bush varieties are compact and require little work to maintain them, while vine tomatoes are generally grown up supports and require more work to produce a crop. In more temperate climates, it is important to look at early cropping varieties for outdoor conditions and unheated greenhouses or tunnels. For heated greenhouses or in hotter climates, later cropping varieties can be used, as they will have the heat available for the tomatoes to ripen late in the season.

243

DATES

Sowing/Planting January–April

Harvesting June–October

SOWING/PLANTING METHOD

Whether the crop is going to be situated inside or out, it needs to be sown in a greenhouse or on a windowsill. However, indoor varieties will be started much sooner than outdoor varieties. Sow into seed trays and cover with a thin layer of vermiculite. At the seed-leaf stage, prick out the seedlings into 8 cm (3 in) pots. Grow on at a minimum temperature of 21°C (70°F). When the last sign of frost has passed, they can be planted out. Alternatively, if the tomatoes are to be grown under protection, they can be potted on until they reach their final pot size, as for aubergines, or planted into the greenhouse soil, or a growbag.

MINIMUM TEMPERATURE

For germination 16°C (60°F)

SITE AND SOIL

Site Sunny and moisture-retentive soil, containing plenty of organic matter.

pH 5.5–7.0

Fertilizer Blood, fish and bone meal or pelleted chicken manure prior to planting.

Water Plants in containers will need regular watering. Water outdoor plants during dry weather.

DIMENSIONS

Planting depth Plant to top of rootball.

Space between plants *Bush* 45 cm (18 in); 45 cm (18 in) rows *Vines* 45–60 cm (18–24 in); 45–60 cm (18–24 in) rows

Both types can be planted a fraction closer, if being grown in beds.

AFTER CARE

Once planted, vine types will need the support of a cane if outside, or string, wire, trellis or a cane if under protection. If a frost is forecast, protect outdoor tomatoes with fleece or a cloche. Once the first truss has set its fruits, water every 10–14 days with a high-potash, seaweed liquid feed. Mulch outdoor varieties with well-rotted organic matter. Remove sideshoots from vine types, but not from the bush varieties. In temperate areas, allow plants to reach four to five fruit trusses outside and six under cover, before removing the growing tip. Tie to supports regularly. Remove leaves around the lowest truss, to aid air circulation and help to prevent disease. Damp down the floors daily in a greenhouse during hot weather. To aid pollination, regularly tap the supports to release pollen from the flowers.

SPECIAL TIP

When growing the crop under protection, plant the tomatoes with one end of the supporting string under the rootball to anchor it and tie the other end to an overhead, supporting wire.

COMPANION PLANTS

Cucumber, squash, pumpkin, melon, carrot, potato, marrow, courgette, beetroot, parsnip, scorzonera, salsify, Hamburg parsley, celeriac, onion, shallot, leek, garlic, celery, Florence fennel, aubergine and pepper.

HARVESTING

Weeks to maturity: 16–18 weeks

Remove the fruits as soon as they are ripe. This will give the best flavour and minimize disease from rots associated with overripe fruits. Remove fruits, with the calyx still attached, to lengthen the life of the tomato. At the end of the season, lay outdoor plants onto straw and cover them with a cloche to ripen the last remaining fruits before the hard frosts start. The whole plant can also be lifted and hung by the roots in a cool shed or garage, where the fruits will slowly ripen on the plant. Alternatively, the fruit can all be picked from the plant, calyx intact, and placed into a drawer to slowly ripen.

HEALTH BENEFITS

High in vitamins A and C, as well as lycopene.

STORAGE

They can be bottled, frozen or made into chutney.

PESTS

Whitefly, aphids and red spider mite.

DISEASES

Potato blight, tomato mosaic virus, botrytis, mildew and greenback.

SELECTED VARIETIES

Ailsa Craig Medium-sized fruits. Vine type. Strong red colour and flavour. Grow inside and out. Harvest from July to September.

Alicante Medium-sized. Vine type. Early cropper. Excellent flavour. Resistant to mildew and greenback. Grow inside and out. Harvest from July to September.

Aviro F1 Medium-sized. Vine. Heavy cropper. Orange fruits. Virus resistant.

Beefsteak Large fruits. Bush. Pink-red fruits up to 250 g (8 oz) each. Grow inside and out. Harvest from July to September.

Big Boy F1 Large fruits. Vine. Huge scarlet fruits up to 450 g (1 lb) in weight. Grow inside and out. Harvest from July to September.

Black Russian Large fruits. Vine. Irregularly shaped, mahogany-skinned fruit. Reddish-black flesh. Grow inside and out. Harvest from July to October.

Cream Sausage Small fruit. Bush. Cream-coloured, elongated plum fruits. Grow inside and out. Harvest from August to September.

Gardener's Delight Small fruit. Vine. Long trusses of red cherry tomatoes. Grow inside and out. Harvest from July to September.

Green Grape Medium-sized fruit. Vine. Green- and yellow-coloured sweet fruit. Harvest from July to September.

Green Zebra Medium-sized fruit. Vine. Green and yellow striped very sweet fruit. Grow inside. Harvest from July to September.

Moneymaker Medium-sized fruit. Vine. Reliable cropper. Red fruit with an excellent flavour. Grow inside or out. Harvest from July to September.

Sungold F1 Small fruit. Vine. Orange cherry tomatoes. Grow inside. Harvest from July to September.

Supersteak F1 Large fruits. Vine. Massive red fruits, up to 900 g (2 lbs) in weight. Grow inside. Harvest from August to September.

Sweet Million F1 Small fruits. Vine. Heavy cropper. Cherry type, red fruits. Harvest from July to October.

Tigerella Medium-sized fruits. Vine. Red- and yellow-striped fruit. Early maturing. Grow inside and out. Harvest from July to September.

Tumbler F1 Small fruits. Bush. Ideal for baskets and containers. Heavy cropper. Small, cherry-red tomatoes. Harvest from July to September.

Tumbling Tom Yellow Small fruits. Bush. Ideal for baskets and containers. Heavy cropper. Small, cherry-sized yellow tomatoes. Harvest from July to September.

White Beauty Large fruits. Vine. Milk-white fruits turn yellowish in sunlight. High-yielding. Harvest from August to September.

Yellow Pear Small fruits. Vine. Pear-shaped yellow fruits with a sweet flavour. Harvest from July to September.

chapter 4

plant organic
HERBS

Basil • Bay • Chives

• Coriander • Dill • Fennel

• Mint • Oregano • Parsley

• Rosemary • Sage • Thyme

The growing of herbs for culinary and medicinal

purposes has been practised for thousands of years. It is not for this historical precedent, however, that they should be incorporated into every organic garden, but for more practical reasons. For the purposes of this book I have highlighted varieties that can be used primarily for their culinary properties although there are literally hundreds of plants classed as herbs that have medicinal properties. Both culinary and most medicinal herbs are essential elements of any organic garden, primarily because of the beneficial insects that they encourage into the garden, which are not only needed for pollination in the fruit garden, but the larvae of many of these insects will also feed on common pests. We all love to see ladybirds indulging themselves on the nectar from the flowers of our herb plants without realizing the good work their larvae have done on our aphid population.

Less lovely but still as important are the lacewings and hoverflies that are also attracted by these plants. Most herbs like an open and sunny position with good drainage, because these are the conditions of their natural habitat. And because of this sharp drainage they do not have a great deal of nutrients available. Therefore their feed requirement in the garden is minimal and an application of pelleted chicken manure in the spring will suffice. Sunny positions are usually possible, but if your soil is not well drained then it can be improved by digging in plenty of organic matter and coarse grit. I like to use a mix that consists of equal parts soil, garden compost and coarse grit. It does not have to be dug down to a great depth as most herb varieties are fairly shallow rooted.

If your soil really is not suited to some varieties do not despair, as they are all easily grown in containers, and I have used a variety of containers for this purpose. The classic terracotta pot will provide an excellent home for a wide range of herbs, but do not stop there, as I have also used old chimney pots, drainage pipes set into the ground on their end, stainless steel pots, copper containers, fake stone troughs, window boxes and even hanging baskets. The most important factor to bear in mind with herbs grown in containers is to ensure that the drainage holes are large enough and plentiful enough to ensure excessive water flows away quickly. In the winter when conditions may not suit these containerized plants they can be moved into a greenhouse or conservatory until late spring.

Maintenance of most herb varieties takes place in early spring, once the risk of severe frost has passed. This is the time to tidy up plants and cut back hard any that require it, such as rosemary, sage and lavender. If these tasks are carried out in the autumn there is a risk that new shoots can be severely damaged by frosts, which will definitely set the plants back and may even kill them altogether. Once cut back they can be fed to get the plants growing strongly.

There are many varieties that need to be planted in areas where they can be touched or brushed against to release their wonderful scents, which makes them excellent subjects for planting in a sensory garden. I have found that leaving planting pockets in paved areas for very prostrate herbs, such as thymes, gives a wonderful effect with certain varieties showing no harm when trodden underfoot. If being grown solely for culinary purposes then it is a good idea to have the herb area close to the kitchen, so that when herbs are picked their freshness is maximized in the food they are accompanying. The diversity of scents produced from this wide variety of herbs makes the majority of them vital ingredients of potpourri, as well as excellent scented bouquets in their own right.

There is no doubt that a well planned and planted organic herb garden, with all the different leaf and flower colours and textures will be as beautiful as any ornamental garden.

BASIL
Ocimum basilicum

Lamiaceae

Basil is a warm-climate annual that originates from tropical
Asia and is an essential in the kitchen. It is easy to grow in the
greenhouse, conservatory or outside, but it will not tolerate any
frost. It requires a sunny and well-drained position and is
ideally suited to culinary uses, as regular picking stimulates the
plant to put on extra growth. The strongly aromatic leaves
produce a distinct clove-like flavour. There are various different
varieties that will add a multitude of flavours, as well as colour,
to many dishes. It is particularly good with fish, egg, meat,
pasta and tomato dishes. If allowed to, the plant will produce
small white flowers during late summer.

DATES

Sowing
Inside March–April
Outside April–May

Harvesting July–October

SOWING METHOD

Sow into seed trays in the greenhouse. Prick out into 8 cm (3 in) pots for planting outside from the end of May.

TEMPERATURE

For germination 20°C (68°F)

SITE AND SOIL

Site Sunny, sheltered and well-drained position.

pH 5.0–8.0

Fertilizer Light feeder

Water No special requirements, just water as necessary.

SPECIAL TIP

If containerised and bought into a light, frost-free place such as a greenhouse, conservatory or window sill, basil will continue to grow during the winter months.

DIMENSIONS

Planting depth 1 cm ($1/2$ in)

Space between plants 30 cm (12 in)

Height of plants 30–45cm (12–18 in)

Spread of plants 30–45cm (12–18 in)

AFTER CARE

Pinch out the growing tips on a regular basis to encourage the plant to bush.

COMPANION PLANTS

Other herbs, tomatoes and peppers.

HARVESTING

Weeks to maturity 12–14 weeks

HEALTH BENEFITS

As well as having many uses in aromatherapy, if basil is brewed as a tea it aids digestion, while basil oil on a handkerchief or sleeve can be used to alleviate mental fatigue. The leaves can also be infused in water to provide an invigorating bath and it is also said to be a natural tranquilizer.

STORAGE

It can be frozen, as with chives (see page 261), but paint the leaves with olive oil first. They can also be dried and kept in an airtight jar or infused in olive oil or vinegar.

PESTS

Whitefly, slugs and snails.

DISEASES

Botrytis and damping off.

SELECTED VARIETIES

americanum (basil lime) Green-leaved with a citrus taste. Used in savoury or dessert dishes.

basilicum (basil sweet) Common, sweet basil. Strongly flavoured, oval bright green leaves.

Cinnamon Strongly flavoured basil, with faintest hint of cinnamon and lovely purple flowers. Use with fresh fruits.

var *citriodorum* (basil lemon) Strong lemon flavour. Ideal to flavour meat or fish and is widely used in Indonesian cooking. It also makes a lovely cup of tea.

Purple Ruffles Mainly a decorative form, with less flavour but large, purple ruffled leaves. Use with salads, pasta and tomato dishes.

BAY
Laurus nobilis

Lauraceae

This dual purpose tree is ideal for any garden and can be grown as an ornamental that also has culinary uses. The small, star-shaped, creamy-yellow flowers are followed by small black fruits, but this plant is primarily grown for its aromatic, dark green foliage. It can be grown as a shrub, large tree, clipped into a hedge or even used as topiary, because it takes very readily to regular clipping. Growing in all of these forms will mean that leaves can still be removed as and when they are required for the kitchen without any harm to the plant; as it is evergreen, this means that bay leaves will be available all year round. These tough leaves are used to flavour many dishes and are one of the basic ingredients of bouquet garni. Being a member of the laurel family, and often having laurel mentioned in its name, it is not to be confused with other laurels whose leaves are all inedible.

256

DATES

Sowing Outside in the autumn or inside in spring at 20°C (68°F).

Harvesting All year round.

SOWING METHOD

Sow into seed trays and cover the seed with coarse grit. Place the seed tray in a sheltered part of the garden. If sowing in spring store the seed in a cool and dry place before sowing into a seed tray and covering with vermiculite. Bay can also be easily propagated from semi-ripe cuttings taken in June or July.

TEMPERATURE

For germination Inside 18°C (65°F)

SITE AND SOIL

Site Sunny, sheltered and well-drained spot, although they will take semi-shade. Bay can be frost-tender in colder areas, so they make great container plants which can then be moved into a more sheltered area or greenhouse for the winter.

pH 6.0–7.5

Fertilizer Annual application of pelleted chicken manure in the spring. Container grown plants need a regular balanced seaweed feed throughout the growing season.

Water Water during very dry spells. Regularly water container plants.

DIMENSIONS

Planting depth To top of rootball.

Space between plants 3–5 m (10–15 ft), if not clipped.

Height of plants 5–6 m (15–20 ft)

Spread of plants 2.4–3 m (8–10 ft)

AFTER CARE

In cold weather, wrap the plant with fleece. Clip into shape in late May or early June and again, if necessary, in August. Water in dry weather.

COMPANION PLANTS

Other herbs.

HARVESTING

Pick fresh leaves for the best flavour.

HEALTH BENEFITS

Infuse to aid digestion and stimulate appetite.

STORAGE

The leaves can be dried and frozen, but they do lose some flavour in the process.

PESTS

Aphids, whitefly and scale insect.

DISEASES

No real disease problems.

SELECTED VARIETIES

nobilis Common bay, sweet bay or bay laurel, all three relate to the same plant.

nobilis Aurea The yellow-leaved form. Not as hardy, with much less flavour.

nobilis f. angustifolia Willow leaf bay has much narrower leaves than others of the type.

CHIVES
Allium schoenoprasum

Alliaceae

Chives are a hardy perennial plant that will thrive in most soil types and, although it prefers to be in an open and sunny position, it will tolerate a certain amount of shade. They are an excellent starter herb as they suffer no pests or diseases and are easily grown from seed, with parent plants gently seeding themselves into pathways, paving and surrounding bare soil patches. Once the herb has outgrown its allocated space it can be lifted (in either autumn or spring) divided and smaller pieces replanted. This plant is of great importance to the herb area, as the flowers are beautiful. They are globular and pale mauve in colour, and are very attractive to bees and other essential insects. In the autumn a clump can be lifted, potted and moved into the greenhouse to be cropped during the winter months. The leaves have a mild onion flavour and can be used as flavouring in cooked dishes, with the leaves and flowers being used in salads. The bulbs can even be pickled in wine vinegar.

259

DATES

Sowing April–May

Harvesting April–November; longer if plants put in greenhouse for winter.

SOWING METHOD

Sow into shallow drills outside and into seed trays or modules in the greenhouse.

TEMPERATURE

For germination 15–21°C (60–70°F)

SITE AND SOIL

Site Sun or semi-shade in well drained, but moisture-retentive soil.

pH 5.5–8.5

Fertilizer Pelleted chicken manure each spring.

Water During dry spells.

DIMENSIONS

Planting depth 1 cm ($1/2$ in)

SPECIAL TIP

If left to flower, the clump can be cut back to within 1 cm ($1/2$ inch) of the ground to encourage a flush of new shoots.

Space between plants 30 cm (12 in)

Height of plants 30 cm (12 in)

Spread of plants 23 cm (9 in)

AFTER CARE

Chives will very much look after themselves, although the clump will need to be lifted and divided every three years, with fresh organic matter dug into the soil before replanting.

COMPANION PLANTS

Other herbs, tomatoes, carrots, celery, onions, shallots, leeks, potatoes, beetroot, potatoes, parsnips, garlic, courgettes, marrows, pumpkins, Florence fennel, aubergines, peppers, melons, celeriac, Hamburg parsley, salsify and scorzonera.

HARVESTING

The plants thrive on being cut back, so regular removal of leaves down to 5 cm (2 in) will be beneficial to the plant and encourage production of soft, new leaves.

HEALTH BENEFITS

They contain some iron, sulphur, vitamins and also aids digestion, can be used as a mild laxative and have mild antibiotic properties.

STORAGE

They are best cut up and stored frozen in ice cubes because, although they do dry, they do not dry particularly well. Can be refrigerated for up to a week in a plastic bag.

PESTS

None.

DISEASES

None.

SELECTED VARIETIES

nutans Large blue-mauve, star-shaped flowers and flat leaves, with mild onion-garlic taste.

schoenoprasum **(common chives)** Common chives.

schoenoprasum **"Forescate"** Attractive form with clear, bright, rose-red flower heads. Good flavour for culinary use.

tuberosum **(Garlic chives)** White flowers. Mild garlic flavour to the flat leaves.

CORIANDER
Coriandrum sativum

Apiaceae

A hardy annual that has really come to prominence with the increased popularity of Oriental food. It adds a curry flavour to dishes, where both the leaves and the seeds are used, with the leaves eaten raw or cooked, although if large quantities are eaten it can have a narcotic effect. It can be grown outside in temperate climates for summer use, with an autumn sowing producing leaves for winter dishes as long as the plants are given frost-free protection. To give a good supply right through the summer, start sowing in early spring and sow in succession until late summer. Some of the plants can be used in a similar fashion to cut-and-come-again lettuce. When left to flower, they produce small umbels of tiny white flowers and at the end of the summer the roots can be dug up and cooked as a vegetable.

DATES

Sowing *Inside* April
Outside May

Harvesting Early summer–mid-winter.

SOWING METHOD

Sow into seed trays in the greenhouse, prick out into 8 cm (3 in) pots, harden off and plant out. Outside, sow thinly into shallow drills and thin when the leaves get big enough to use.

TEMPERATURE

For germination 18–20°C (65–68°F)

SITE AND SOIL

Site Semi-shade for leaf production, but full sun for harvesting seed. Both need a well-drained, but moisture-retentive soil.

pH 5.5–7.5

Fertilizer Pelleted chicken manure prior to sowing or planting out.

Water Water during dry weather.

DIMENSIONS

Planting depth 1 cm (½ in)

Space between plants
15 cm (6 in);
30 cm (12 in) rows.

Height of plants 45 cm (18 in)

Spread of plants 20 cm (8 in)

AFTER CARE

Do not let the plants dry out, otherwise they will bolt. Pick leaves regularly to encourage production.

COMPANION PLANTS

Grows particularly well with dill and chervil and is said to help repel aphid and carrot fly.

HARVESTING

Cut leaves on a regular basis as and when they are needed. Seeds can be collected when they are ripe by tapping them into a paper bag or envelope.

For winter leaves, do not be tempted to keep the plants on the windowsill as they have an unpleasant odour.

HEALTH BENEFITS

Used to help with stomach ailments; assists with flatulence, and is also a mild sedative.

STORAGE

Fresh leaves can be frozen. Seeds can be stored in a dry and cool place until they are needed.

PESTS

No real pest problems.

DISEASES

No real disease problems.

SELECTED VARIETIES

Coriander There are no better varieties than this.

DILL
Anethum graveolens

Apiaceae

A hardy annual closely related to fennel, with the same flower colour and structure. It is just as much at home in the ornamental border as the herb garden. It is grown primarily for the culinary uses of its feathery, blue-green leaves and seeds, with both having a mild, but distinctive flavour. The plant will gently seed itself most years, but as a precaution it is worth saving a few seeds just in case nothing appears in the spring. Do not plant closely to fennel, as the two plants may cross-pollinate.

DATES

Sowing April–May

Harvesting June–October

SOWING METHOD

Sow into shallow drills outside, as dill does not like to be transplanted, although sowing into module in April will counter that problem, as there is no pricking out to be done.

TEMPERATURE

For germination 18–20°C (65–68°F)

SITE AND SOIL

Site Sunny and moisture-retentive, but well-drained position out of the wind.

pH 5.5–8.5

Fertilizer An annual application of pelleted chicken manure in the spring.

Water Water in dry weather.

SPECIAL TIP

To prevent this plant seeding around, remove the flower heads as the flowers go over.

DIMENSIONS

Planting depth 1 cm ($1/2$ in) drills.

Space between plants
30 cm (12 in);
30 cm (12 in) rows.

Height of plants 120–150 cm (4–5 ft)

Spread of plants 30 cm (12 in)

AFTER CARE

Water in dry weather and keep weed-free.

COMPANION PLANTS

Other herbs, except fennel, and most ornamental plants.

HARVESTING

The leaves can be picked fresh as required, with the seeds harvested when they have ripened and turned brown.

HEALTH BENEFITS

Aids indigestion, flatulence, stomach cramps and insomnia.

STORAGE

Fresh dill can be frozen or dried. Seeds can be collected when ripe and stored in a paper bag or envelope in a cool, dry place.

PESTS

Aphids.

DISEASES

No real disease problems.

SELECTED VARIETIES

Anethum graveolens This is the only variety available.

FENNEL
Foeniculum vulgare

Apiaceae

This vigorous, hardy-perennial herb would not be out of place
in the ornamental garden as well as the herb area, having green
or purple filigree foliage. Not to be confused with the vegetable
(Florence fennel, grown for its swollen stem) this herb is tall
and impressive, with the foliage topped by umbels of bright
yellow flowers held at the ends of stiff stems. If left to set seed,
the plant will freely seed around. The foliage, stems and seeds
all have a delicate aniseed flavour.

DATES

Sowing *Inside* March
Outside May

Harvesting June–October

SOWING METHOD

Sow into seed trays in the greenhouse, prick out into 8 cm (3 in) pots before hardening off and planting out. Outside, sow thinly into shallow drills and thin when the leaves get big enough to use. Established clumps can also be divided in the autumn or spring.

TEMPERATURE

For germination 18–20°C (65–68°F)

SITE AND SOIL

Site Sunny, fertile soil, rich in organic matter, with plenty of moisture retention, although not waterlogged.

pH 5.5–8.5

Fertilizer An annual application of pelleted chicken manure in the spring.

Water Water in dry weather.

DIMENSIONS

Planting depth 1 cm ($^1/_2$ in) drills.

Space between plants 60 cm (24 in)

Height of plants 1.5–1.8 m (5–6 ft)

Spread of plants 60 cm (24 in)

AFTER CARE

Keep harvesting the leaves to encourage plenty of young and tender leaves and shoots, but allow some shoots to flower and set seed, if these are required.

SPECIAL TIP

If seed is not required, keep removing the flowering stems to maximize leaf production.

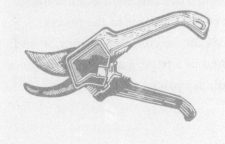

COMPANION PLANTS

Will grow with most plants and herbs, but keep well away from coriander, caraway and dill as they will cross-pollinate.

HARVESTING

Pick young leaves and stems as required. Seeds can be collected when ripe.

HEALTH BENEFITS

Infuse to aid constipation and help with digestion. If chewed, fennel can also help with indigestion and some say it can alleviate the toxic effects of alcohol.

STORAGE

The fresh leaves and stems can be frozen. They can be dried, but lose a lot of their flavour in the process. Seeds can be collected when ripe and stored in a paper bag or envelope in a cool, dry place.

PESTS

Aphids.

DISEASES

Mildew.

SELECTED VARIETIES

vulgare **(common sweet fennel)** with green, filigree leaves and bright yellow flowers.

vulgare **Purpureum** The purple form of the above.

MINT
Mentha spp.

Lamiaceae

As these plants can become rampant in a garden situation it is often advisable to plant them in containers, which can then be placed close to the house for ease of picking. Leaves and stem tips can be removed as and when they are required, without any detriment to the plant. They have a wide range of culinary and medicinal uses, as well as being excellent ornamental plants.

271

DATES

Sowing
Inside February–March
Outside March–April

Harvesting All year round

SOWING METHOD

Softwood cuttings or division are the preferred propagation methods.

TEMPERATURE

For rooting No heat required.

SITE AND SOIL

Site Any soil and best in semi-shade, but will grow almost anywhere.

pH 6.5–8.0

Fertilizer Layer of well-rotted organic matter around the plants in the spring.

Water Only water in dry weather.

DIMENSIONS

Planting depth To top of rootball.

Space between plants 30 cm (12 in)

Height of plants 2–90 cm ($^{3}/4$–36 in), dependent on variety.

Spread of plants Indefinite spread.

AFTER CARE

Control by regular harvesting. Water in dry weather.

COMPANION PLANTS

Suitable for growing with all other herbs.

HARVESTING

The leaves can be harvested as and when required. They are much better when picked straight from the plant, as they will wilt very quickly. Pick individual leaves or shoot tips. The plants are vigorous and will regenerate very quickly.

HEALTH BENEFITS

Relieves heavy colds, as well as aiding digestion and helping with muscular aches, pains and migraines. Do not

SPECIAL TIP

Dig up a small clump in the autumn, which can be potted up and brought inside for cropping after the outdoor plants have died back.

take large quantities of Pennyroyal mint if pregnant or suffering from kidney problems.

STORAGE

Leaves can be frozen, as with chives (see page 261), dried and kept in an air-tight container or infused in oil or vinegar.

PESTS

Aphids.

DISEASES

Rust.

SELECTED VARIETIES

x *gracilis* Variegata (Ginger mint) Gold-splashed, green leaves with a spicy flavour.

x *piperata* (Peppermint) Strong leaf flavour, with reddish black tinges to the stems and leaves.

***pulegium* (Creeping Pennyroyal)** Will root as it goes. Peppermint-flavoured, bright green leaves.

***requienii* (Corsican mint)** Tiny green leaves. Strong peppermint flavour.

***spicata* (Spearmint)** Spearmint-flavoured green leaves.

***suaveolens* Variegata (Variegated apple mint)** Green and white leaves, with an apple flavour.

OREGANO
Origanum vulgare

Lamiaceae

Also known as wild marjoram, oregano is a favourite in the kitchen. It is a hardy perennial that can be grown in the herb garden or at the front of an ornamental border. The yellow-leaved varieties are more ornamental, with slightly less flavour to the leaves, while the pale, lilac flowers of all varieties will attract many beneficial insects.

274

DATES

Sowing March–April

Harvesting June–October

SOWING METHOD

Sow into trays or modules. Mix seed
with silver sand to make it easier to
sow. Do not cover seed. Roots well
from softwood cuttings.

TEMPERATURE

For germination 18–20°C (65–68°F)

SITE AND SOIL

Site Sunny and well-drained, moisture-
retentive position. Dig in plenty of
organic matter prior to planting.

SPECIAL TIP

Plant among vegetable crops to encourage
beneficial insects, which will feed on
potential pests.

pH 5.5–8.0

Fertilizer Pelleted chicken manure
in spring.

Water Water during dry weather.

DIMENSIONS

Planting depth Just bury the rootball.

Space between plants 30 cm (12 in)

Height of plants 60 cm (24 in)

Spread of plants 60–90 cm
(24–36 in)

AFTER CARE

Remove growing tips regularly to keep
the plant bushy. Keep weed-free.
Divide the clump in autumn or early
spring, when it gets too big for its
allocated spot.

COMPANION PLANTS

Grows well with other herbs,
vegetables and ornamental plants.

HARVESTING

Harvest regularly by removing growing tips, to encourage more growth.

HEALTH BENEFITS

Helps with respiratory conditions and toothache, as well as having antiseptic properties. Do not take medically if pregnant.

STORAGE

It dries and freezes well for use in the winter.

PESTS

Aphids.

DISEASES

No real disease problems.

SELECTED VARIETIES

Aureum Yellow-leaved variety. Good in herb and ornamental gardens.

County Cream Cream and green variegated leaves.

Gold Tips Green leaves with golden tips.

vulgare Common oregano or sweet marjoram.

PARSLEY
Petroselinum crispum

Apiaceae

This is an incredibly popular herb for garnishing and flavouring
hot and cold dishes. It is an easy-to-grow, hardy biennial that
should be grown as an annual to get the best results. It will do
equally well in the ground or in containers. There are two main
types, with the first having curly, decorative leaves and the
second being flat-leaved, but with more flavour. As well as
being very useful in the kitchen, if it is chewed raw it is also a
very useful antidote for freshening breath, particularly after
eating garlic. It can be harvested throughout the summer and
then the whole plant can be lifted and brought under
protection to provide leaves for winter use.

DATES

Sowing February–March and again in June

Harvesting June–March

SOWING METHOD

Sow early into modules; inside in February and plant out during April. Sow outside into shallow drills. Parsley is slow to germinate and it is important that the compost or soil does not dry out during this time. For winter use, sow in June, either into modules and then planted out, or directly into the soil.

TEMPERATURE

For germination 18°C (65°F)

SITE AND SOIL

Site Fertile and well-drained, moisture-retentive soil. If the soil is allowed to dry out, the plants will quickly run to seed. Best in semi-shade, but will grow in full sun.

pH 6.0–7.5

Fertilizer Incorporate well-rotted manure or compost into the soil before planting and apply pelleted chicken manure.

Water Keep the compost and soil moist during the life of the plants.

DIMENSIONS

Planting depth Sow into 1 cm (½ in) drills.

Space between plants
15–23 cm (6–9 in);
45 cm (18 in) rows

To speed up germination, boiling water can be poured over the seeds to break their dormancy. This is usually easier to do once they have been sown.

Height of plants 30–60 cm (12–24 in)

Spread of plants 30–45 cm (12–18 in)

AFTER CARE

Keep the plants well-watered and weed-free. In the autumn, lift plants, pot them up and move them into a greenhouse, polythene tunnel or kitchen windowsill for cropping through the winter.

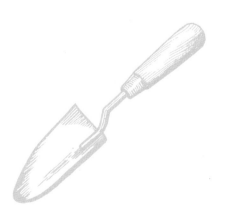

COMPANION PLANTS

Suitable for growing with all other herbs.

HARVESTING

Pick leaves regularly, from mid-summer onwards, to encourage more leaf production and to prevent the plant running to seed. Pinch off at the base of the stem, as both leaves and stems can be used.

HEALTH BENEFITS

High in vitamin A, B and C as well as calcium, magnesium, sodium and fatty acids. It can also be used as a digestive tonic and as a mild antiseptic. To freshen breath, chew raw leaves and stems.

STORAGE

Once harvested, parsley will last for several days if stood in a jar of water, and it can be dried or frozen for later use.

PESTS

Slugs and carrot fly.

DISEASES

Mildew.

SELECTED VARIETIES

Aphrodite Hardy and compact variety. Tightly curled green leaves. Ideal for containers and, under protection, will crop through the winter.

Curlina Compact variety. Tightly curled leaves.

Forest Green Vigorous, deep-green curled parsley. Does not yellow in adverse weather.

Italian Giant Hardy, plain-leaved parsley. Large, bright green leaves. Protect with a cloche to crop into winter.

Moss Curled 2 Tightly curled green leaves.

Plain Leaved 2 Flat, bright green leaves. Stronger flavour than curled varieties.

ROSEMARY
Rosmarinus officinalis

Lamiaceae

A plant that is used as much as an ornamental as it is in the herb garden. The breeding of new flower colours has made this a sought-after plant and, with its excellent drought tolerance, it fits very nicely into modern gardens. The narrow green leaves have a waxy coating that prevents too much water loss, which helps greatly with their usually sunny, sheltered and hot planting position. In temperate climates, some of the varieties available are not reliably hardy. However, all rosemary varieties grow well in containers, so they can be moved under protection for the winter. As well as a multitude of culinary uses, the aromatic leaves of rosemary are also used as an essential ingredient of potpourri.

DATES

Sowing March–April

Harvesting All year round

SOWING METHOD

Sow into a seed tray on heat, prick out into an 8 cm (3 in) pot and harden off before planting out. Although successful from seed, it is easier and quicker to grow from softwood cuttings taken in spring and when rooted, pot them into 8 cm (3 in) pots and plant out when ready.

TEMPERATURE

For germination 21°C (70°F)

SITE AND SOIL

Site Well-drained soil in full sun.

pH 5.5–8.0

Fertilizer Pelleted chicken manure in the spring after pruning.

Water Water in dry weather.

DIMENSIONS

Planting depth Just bury the rootball.

Space between plants
Specimen plants 60–90 cm (2–3 ft)
For hedging 45 cm (18 in)

Height of plants Up to 150 cm (5 ft)

Spread of plants Up to 90 cm (3 ft)

AFTER CARE

Prune back plants after flowering to prevent the bushes becoming leggy and short-lived.

COMPANION PLANTS

Grows well with all plants and herbs, attracting beneficial insects.

HARVESTING

After pruning, the large amount of clippings can be dried for use later. Pick fresh tips or leaves as required. Harvesting can continue for 12 months of the year.

In colder winters, wrap established, specimen rosemary plants in fleece to prevent damage.

HEALTH BENEFITS

Helps to alleviate stress and hangovers. It stimulates blood circulation and aids in fat digestion. If gargled, it can act as an antiseptic mouthwash.

STORAGE

Leaves can be dried, but as the plant can be picked from all year round it is only worth drying the early summer clippings.

PESTS

No real pest problems.

DISEASES

No real disease problems.

SELECTED VARIETIES

officinalis Common rosemary.

Beneden Blue Smaller variety, reaching 90 cm (3 ft), with gentian-blue flowers.

Lady in White White-flowered form.

Miss Jessop's Upright Excellent hedging plant. Will survive most winters. Erect, with light mauve-blue flowers.

Roseus Lilac-pink flowers.

SAGE
Salvia officinalis

Lamiaceae

This hardy, evergreen shrubs comes in several forms, most of which are highly decorative. It's ideal for planting in the ornamental garden, which can save space in the herb garden for something less beautiful, but equally useful. *Salvia officinalis* has lovely aromatic, grey-green leaves, which are soft to the touch and topped by small blue flowers. There are various named varieties that have purple, multi-coloured and yellow-green leaves which stand out much more, but have less of a flavour. Sage has very important culinary uses, as well as being a widely used medicinal herb. Sage is an excellent plant to have in the organic garden, as it attracts a lot of beneficial insects to its flowers.

DATES

Sowing March

Harvesting All summer

SOWING METHOD

Sow into a seed tray, prick out into 8cm (3 in) pots, harden off and plant out. Also easy from softwood cuttings in early summer.

TEMPERATURE

For germination 18–20°C (65–68°F)

SITE AND SOIL

Site Full sun and well-drained soil.

pH 5.5–8.0

Fertilizer Pelleted chicken manure in the spring after pruning.

Water Water in dry weather.

DIMENSIONS

Planting depth Just bury the rootball.

SPECIAL TIP

If plants do become tall and bare at the base, you can cut them back hard in the spring

Space between plants 45–60 cm (18–24 in)

Height of plants 60 cm (24 in)

Spread of plants 90 cm (3 ft)

AFTER CARE

Keep pinching back shoots as they grow to prevent the plants becoming leggy. If flowers are not required remove them.

COMPANION PLANTS

Put with plants that will benefit from the insects the flowers will attract.

HARVESTING

Pick leaves as required through the summer. If leaves are to be picked and dried, or picked fresh, this must be done before flowering starts, as the flavour then becomes impaired.

HEALTH BENEFITS

Can help with sore throats if gargled, and also aids digestion.

STORAGE

After picking, leaves can be hung and dried slowly in an airy shed.

PESTS

Capsid bugs.

DISEASES

Powdery mildew.

SELECTED VARIETIES

Icterina Green leaves, marbled primrose-yellow and gold, with blue-purple flowers.

Kew Gold Bright, golden leaves. Very few flowers.

Purpurescens Purple-leaved form. Hardy.

Tricolor Bright-white, deep-pink and purple leaves; will darken as the summer progresses.

THYME
Thymus spp.

Lamiaceae

The range of thyme varieties is continually extending, with many being very ornamental, while others have differing flavours that add interest to food. As they are evergreen, this interest is all year round. The lilac-pink flowers will attract many beneficial insects and can therefore be planted in lots of productive areas. Many varieties are low-growing or prostrate, which makes them ideal as edging or for growing among paving slabs, where they can be trodden on and their scents released. They are very easy plants to get growing and keep, so they deserve a place in any garden.

DATES

Sowing March–April

Harvesting May–October

SOWING METHOD

Mix seed with silver sand before sowing into a seed tray. Do not cover seed. Varieties of common thyme have to be propagated by softwood cuttings.

TEMPERATURE

For germination 18–20°C (65–68°F)

SITE AND SOIL

Site Sunny and well-drained position.

pH 6.5–8.0

Fertilizer Light feeder.

Water In dry weather only.

DIMENSIONS

Planting depth Cover the rootball.

Space between plants 30 cm (12 in)

Height of plants 1–30 cm (^{1}/2–12 in)

Spread of plants 30 cm + (12 in +)

AFTER CARE

Pinch out growing tips regularly to keep plants compact and cut back hard after flowering.

COMPANION PLANTS

All herbs, vegetables and ornamental plants.

HARVESTING

Pick growing tips or stems throughout the growing season.

HEALTH BENEFITS

Helps with digestion and relief from hangovers. Excellent antiseptic qualities, as well as aiding in the

SPECIAL TIP

For more flavour in cooking, use dried thyme, as the flavour intensifies when dried. Use fresh sprigs as a garnish.

breakdown of fats. Essential ingredient of bouquet garni.

STORAGE

Cut sprigs before flowering and hang in an airy shed.

PESTS

No real pest problems.

DISEASES

No real disease problems.

SELECTED VARIETIES

x *citriodorus* (Lemon thyme) Upright, lemon-scented, green leaves.

x *citriodorus* Aureus Yellow-leaved variety of lemon thyme.

x *citriodorus* Silver Queen Grey and silver-white leaves.

Doone Valley Semi-prostrate. Large green leaves, erratically marked with golden-yellow.

***herba-barona* (Caraway thyme)** Strongly caraway-scented, dark-green leaves.

Orange Spice Semi-prostrate with orange-scented, green leaves.

pseudolanguinosus Prostrate. Hairy leaves. Little scent. Good between paving.

***serpyllum* Pink Chintz** Pink flowers. Scented leaves. Good between paving.

***vulgaris* (Common thyme)** Strongly scented green leaves.

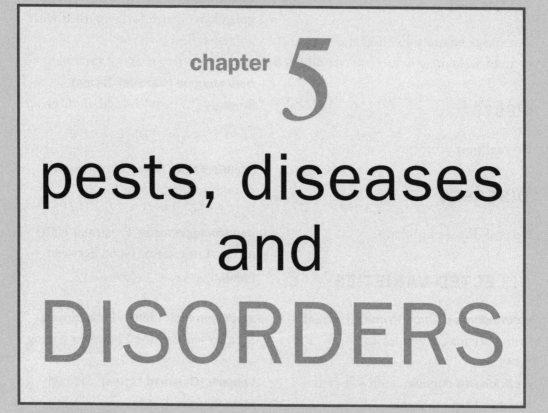

chapter 5

pests, diseases and DISORDERS

It is a devastating occurrence for any organic gardener when a perfectly healthy crop succumbs to a pest or disease. In this chapter, I have brought together a reasonably comprehensive guide to the more common problems encountered when growing fruit, vegetables and herbs organically. All the control methods are organic, with many being simple to implement, although the organic gardener's main weapon is to work in harmony with nature in defeating pests and diseases.

NATURAL PREDATORS

Spraying, even with organic sprays, should always be the last line of defence, as it will usually also kill some beneficial insects. In the wild, most insects – whether pest or beneficial – will have a predator. Fortunately for us gardeners, it is very often already in our gardens or can be tempted in very easily by companion planting in our productive areas. We should look very carefully at what we can do in our ornamental areas, so that they act as a nursery for these natural predators. It is important that once these predators have been tempted into our productive areas, they are given enough reason to stay. One reason would be plenty of food, in the shape of pests, for them to consume, with the flip side being that our pest levels will generally be kept at a very manageable level instead of being completely eradicated. If we eradicate the pest, then we also eradicate the predator, as they then have nothing to feed on. It is vital to be vigilant, as early detection of pests, diseases and disorders is the answer. An early response should result in only minimal depletion in the final yield.

HYGIENE AND CROP ROTATION

As far as diseases and disorders are concerned, a lot of the control methods require a combination of good husbandry and common sense. There are only a few diseases and disorders that should cause us to lose sleep, although that does not mean we can become complacent. Even though there are only a handful of serious dangers to the crop, these sleep deprivers can be absolutely devastating in the productive garden. Two factors keep reccurring in the control sections of these diseases and disorders. The first is hygiene and the importance of maintaining as clean a productive area as possible. This involves removing discarded plant material, including debris dropped by the plants themselves. Removing the potential pest overwintering site will limit re-infection in the following year. Secondly, implement a good crop-rotation plan, as the moving of plants so that they do not grow in the same place year on year will prevent the build up of diseases, as well as pests.

START AS YOU MEAN TO GO ON

Make sure that your plants start off in the right way and keep them growing strongly, so that if they are attacked by any pest or disease they are much better equipped to cope with it, and ultimately produce the yield they were grown for. Pick F1-hybrid varieties, as these are first generation of a cross between two different parents and have increased vigour, which will help them through an early attack. Do not buy or use substandard plants or seed, as they will always be inferior and will act as a magnet for pests and diseases that may ultimately infect other perfectly healthy plants growing nearby. Another way of minimizing both pest and disease problems is to grow resistant varieties. For example, some potatoes are more resistant to blight than others, such as Cara and Maris Peer or carrot Maestro, a carrot-fly-resistant variety. This does not mean that they are immune to the particular pest or disease, but that they are less likely to suffer the damage to which other varieties are susceptible. Be assured that seed catalogues will be only too keen to point these varieties out to you.

CUT DOWN THE COMPETITION

Keep weeds at bay, as they not only remove vital nutrients and water from the soil, producing weaker plants, but they are also excellent hosts for pests. The use of mulches will not only help to keep the weed population down but also conserves water, as well as providing shelter for beneficial animals. If growing on 120 cm (4 ft) beds, then placing plants closer together will also prevent water loss from the soil, as covering it reduces water evaporation from the surface, and also blocks out light, therefore preventing weed growth.

The cultivation methods already discussed in previous chapters of this book, coupled with the detailed descriptions of control and prevention methods, mean that all organic gardeners can now start the growing year in the confidence that they can win the battle against pests and diseases.

APHID *(Greenfly, blackfly etc)*

These sucking insects are a prolific, common pest. Once they arrive on a crop, it is not long before the colony has grown considerably, as the females can give birth to live young when only a week old. Their favourite victims are **young, tender and sappy shoots**, where they will cause stunted, distorted growth. A severe attack will cause the plant to produce little or no crop, and even die.

Control Grow susceptible plants in and around a crop that will attract beneficial insects, such as hoverflies, ladybirds, lacewings etc. It is important to provide a home for all these insects to overwinter, once they have been attracted. Birds, bats, ground beetles, earwigs and spiders are also very vigorous predators of aphids and will require places to live and overwinter. Where the colony of aphids can be tolerated, use this as a feeding and breeding station for the beneficial insects, so that their numbers can be increased in case of further attack. It is also feasible to grow a dummy crop, just for the purpose of attracting aphids away from the more prized crop next door. As soon as any aphids are spotted, they can be rubbed off with finger and thumb, or remove badly infested shoots completely. As far as sprays are concerned, insecticidal or soft soap can be used at regular intervals, as can pyrethrum-based sprays. In a greenhouse situation, the natural predator *Aphidius* can be used once the temperatures begin to rise beyond 10°C (50°F).

APPLE AND PEAR SCAB

An easily identifiable disease, causing dark brown blotches to appear on **leaves and fruit**, with the fruit blotches eventually becoming corky and sometimes cracked. It is a disease that is prevalent in damp, cool weather, where there is poor air movement – particularly in spring. It only affects the skin of the fruit, not the flesh beneath. It overwinters on plant material and is spread in the spring by wind or rain. In more severe attacks, it can cause premature leaf drop.

Control Rake up all fallen debris from around the trees and compost it. The debris can also be collected using a lawnmower, which will shred the leaves in the process thus giving a quicker decomposition in the compost bin. The spotted leaves can be picked off the tree, as this appears to prevent the disease spreading, but be careful not to defoliate the tree. Cut out diseased twigs and prune well to maintain good air circulation around the tree. If the position of your apple or pear trees is not ideal, then grow scab-resistant varieties.

APPLE AND PEAR SUCKER

This tiny insect lives and feeds in the **flower buds** of these trees, having moved there after overwintering in the fruiting spurs. The adults then lay their eggs on the buds in May. The hatched nymphs and adult insects then feed on the blossom, which may fail to develop as a result.

Control Check the buds in spring for the eggs and squash any that are found. Spray with insecticidal soap or derris about three weeks after the petals have fallen. If the attack is fairly light, then remove the infected blossom and burn it.

ASPARAGUS BEETLE

The 6 mm ($1/4$ in) adult beetles have very distinguishable yellow and black bodies. They emerge from hibernation in the spring to lay their eggs. The first batch of eggs are laid in June, with maybe one or two more to follow. The larvae then emerge, grey-black in colour. Both the adults and the larvae feed on **asparagus ferns**, very often stripping them completely and sometimes ringing the stem totally, which in turn kills the shoot.

Control Examine the plants carefully and pick off the adults, and larvae. As soon as signs of attack are spotted, spray the plants with derris. In the autumn, remove any surrounding plant debris where the adults might hibernate.

BACTERIAL CANKER

This disease spreads from spores in dark brown spots on the **leaves of plums and cherries**, and then moves to the twigs and branches, via wounds and open cuts. It first becomes obvious when the brown spots in the leaves drop out, causing a "shot hole" appearance. Later in the year, an amber gum will exude from slight depressions in the trunk or branches. On infected branches, the leaves will become yellow and the branch will die back, but on infected trunks it is likely that the whole tree will be lost.

Control There are no fully resistant varieties, although some seem to be less susceptible than others. This is not an easy disease to control. Cut out affected branches and twigs below the point of the disease into clean wood. Ensure that all pruning cuts are clean and tidy, so that the trees heal quickly and that stakes do not rub on the tree trunks. Avoid damaging the bark of the trees (particularly mechanical damage).

BIG BUD MITE

A pest whose presence is obvious to spot. It enters the **buds of blackcurrants**, feeding on them and causing the whole bud to swell well beyond its usual proportions. This infestation will occur in the summer, although it is not easy to spot with the leaf coverage, so they are usually noticed from early winter. The mite will live and breed in the swollen bud until spring, when it emerges as an adult. Although the damage caused is not wanted, it is not as bad as the blackcurrant reversion disease that this mite can carry and transmit.

Control Remove any shoots that have infected buds and burn them. Always buy certified stock.

BITTER PIT

This only becomes apparent during the **storage of fruit**, but in severe cases there may be some signs on the fruit prior to this. Small sunken areas begin to appear on the fruit, turning brown at the bottom of these individual pits and it is caused by deficiency of calcium in the soil and an imbalance of magnesium or potassium.

Control In a well-maintained fruit area, this should not be a problem. If it does happen, ensure that trees are watered during dry spells in following years and that they are mulched with manure, so that the uptake of calcium is not inhibited in the dry weather.

BLACKCURRANT REVERSION

This common virus is transmitted by the big bud mite and is very difficult to detect, as the signs are **narrower mature leaves**, with less than five pairs of veins. The flower buds will become a bright magenta colour and the bushes will ultimately lose vigour, and therefore the crop will be reduced.

Control There is no cure for this disease, so ensure that bushes are obtained from a reputable supplier and are from certified stock. Control big bud mite by checking the buds regularly and particularly before the bushes burst into growth. Dig up any infected bushes and burn them.

BLOSSOM END ROT

Quite a common and easy-to-identify problem, which causes a sunken, black area to form at **the base of the fruit**, although it does not affect all fruit on the plant. It is caused by a lack of calcium in the soil or compost, and is exaggerated in dry weather and acidic soils.

Control Make sure that adequate water is applied on a regular basis, as irregular watering will add to the problem, causing the soil or compost to dry too much before being heavily watered. Remove infected fruits, as they will not be edible.

BOTRYTIS

This is also known as "grey mould" and is present as a greyish mould growing on a wound. This mould will gradually eat into the infected area and cause all parts of the plant above it to wilt and die. It can survive on plant debris and even overwinter on it. It is generally more prevalent in hot and humid atmospheres and areas where there is little air movement, so it is often found in **greenhouse crops**.

Control Good hygiene is vital. Remove all dead and discarded plant material, as well as removing the infected part of plants as soon as they are spotted. If a plant becomes badly infected, then it must be removed before the mould releases spores that can infect other plants. Ensure good ventilation around plants and space plants well.

BRASSICA WHITE BLISTER

This fungal diseases manifests itself as small, white spots on the **leaves and stems** of susceptible plants. These areas then become distorted and inedible. It is spread by wind, water splashes and insects, and can stay in the soil for several months – including over winter – until a suitable host is planted.

Control There is no real control, except to destroy the infected plants and to practise good crop rotation.

BROAD BEAN RUST

A colourful disease that occurs during warm, damp weather, when orange-brown pustules appear on the **undersides of the leaves.** It is rarely damaging to the plant, but causes the upper part of the leaf to yellow and may therefore become unsightly.

Control Remove infected parts and compost them. As it is spread by rain splash, avoid using overhead irrigation. Clear all plant debris at the end of the crop.

BROWN ROT

A disease that **affects tree fruit** and attacks via wounds in the bark, as it is airborne. Once affected, the fruits will show soft brown patches that will quickly become white and fluffy. The fruit may drop prematurely, or stay mummified on the tree throughout the winter. If stored, affected fruit will rot and infect other perfectly healthy fruits.

Control Remove any diseased fruit from the tree as soon as it appears, and burn it with the windfalls. Do not store any fruit that may be infected and check fruit in store regularly, in case any have slipped through.

BULB EELWORM

These microscopic pests affect **the bulbs of onions** and plants within the onion family, burrowing into the bulbs and causing distortion and swelling.

Control Dig up any affected plants and implement a good crop rotation, as no onion-related plant should then be grown on the area for at least two years.

CABBAGE ROOT FLY

This has to be the most devastating of all brassica pests, as it causes the collapse and death of the plants infected. The adult fly resembles a small horsefly in appearance and lays its eggs on the soil surface right next to **the stem of young brassica** plants. When the larvae emerge, they burrow down into the root to feed. The legless larvae are white and the symptom of attack is the complete collapse of the young plant, by which time control is too late. The pupae will also overwinter in the soil, ready to re-infect in the spring. Although the first attack in the late spring is usually the worst, there can also be another two or three generations within the season.

Control The favoured method is to prevent the female adult from laying its eggs in the first place by placing a physical barrier such as fleece over the crop after planting and leaving it in place until the plants become more mature and less liable to attack. Just as good is to place a barrier around the root of each plant to prevent the female from laying her eggs on the soil surface and a piece of underlay will do

the job very nicely. This cabbage root fly mat is made from a 15 cm (6 in) square of old carpet underlay, or off-cuts from the local carpet shop, that has a slit cut into the centre from one side. At the top of this slit make a small cross cut at the top to create a "T". This can then be slipped around the stem of each plant and closed, so that it sits snugly around the stem of the newly planted brassica, preventing the adult female from getting to the soil around the stem. As they prefer to attack younger plants, brassica raised in modules or pots will survive much better, although I would still advise using one of the above methods as a precaution.

CABBAGE WHITE BUTTERFLY

It is the caterpillar, not the butterfly, that causes the problem, **eating the leaves of all brassicas** voraciously. They appear in April and May and can produce up to three generations a year, with the last one (in late summer) often being the most severe. There are two types of butterfly: the cabbage white and the small cabbage white, with the caterpillars of both being capable of stripping a brassica of all its leaves very quickly. The eggs are generally laid on the undersides of leaves, with the caterpillars growing up to 3.5 cm (1^1/2 in) long. They are green in colour and can be difficult to spot. Usually, they will feed at night, so they are rarely seen by the gardener working in the vegetable area during the day.

Control From dusk, the caterpillars can be seen feeding, so pick them off and squash the bright orange eggs. Spray with *Bacillus thuringiensis* as soon as the caterpillars are spotted. The caterpillars then eat the brassica leaf that has been covered with Bacillus and are killed. The spray is harmless to everything except the caterpillars, and has to be applied every 10–14 days from the first sighting. The best prevention method is to stop the butterflies laying their eggs on the crop in the first place. This can be done by covering the brassica crop with a mesh that will not allow the butterfly to pass through it. As they lay eggs through the summer, this netting will invariably stay on for the life of the crop. Blue tits are an excellent predator, and so are wasps.

CANKER

Related to bacterial canker, but affecting a much wider variety of trees. The **sunken lesions on twigs, branches and trunks of trees** will become discoloured and ooze a sticky amber liquid. In summer, small white pustules may also appear, with their winter-fruiting bodies being red.

Control As for bacterial canker (see pages 295–6).

CAPSID BUGS

A difficult pest to see, as the winged adults quickly fly off when disturbed. They are sap-sucking pests that cause very **distinctive, small, ragged holes in leaves**. As they grow, these leaves take on a ragged appearance, but damage is not usually severe and often not worth worrying about.

Control Tidy all fallen leaves from affected trees, to remove any overwintering pests. Encourage natural predators, such as birds, to the trees in winter.

CARROT FLY

The insignificant, small, black flies lay their eggs close to the shoulders of the susceptible crop from late May/early June, and once the 1 cm (½ in) larvae hatch, they burrow into the host plant and generally render it inedible. There are usually three generations a year, with the first one doing the most damage. They **tend to attack younger plants**. The first sign of attack is often a reddening of the foliage, along with the obvious tunnelling into the root once the crop has been lifted.

Control The carrot fly is a weak flier and usually flies less than 30cm (12 in) from ground level, so the obvious defence is to surround the crop with a barrier – such as a hedge or low fence – of at least 45 cm (18 in). Also, do not grow a susceptible crop in a sheltered part of the garden where there is no wind. Delay the first sowing until early June to avoid the most severe attack. The flies are usually attracted to a crop by smell, so delay any thinning until the middle of June. Probably the most effective control is to place a physical barrier in the way, so the crop can be covered with fleece, which will also – as a bonus – bring the crop forward. You could also use a cloche covered with enviromesh or a very fine netting that the fly cannot pass through. To help prevent attack, carrot-fly-resistant varieties can be grown, such as carrot Resistafly. Finally, as the larvae overwinter in the soil, dig over the ground in the late autumn/early winter to expose the larvae for birds to feed on.

CELERY LEAF SPOT

Numerous brown spots will appear on older leaves at first, quickly spreading to younger leaves and even the stalks. It is usually carried in the seed, although most seed is treated against it. However, remember that this initial treatment is not organic.

Control Remove the infected leaves and never save seed from infected plants, even after they have had all the infected leaves removed. After the plants have been cleaned up, they can also be sprayed every 14 days with Bordeaux mixture until two weeks prior to harvest.

CHOCOLATE SPOT

A disease that appears, as its name suggests, as brown spots and streaks on the **leaves and stems of broad beans**. The spots, in a severe attack, may become joined, making the leaves and stems completely black. At this point, they will die.

Control It is rarely a problem on a well-cultivated vegetable plot that has been well manured and adequately fed. It is best to pull up and burn infected plants, but minor attacks can be controlled with a copper fungicide spray.

CLUB ROOT

This is, without question, the worst possible disease for **any brassica** to have. Not only does it cause a severe reduction of the crop, but it can also survive in the soil for up to 20 years without having to live on a host. It thrives in acidic soils that are damp and poorly drained. The first sign of infection is a wilting plant in hot weather, making a partial recovery during the cooler night time. The leaves also take on reddish tints. Plants will become stunted as the roots fail to develop. They become distorted and covered in swollen galls. It is spread by infected plant material; usually on bought-in brassica plants or on tools used in infected soil.

Control If your soil is acidic, apply plenty of lime before growing any brassica crop and improve the drainage of the soil. Always raise your plants yourself, using seed obtained from a reputable supplier. If you have the infection in your soil, it can be partially overcome by raising brassicas in pots and then transplanting more mature plants. These will still become infected, but will be stronger on planting and therefore able to grow away, producing some sort of crop. This is applicable to all brassicas, except for cauliflowers. Grow varieties that have a proven resistance to the disease and rotate crops regularly.

CODLING MOTH

The mottled grey female adult lays its eggs on the **developing fruits and leaves** of susceptible fruit trees during early and midsummer. The caterpillars emerge and burrow into the fruit, usually undetected, as they tend to go through the eye of the fruit and less regularly through the more visible side. Usually, the first sign of damage is half a maggot seen after taking a bite from an apple, but a less dramatic sign is premature apple drop. Check fallen apples for tunnels, as a good indicator of prospective damage.

Control The best control method is to use pheromone traps that can be hung among the trees from mid May, at a rate of one trap per five trees. These triangular traps have a sheet of sticky paper in the bottom, in the middle of which is a capsule containing the pheromone, which is what the female moths use to attract the male moths at mating time. The male moths will fly into the trap, attracted by the pheromone, and become stuck to the paper, leaving the females eggs unfertilized and therefore unable to produce caterpillars. The traps can not only be used as a control measure, but also as an indicator of when the moths are about, so that spraying can be timed correctly. Once the moths are laying, *Bacillus thuringiensis* can be used, but it is not totally effective. You can also use the contact insecticide

derris, but the timing of this is crucial, so that it gets the larvae before they burrow into the fruit. Earwigs and blue tits will also feed on the larvae, but earwigs will also be killed by the derris.

CROWN ROT

This fungal disease **only affects celery** and is present on damp soils, causing the crown, roots and stalks to rot. It is first noticed by stunted plants with yellow leaves. It will spread in the ground, but does not affect other plants once harvested.

Control Implement a good crop rotation and grow celery on a well-drained site.

CUCUMBER MOSAIC VIRUS

This viral disease is not specific to cucumbers but **can infect any member of the *Cucurbitaceae* family, as well as beans, peppers and celery.** Spread primarily by aphids, this disease will cause the plants to become stunted and to develop mottled, yellow, puckered leaves.

303

Control As there is no cure, grow resistant varieties and control aphid populations. Remove and destroy infected plants as soon as the disease appears.

CUTWORM

A problematic pest, with larvae that will feed on crops all through the year. The larvae live in the soil and are usually brown, yellow or green in colour, curling up into a characteristic "C" shape when disturbed. The main damage is caused by the **larvae eating through the stems of seedlings** at ground level.

Control Keep weeds at bay, as they are a favourite egg-laying crop for the adults. Cultivate the soil close to seedlings that have been attacked, exposing the larvae, which will then be eaten by birds. Chickens allowed to scratch over the soil surface will do the same job, although this will be on crop-free land. In a greenhouse environment, soaking the soil and then covering it overnight will bring the larvae to the soil surface, where they can be picked off in the morning.

DAMPING OFF

This is generally shown as the **rotting of the stem** at soil level or just below, or the seeds failing to germinate. The seedling succumbs to the disease before it breaks through the compost.

Control The disease is more prevalent in waterlogged conditions, so make sure the compost is well-drained and clean pots and trays before use. Ensure good ventilation around seedlings in the greenhouse and sow susceptible crops outside when the weather has improved, so that the seedlings can germinate in a warmer soil.

DOWNY MILDEW

This disease attacks **the undersides of leaves** in a wide range of plants with the signs being yellowish patches on the leaf surface confirmed by the mould growing beneath. It is particularly bad in lettuce and onion crops, although it attacks other plants, and will cause infected onions to rot in store.

Control It is prevalent in damp and humid growing conditions, so it can be prevented by improving the air flow and ensuring adequate ventilation in greenhouses. Infected leaves can be removed and destroyed, but if the plant is badly infected then remove the whole plant. Grow resistant varieties and implement a good crop rotation. If onions are infected, then it can stay in the soil for up to four years, so the crop cannot be grown on the infected land for five years.

FIREBLIGHT

Once a notifiable disease, but now so common that there is no requirement to contact the authorities if a tree becomes infected. This bacterial disease **enters the tree via wounds or cuts** and will cause the tips to droop, turn brown and wither.

Control As soon as it is identified, cut out infected shoots into clean wood and burn the diseased material. In severe cases, the whole tree will need to be removed and burned. As the disease can pass from tree to tree, it is not wise to wait too long before taking action.

FLEA BEETLE

These small, shiny black beetles make hundreds of tiny "shot holes" in **the leaves of susceptible seedlings**. In a normal growing year, this does not cause too many problems, as the seedlings will usually overcome the damage; but in a bad year, it will cause a greatly reduced crop.

Control This pest is very aptly named because, when touched, it jumps. This gives an indication as to one of the forms of control. Grease a piece of card on one side and then hold it about 2.5–5 cm (1–2 in) above the infected crop. Pass the card along the row of seedlings, with the greased side facing downwards, while running a stick along the very top of the leaves directly under the card. The stick touching the leaves will make the flea beetles jump directly upwards onto the greased card where they will become stuck. The crop can also be covered with fleece, to prevent the beetles from landing on the crop. As there is only one generation per year, once the seedlings have become established, the fleece can be removed.

FOOT AND ROOT ROTS

These two diseases have similar symptoms and can be treated in identical fashion. The first signs of these diseases are often **wilting of the top growth, discolouration of the leaves and dying back of shoots**. The base of the stems, very often at ground level, darken and soften, as do the roots.

Control There is no control for organic gardeners, except to remove infected plants, along with the soil or compost from directly around the roots. Good hygiene will help to restrict the possibility of initial infection, as will cleaning pots and equipment on a regular basis.

FUSARIUM AND VERTICILLIUM WILT

Although two separate diseases, they are almost identical in their symptoms and control measures. These devastating and fatal diseases can only be spotted once **the plant has wilted and the stem is cut open to find either a brown or black discolouration of the stem tissue**, well above soil level. The wilting is caused by the fact that the diseases block the water vessels, preventing vital water from reaching the upper parts of the plant. They are thought to be primarily soil-borne diseases, entering the plant via wounds. They can stay in the soil for several years and it is recommended that if a crop has been infected, no similar crop should be grown in the area for at least six years.

Control If there is only a slight attack, earth up outdoor plants or pack compost around greenhouse plants. This will encourage new root growth above the diseased area. With more severe infections, remove the diseased plants immediately and destroy them. Do not compost any plant infected with either of these wilts.

HONEY FUNGUS

Generally a problem for **tree fruits and currants**. This fungus usually inhabits dead tree stumps, but can move onto live subjects by means of black, "shoelace-like" mycelium, predominantly attacking young trees. It is a strange problem, as it can cause death very rapidly or can take several years. Initially, it will demonstrate itself when leafy shoots begin to die back. Under the bark of this infected shoot, you will find black shoelace growths, confirming that honey fungus is present. At the base of the trees or bushes, honey-coloured toadstools may appear in the summer and autumn.

Control There is no real control, except for removing infected trees and bushes, taking as much of the root as possible and burning all parts. It is worth noting that strong-growing fruit trees and soft fruit bushes seem to be less prone to attack.

LEAF MINER

The larvae of this pest tunnel into **the leaves** and create very noticeable tunnels. The damage tends to be unsightly, but will not be too detrimental to the crop, unless the case is extremely severe.

Control Remove infected leaves or squash the larvae in situ.

MICE

These small rodents can cause great problems in the productive garden by **digging up freshly sown seed for food.** They are particularly fond of the seeds of peas, beans and sweetcorn, as well as stored produce.

Control The only real answer is to trap them, using either humane traps or traps that kill instantly, depending on your personal preference. Humane traps do need to be checked regularly, otherwise they become far from humane, as mice can quickly die from starvation or stress.

ONION FLY

The adults of this pest lay their eggs on the soil or on the **young leaves or stems of susceptible plants**. In early summer, white larvae emerge that will feed on the roots and bulbs – or even in the stems – for about three weeks. It is possible for up to four generations to be hatched each year. The obvious signs of attack are the top growth wilting and white maggots being found when the soil around the bulbs is removed.

Control Cover the crop with fine netting or fleece as soon as it is planted. Hoe regularly around the crops and cultivate any infected areas in winter, to bring any maggots to the surface and expose them to predatory birds. The female fly is attracted by the smell of young onions, so do not directly sow and thin young plants. Instead, multi-sow into modules or grow from sets that do not require thinning. Remove infected plants as soon as the pest is detected. Implement a good crop rotation.

ONION NECK ROT

Generally, this disease does not show itself in the top growth although, in severe cases, the leaves may turn yellow. The fungal disease occurs in cool, wet summers, beginning in the neck of the bulb and then spreads downwards, **infecting the whole of the bulb**. When lifted, white, fluffy fungal growth is often apparent on the roots and the bulbs are soft at the neck, but not always at the sides. It is a seed-borne disease that will also survive in the ground for up to four years, but does not spread in store.

Control: Always buy seeds and sets from a reputable supplier and ensure correct spacing between the crops, so

that there is adequate ventilation. Make sure that there is good drainage and improve the soil by incorporating well-rotted organic matter prior to planting. Check stored bulbs regularly and remove infected ones. Rotate crops on at least a four-year rotation.

ONION WHITE ROT

A very persistent disease that can stay in the soil for up to 15 years and will cause bulbs to rot in store. Generally recognizable as a **mouldy growth near the neck** of stored onions. If the disease takes hold while the onions are in the ground, the plants suddenly start to die. This disease is most active in early spring, so autumn-sown sets are more susceptible. By spring, they are at an ideal stage for the disease to attack.

Control Grow plants from seed and avoid using sets. Remove affected bulbs as soon as the disease is spotted, and thoroughly clean all equipment and boots that have come into contact with the infected soil. Use a wider spacing as the disease can spread through the soil, so closer spacings will cause greater damage to the crop. Never bend the tops of onions manually, as this may encourage the disease. Only store undamaged and uninfected bulbs. If growing onion-related crops on infected ground, you can replace the soil around garlic and leeks with uncontaminated soil to a diameter and depth of about 10 cm (4 in).

PARSNIP CANKER

A disease that causes the shoulders of parsnips to initially turn a reddish-brown before it **spreads into the rest of the root causing it to rot**. This problem is usually found on poorly drained sites. Carrot-fly damage can create an entry point for the canker spores.

Control If not growing on a well-drained site, then improve the soil condition and try growing canker-resistant varieties. Controlling carrot fly will help to minimize the disease, as will growing and harvesting smaller, younger roots that seem to be less susceptible.

PEA AND BEAN WEEVIL

This weevil **takes characteristic 'U'-shaped chunks out of the edges of leaves on susceptible plants**. It is the greyish-brown adult beetle that does the damage, feeding in the spring and again from June or July onwards.

Control Established plants do not generally suffer from the damage caused by this pest, so there is no real need to control it, unless it is attacking young seedlings, in which case it can be sprayed with derris. Susceptible crops can also be covered with fleece, to prevent the adults from reaching the crop.

PEA MOTH

A devastating pest, because the affected crop still looks healthy. Having produced an excellent crop of pea pods, they can sometimes be rendered useless by **larvae inside the pods**. The adults lay their eggs on the plants while they are in flower with the resulting larvae entering the pods via a very small hole in each pod.

Control Cover the peas prior to

flowering, and leave them covered until flowering has finished. Sow early and late, so that the peas in flower fall outside the moth's natural life cycle. Derris can be used as a last resort, if the attack is severe, to prevent subsequent adults overwintering and affecting later crops.

PEACH LEAF CURL

A visually disturbing disease that **causes the leaves to blister and swell**, eventually falling from the tree. It is a fungal disease that affects all trees in the *Prunus* genus and is spread by rain splash. In a bad attack, the loss of leaf and the subsequent loss of leaf area able to convert sunlight will reduce the vigour of the tree and cause a lower yield. Worse in cold and wet springs, the red blisters will eventually produce spores that will readily spread to other leaves, as well as other trees.

Control Remove infected leaves as soon as they appear, and keep trees well-fed and watered to promote healthy new growth. Trees that have been affected during the previous year can be sprayed with Bordeaux mixture just after leaf-fall in the autumn, and

again in early spring when the buds begin to swell. As the spores are spread by rain, the trees can be covered from mid winter until early spring to prevent rain from getting to the emerging leaves. This method is easier with fan-trained specimens, than free standing trees.

PEAR LEAF BLISTER MITE

The damage caused by this mite on pears and sometimes apples resembles that of peach leaf curl. The **leaves becoming blistered and misshapen**, with the blistering turning from pink or yellowish-green to black by mid-summer.

Control As with peach leaf curl, the effects of this mite are unsightly, but unlike peach leaf curl it does not have a detrimental effect on the tree. When spotted, remove the leaves by hand.

POTATO AND TOMATO BLIGHT

This very serious disease is first noticed when **brown patches appear on the leaves** of susceptible plants, mainly on the edges and tips. These patches will spread into the stems of the plants and turn black, often with white mould growing on the undersides of the infected leaves. The whole plant will then collapse and in the case of potatoes, the tubers will rot and turn black inside. Tomato fruits will show dark markings and become dry and leathery. The disease will overwinter on infected tubers and tomatoes, and is more prevalent in warm and wet weather, when it will spread rapidly.

Control Always buy good quality tubers and plants from a reliable source, and look for blight-resistant varieties. Spray the foliage with Bordeaux mixture every 14 days, from mid-summer until harvest. Remove all infected foliage as it appears and put it onto a hot compost heap. Do not save tubers or tomato seeds from infected plants to use as seed for the following year.

POWDERY MILDEW

A **white powdery coating on any part of a plant** usually appears during warm and dry days, particularly on dry soils.

Control Ensure the crop is supplied with enough water and mulch as much as possible. Good preparation of the ground, incorporating organic matter, will also help to retain moisture. Cut out infected shoots as the disease appears, or remove infected plants of a crop to prevent it spreading. Grow varieties that are listed as having some resistance to the disease if it has been a problem in the past.

RASPBERRY BEETLE

This pest is usually noticed when **fruits appear malformed** and it attacks all types of cane fruit. The 6 mm (¼ in) long, yellowish larvae feed on ripening fruit, potentially ruining a good yield.

Control Once they have fed on the fruit, the larvae will fall to the ground and overwinter as pupae, so hoeing the ground regularly will bring them to the surface and expose them to predators such as birds. If grown in a cage, chickens can be put in among the canes in winter and they will scratch out the pest. It is also possible to control this pest by spraying with derris, but this would usually be at a time of year when bees are flying, so spraying may be more detrimental in the long run.

RED SPIDER MITE

This is a small pest, which isn't visible to the naked eye. It is only really a problem in the greenhouse, or outside in very dry and warmer summers. It shows its presence when the **leaves take on a mottled appearance** and visible webs appear. The red spider mite is misnamed really, as it is a green-yellow colour when it causes most damage, only becoming red during the autumn and winter. During a bad attack, the leaves may turn a bronze colour, eventually withering and dying. The mites live and reproduce under the leaves and crawl, as they cannot fly, from one plant to another when the leaves are touching.

Control As red spider mites like a dry environment, keep the air moist by damping down greenhouses on hot days and spraying susceptible plants with a mist of water at least twice a day. If plants become infected, then some of the worst leaves can be removed to minimize the damage. In severe attacks, the only remedy is to remove the worst plants and destroy them. If you are growing in a greenhouse or conservatory, then you could use the predatory mite *Phytoseulus persimilis* as a biological control. However, it needs a temperature of 18–24°C (64–75°F) to work properly. Insecticidal soap can also be used, spraying at 10–14 day intervals. The red spider mites will overwinter in the cracks and crevices of greenhouses, so pressure-wash the inside when it is empty and scrub down where possible. Clean up and discard all debris.

RUST

Orange-brown spores usually appear on the undersides of leaves, but can also infect the stems of plants. These **infected areas becoming discoloured** and sometimes wither. It is a disease that will be more prevalent in damp weather, as the spores need moisture to become infectious.

Control Remove infected parts and compost. As the spores are spread by rain splash, avoid using overhead irrigation. Clear all plant debris at the end of the crop. Gooseberries and currants can be sprayed with Bordeaux mixture.

SAWFLY

The small adult flies, only 1 cm ($1/2$ in) long, lay their eggs on the undeveloped fruit at flowering time. The larvae hatch and they feed on the surface, **leaving ribbon-like scars**, before burrowing into the developing fruits. The damaged fruits do not become ripe, but fall from the tree prematurely. If left, the sawflies will overwinter in the soil and re-emerge in the spring.

Control Pick up and compost the infected fallen fruits as soon as possible. If the trees have been mulched, remove this for the winter and lightly fork over the soil to expose the overwintering cocoons. If there is a sign of potential infestation, the trees can be sprayed with derris a week after the blossom has fallen.

SCALE INSECTS

These are quite easy to spot as **small, oval, brown waxy scales on the undersides of the leaves**. When newly hatched, these small insects crawl to a suitable feeding spot and then settle there, never moving again. They feed on the sap of the plants weakening them and even cause leaf drop. They excrete "honeydew" which falls onto the leaves below. This often has a sooty mould growing on it, which not only spoils the appearance of the infected plant but also prevents it from growing well by reducing the leaf surface area able to convert sunlight into food.

Control The only really effective organic control for all plants is to check susceptible plants regularly. If any scale insects are found, remove them with a fingernail, cotton bud, or something similar that will not also damage the leaf. If the plants are growing in a warm greenhouse or conservatory, then biological control can be used in the form of the parasitic wasp *Metaphycus helvolus*, which not only needs plenty of sunshine to work effectively but also a regular temperature between 20–30°C (68–86°F).

SCLEROTINIA

This fungal infection affects both **stems and fruit, which become brown and slimy** as they rot. It is usually found in damp and cool conditions, overwintering in the soil.

Control Remove all infected plants before they spore if possible, and utilize a four-year crop rotation plan to avoid re-infection.

SILVER LEAF

A potentially fatal disease, with plums being particularly susceptible. This fungal disease usually infects the tree when it is dormant and enters via wounds or cuts. The **leaves take on a very noticeable silvery sheen** and may then turn brown, while the shoots supporting these leaves progressively die back. Purple, brown or white fungi will then appear on these dead shoots and, if the shoots are cut through, they will show a purple or brown ring of stain running through the wood.

Control To minimize open wounds into which the disease can enter, only prune susceptible plants once the sap in the tree starts to rise (when the buds begin to show signs of life). Cut back all infected branches to at least 15 cm (6 in) past the last point of infection, and burn all infected branches immediately. There are some cases where the individual trees naturally recover from the disease, without the infected wood being removed, but removal is by far the better option.

SLUGS AND SNAILS

The bane of most gardeners' lives, these pests feed on plants mainly during the night and thrive in damp conditions. The vegetable plot or fruit-growing areas are an ideal environment, due to the regular watering and the high organic content of the soil. It is usually the garden snail that causes the most damage, as research has shown that it eats faster than even the hungriest slug. They are usually a grey-brown colour, with a shell about 3 cm (1^1/4 in) across. With slugs, the light-greyish field type and the dark-grey or black garden slug cause the most damage. Both are about 3–4 cm (1^1/4–1^1/2 in) long. As a general rule, the larger the slug, the slower and the less it eats. Both of these slugs will inhabit areas above ground, as well as below, so **most vegetable, herb and fruit crops can be susceptible**.

Control Organic slug pellets can be applied when the crop is planted or on emergence of seedlings. They are not harmful to wildlife and are based on ferrous phosphate, which biodegrades into the soil as iron and phosphates. They are usually supplied in 750 g containers. There are a number of physical barriers that can be used. Wood ash is very good, as it prevents slugs and snails from travelling if applied in a wide band. It is free, as it is a by-product of wood burning, but has to be replaced after rain or a heavy dew. Do not use a wood and coal ash mix, as it contains too much sulphur. Egg shells, when crushed, are uncomfortable for the slugs and snails to travel on. They also avoid travelling across copper, so copper in bands around pots proves very effective. Vaseline in a band around the pot is also difficult for them to pass over. As an accompaniment to these methods, nematodes can also be used. These are microscopic insects that are specific to slugs and snails. They are obtained in powder form and are reconstituted by adding to water. They are very easy to apply with a watering can, although they need a soil temperature of 5°C (41°F) as a minimum to work, so they are usually applied from March or April. Finally, wildlife such as frogs, birds and hedgehogs are just a few natural predators that can be encouraged into the garden as natural predators.

SPUR BLIGHT

Much more prevalent in a wet spring, this fungal disease **causes silver patches to appear on raspberry canes and briars**, followed by black-fruiting bodies. It is spread by rain and wind, and the affected areas will eventually die off.

Control Plant varieties that show some resistance to the disease and thin canes in the spring to reduce overcrowding. If the disease does occur, then spray when the buds begin to open with Bordeaux mixture and again 14 days later.

THRIPS

These small cylindrical insects are pests inside and out, and feed by **sucking sap from the upper surfaces of the leaves.** They vary in colour from a creamy-white to a dark brown/black, with the larvae resembling the adults, except that they are wingless. As the adults fly, they are able to pass easily from plant to plant and feed on buds and flowers of a wide range of plants, as well as the leaves, causing a silvery mottling and distortion of infected

315

parts. They reproduce quite quickly and will overwinter in the soil, and on infected plant debris.

Control As they like a dry environment, keep the air moist by damping down greenhouses on hot days and spraying susceptible plants with a mist of water at least twice a day. Prevention is better and a lot easier than cure, so check all susceptible plants that are introduced into the garden or greenhouse by tapping the foliage over a sheet of white paper to see if any adult thrips fall off. There is a predatory mite that can be introduced into a protected environment that is thrip-specific, but it is not suited to the garden, as the *Amblyseius cucumeris* mite requires an optimum temperature of 25°C (77°F) to be successful.

TOMATO MOSAIC VIRUS

This is **mostly carried by aphids**, so control of these will control the problem, although it can also be spread via infected equipment. The infected plants will have a mottled appearance and possibly some distortion, which will slow down the plant's growth, flowering and ultimate size of fruit, thus affecting the yield.

Control As there is no cure for this problem, it is best to grow resistant varieties and be vigilant. If a plant seems infected, then remove it immediately and destroy it.

VIOLET ROOT ROT

A devastating fungal disease that can stay in the ground without a host for many years, rendering the ground useless for growing susceptible crops. It is usually noticed when the **top growth becomes yellow and stunted**, while the roots and tubers, when lifted, are covered by dark purple strands. It is more prevalent on acid soils.

Control There is no effective control, although removing infected plants before they degenerate and spores are released into the surrounding soil will help enormously. Once removed, the infected material must not be composted; it must be burned. Improving the drainage will help, but it may not be possible to grow susceptible crops on the ground again. After five years, a trial crop can be tested to see if the disease is still in the ground.

WASPS

These volatile insects are a bit of a dilemma in the garden, because they sting us without warning and **eat holes in ripening fruit**. However, they are vigorous eaters of caterpillars, aphids and various other pests.

Control Wasps can be caught by using sweet traps, where jam or sugar is mixed with water and placed into a container that has had several holes pierced into its lid. It is important to pierce the lids inwards, so that when the wasps crawl into the container, attracted by the sweet smell, they find it very difficult, if not impossible, to climb out. To get rid of ground nests, a bowl pushed firmly over the entrance will prevent the wasps getting out and they will starve. For aerial nests, and even possibly ground nests, it is best to get a professional pest expert to deal with them. Ensure that you ask them to use soap or a pyrethroid spray to kill the nest, as these are organically sound.

WHITEFLY

These small sap-feeding insects are easy to spot, as they fly as soon as the plant is touched. They feed on the underside of leaves. If they cannot be spotted flying, the **grey, sooty mould growing on the surface of the leaves** directly below will give them away. The leaves will also develop yellow spots on the surface, directly above where the pests have been feeding and, in severe infestations, the plant growth can be stunted. The whitefly will attack plants outside, as well as greenhouse plants, although they will not be able to overwinter out in the open. They generally survive in a greenhouse and then move out into the vegetable plot in the summer, once the temperatures have risen.

Control Remove badly infected plants. Hang yellow sticky traps that will catch the whitefly on plants nearby. These can be used to monitor the pest population. In greenhouses, a parasitic wasp biological control can be used. *Encarsia formosa* looks like a tiny hover fly and will work at temperatures above 10°C (50°F), although they work best at 18–25°C

(64–77°F). These small parasitic wasps lay their eggs inside the whitefly scales (eggs) and the larvae eat the whitefly larvae before they can hatch. Insecticidal soap can be sprayed onto the whitefly, making sure that it is directed under the leaves early in the morning, every seven to 10 days for three to five weeks.

WINTER MOTH CATERPILLAR

A pest that has the potential to greatly reduce fruit crops by **eating the blossom, as well as the tree foliage and sometimes even the buds**. However, it is a very easy pest to control, as the female moth is wingless and has to crawl from its overwintering home in the soil up the tree to lay its eggs. They are easy to recognize, as they are green with three longitudinal stripes running the full length of their body and they "loop" as they travel.

Control The most effective method of control is to tie a grease band around the stems and supporting stakes of all susceptible trees, any time during the dormant period of the tree, but before March. Check the trees on a regular basis to see if any females have managed to get across the barrier, although this is unlikely.

WIREWORMS

These are the larvae of the click beetle and are a yellow/brown colour and 25 mm (1 in) in length. The adults will lay their eggs in weedy places and grasslands in mid-summer and the larvae can stay feeding for up to five years, but dislike being disturbed. The **larvae will burrow into the tubers**, stems and roots of crops, rendering them inedible and causing reduced crops by weakening the infected plants.

Control Cultivate during winter to bring the wireworms to the surface and provide food for birds. Do not leave potatoes in the ground beyond early autumn, to limit any damage. Decoy potatoes can be sunk into the ground or into pots in the greenhouse to attract wireworms and, once infested, can be removed and destroyed. It is best to spike these potatoes with a small stick, so that you know where they are buried. If the

ground is newly cultivated from
pasture, then a wheat crop can be
grown between the rows of susceptible
vegetables for the first two years. The
wireworms are attracted to the wheat,
which can then be dug up and burned.

SUPPLIERS

Beans and Herbs

Seeds

The Herbary

161 Chapel Street

Horningsham

Warminster

Wiltshire

BA12 7LU

WEBSITE: www.beansandherbs.co.uk

Butterworth's Organic Nursery

Fruit trees

Garden Cottage

Auchinleck House Estate

Cumnock

Ayrshire

KA18 2LR

TEL: 01290 551088

WEBSITE: www.butterworthsorganicnursery.co.uk

Chiltern Seeds

Seeds

Bortree Stile

Ulverston

Cumbria

LA12 7PB

WEBSITE: www.chilternseeds.co.uk

Chris Bowers

Fruit trees and soft fruit

Whispering Trees Nurseries

Wimbotsham

Norfolk

PE34 3QB

TEL: 01366 388752

FAX: 01366 386858

WEBSITE: www.chrisbowers.co.uk

Deacon's Nursery

Fruit trees and soft fruit

Moor View

Godshill

Isle of Wight

PO38 3HW

TEL: 01983 840750 or 01983 522243

FAX: 01983 523575

WEBSITE: www.deaconsnurseryfruits.co.uk

DT Brown Seeds

Seeds, fruit trees and soft fruit

Bury Road

Kentford

Newmarket

Suffolk

CB8 7PR

TEL: 0845 166 2275

Mr Fothergill's Seeds Ltd

Seeds and soft fruit

Gazeley Road

Kentford

Newmarket, Suffolk

CB8 7QB

TEL: 01638 751 161

FAX: 01638 554 084

WEBSITE: www.fothergills.co.uk

Nicky's Nursery

Seeds

33 Fairfield Road

Broadstairs

Kent

CT10 2JU

TEL/FAX: 01843 600972

WEBSITE: www.nickys-nursery.co.uk

Real Seeds

Seeds

Brithdir Mawr Farm

Newport

near Fishguard

Pembrokeshire

SA42 0QJ

TEL: 01239 821107

WEBSITE: www.realseeds.co.uk

Samuel Dobie & Son

Seeds, plants, fruit trees and
soft fruit

Long Road

Paignton,

Devon

TQ4 7SX

TEL: 0870 112 3625

WEBSITE: www.dobies.co.uk

Seeds by Size

Seeds

45 Crouchfield

Hemel Hempstead

Hertfordshire

HP1 1PA

TEL: 01442 251458

WEBSITE: www.seeds-by-size.co.uk

Seeds of Italy

Seeds

C3 Phoenix Industrial Estate

Rosslyn Crescent

Harrow

Middlesex

HA1 2SP

TEL: 0208 427 5020

FAX: 0208 427 5051

WEBSITE: www.seedsofitaly.com

Select Seeds

Seeds

58 Bentinck Road

Shuttlewood

Chesterfield

FAX: 0845 166 2283

WEBSITE: www.dtbrownseeds.co.uk

Edwin Tucker and Sons Ltd

Seeds

Brewery Meadow

Stonepark

Ashburton

Devon

TQ13 7DG

TEL: 01364 652233

FAX: 01364 654211

WEBSITE: www.edwintucker.com

Highfield Nurseries

Fruit trees and soft fruit

School Lane

Whitminster

Gloucester

GL2 7PL

TEL: 01452 740266 or 01452 741309

FAX: 01452 740750

WEBSITE: www.highfield-nurseries.co.uk

Jekka's Herb Farm

Seeds and plants

Rose Cottage

Shellards Lane

Alveston,

Bristol

BS35 3SY

TEL: 01454 418878

FAX: 01454 411988

WEBSITE: www.jekkasherbfarm.com

Keepers Nursery

Fruit trees and soft fruit

Gallants Court

East Farleigh

Maidstone

Kent ME15 0LE

TEL: 01622 726465

FAX: 0870 705 2145

WEBSITE: www.keepers-nursery.co.uk

Ken Muir

Fruit trees and soft fruit

Rectory Rd

Weeley Heath

Clacton-on-Sea

Essex

CO16 9BJ

TEL: 01255 830181

FAX: 01255 831534

WEBSITE: www.kenmuir.co.uk

Medwyn's of Anglesey

Seeds

Llanor

Ffordd Hen Ysgol

Llanfairpwllgwyngyll

Anglesey

LL61 5RZ

WEBSITE: www.medwynsofanglesey.co.uk

S44 6RQ

TEL: 01246 826011

WEBSITE: www.selectseeds.co.uk

S E Marshalls & Co

Seeds, plants, fruit trees and soft fruit

Alconbury Hill

Huntingdon

Cambridgeshire

PE28 4HY

TEL: 01480 443390

FAX: 01480 443391

WEBSITE: www.marshalls-seeds.co.uk

Simpsons Seeds

Seeds

The Walled Garden Nursery

Horningsham

Warminster

Wiltshire

BA12 7NQ

TEL: 01985 845004

FAX: 01985 845052

WEBSITE: www.simpsonsseeds.co.uk

Suttons Seeds

Seeds, plants, fruit trees and soft fruit

Woodview Road

Paignton

Devon

TQ4 7NG

TEL: 0870 220 2899

FAX: 0870 220 2265

WEBSITE: www.suttons-seeds.co.uk

The Organic Gardening Catalogue

Seeds, fruit trees and soft fruit

Riverdene Business Park

Molesey Road

Hersham

Surrey

KT12 4RG

TEL: 0845 130 1304

FAX: 01932 252707

WEBSITE: www.organiccatalog.com

Thompson & Morgan (UK) Ltd

Seeds, plants and soft fruit

Poplar Lane

Ipswich

Suffolk

United Kingdom

IP8 3BU

TEL: 01473 - 695 200

FAX: 01473 - 680 199

WEBSITE: seeds.thompson-morgan.com

Victoriana Nursery Gardens

Seeds, plants, fruit trees and soft fruit

Challock

Nr Ashford

Kent

TN25 4DG

TEL: 01233 740529

FAX: 01233 740030

WEBSITE: **www.victoriana.ws**

W. Robinson & Son (Seeds & Plants) Ltd

Seeds and plants

Sunny Bank

Forton

Nr. Preston

Lancs

PR3 0BN

TEL: 01524 791210

FAX: 01524 791933

WEBSITE: **www.mammothonion.co.uk**

INDEX

Page references in bold type indicate significant mentions.